Big Red's Mercy

The Shooting of Deborah Cotton and a Story of Race in America

Mark Hertsgaard

PEGASUS BOOKS
NEW YORK LONDON

BIG RED'S MERCY

Pegasus Books, Ltd.
148 West 37th Street, 13th Floor
New York, NY 10018

First Pegasus Books cloth edition May 2024

Interior design by Maria Fernandez

Library of Congress Cataloging-in-Publication Data is available.

ISBN: 978-1-63936-675-0

10 9 8 7 6 5 4 3 2 1

Printed in the United States of America
Distributed by Simon & Schuster
www.pegasusbooks.com

To all of slavery's victims, then and now

Contents

	A Note on Language	vii
1	Called	1
2	Coming Out the Door	18
3	Becoming Deborah "Big Red" Cotton	41
4	Like Shooting Up a Church	67
5	"The Blues Came from Slavery, Jazz Came from Freedom"	81
6	The Unblinking Eye	114
7	"Mama, I Don't Wanna Die"	138
8	"This Country Is Still Really Broken"	155
9	Crabs in a Barrel	170
10	The Obama Backlash	189
11	The Lost Boys of New Orleans	209
12	Hard Conversations	234
13	"The Truth Hurts, But Silence Kills"	261
14	One Last Second Line	289
	Further Reading and Listening	305
	Acknowledgments	311

A Note on Language

The following narrative is based on the author's eyewitness observations and hundreds of hours of interviews with people involved in the events described herein, and on extensive research in libraries and museums. The vast majority of quotations in the narrative come from these interviews; where that is not the case, attribution is provided in the text. In the name of factual accuracy and reflecting the world as it is, all quotations are reported exactly as the words were originally spoken or written, without sanitizing abbreviations or euphemisms. The portrayal of the way people actually speak and write—both in the present day and throughout history—in these pages does not mean an endorsement of the expressions quoted.

1

Called

"The great force of history comes from the fact that we carry it within us, are unconsciously controlled by it in many ways, and history is literally present in everything we do."

—James Baldwin

Deborah Cotton and I met by getting shot together.

It was a Mother's Day Sunday early in Barack Obama's second term as the first Black president of the United States. Deb, as her friends called her, was among hundreds of people, almost all of them Black, marching through the streets of New Orleans, marching not in protest but in celebration, celebration of the unique, deeply rooted African American culture of New Orleans as expressed by its iconic ritual, a second line parade.

Like Obama, Deborah Cotton literally embodied America's racial divide, for she, too, descended from a Black father and a White mother. Also like Obama, she was graced with a sparkling smile, good looks, and an effortless charisma that glided her smoothly between the Black and White worlds. Born in Los Angeles, kidnapped (her word) as a toddler, and raised in rural Texas, she had relocated to New Orleans in 2005, three months before Hurricane Katrina put most of the city underwater. Now, she was a veteran racial and social justice activist and an accomplished freelance writer who, under the pen name "Big Red Cotton," wrote about second line parades for the local music paper *Gambit*.

A second line parade is a street party, a musical explosion, a church service, a cultural remembrance, and a political statement all wrapped up in one unforgettable afternoon. Not to be confused with the annual Mardi Gras parades, second lines evolved from the burial rites that enslaved Africans brought with them when they began arriving in Louisiana in 1722. Second line parades are still employed today in New Orleans to grieve and celebrate the recently deceased, but they also take place in one neighborhood or another every Sunday afternoon of the year, except during the summer when it's too hot.

Propelled by riotously percussive music, hundreds of people take over the streets for four hours of dancing, drinking, eating, flirting, and grooving to the beat. One or more brass bands drive the action, their squealing horns and thumping drums channeling the jaunty rhythms and melodic kicks that made New Orleans, in Bruce Springsteen's words, "this great mother city of American music." Specially attired dancers strut their stuff in flamboyantly colored uniforms accented by plumed fans, feathered hats, and parasols. Surrounding the band and dancers are spectators joining the fun—the parade's "second line." Usually the crowd is overwhelmingly African American, but all colors, ages, backgrounds, and beliefs are welcome. In the words of Curtis Mayfield's "People Get Ready," you don't need a ticket for this train; you just get on board. While you're at it, smile at your neighbor and give thanks to be here, now, for one more blessed day of life.

Gunshots were fired into the Mother's Day second line parade at 1:47 P.M. on May 12, 2013. The To Be Continued Brass Band had halted just before entering the intersection of Frenchmen and North Villere streets, a poverty-stricken neighborhood in the Seventh Ward, a ten-minute walk from the free-spending tourists in the French Quarter. The band had played the first four notes of a song by The Hot 8 Brass Band "and then everything went crazy," Joe Maize, a trombonist for To Be Continued, later recalled.

I didn't live in New Orleans, I just happened to be passing through town that weekend and decided to catch an hour of second lining before heading to the airport to fly home. When the gunfire erupted, I was standing on the far side of the intersection from where Deb Cotton and the TBC band had paused. The gunshots were coming from about ten feet behind my left shoulder. The bullets made an oddly muffled *zip, zip* sound as they streaked through the humid afternoon air. People around me started to push, run, and throw themselves to the ground. I did the same, diving like a baseball player sliding headfirst into home plate.

The gunfire lasted about ten seconds. Then, for a moment, all was quiet, as if everyone were holding their breath to see what came next. A woman's voice broke the silence, erupting in a piercing wail: "Oh, my God! Oh, my God!" And then it was bedlam, a cacophony of voices shouting in pain, fear, and alarm.

On the other side of the intersection, right where I'd been standing a few seconds ago, a Black guy lay facedown, motionless, a semicircle of red spreading from his shoulder. Steps away, a thin Black woman with wild, frightened eyes huddled against a building, clutching her belly, grimacing and weeping.

TV satellite trucks reached the scene almost as quickly as ambulances did, and soon live coverage was beaming to television screens around the world. The initial fear was that it was a terrorist attack, perhaps a copycat of the bombing at the Boston Marathon a month earlier that had killed three and wounded hundreds more. Detective Chris Hart, the lead New Orleans Police Department officer at the scene, was pacing the blood-spattered intersection when his cell phone buzzed. "I'm watching you on Al Jazeera *right now*, Chris," a former NOPD cop doing security work in Afghanistan told him. "You're wearing a blue shirt and a baseball cap. What the fuck is happening back in New Orleans?"

Second line parades embody two milestones in United States history—the imposition of slavery and the invention of jazz—that have profoundly shaped the nation's evolution and gave the Mother's Day shooting the quality of a true-crime parable for the Obama-Trump era.

If slavery was America's original sin, as Obama once said (echoing James Madison), New Orleans was an epicenter of that sin. New Orleans hosted the largest slave trading market in North America prior to the Civil War: an estimated one million people were bought and sold here, fueling the Cotton Boom that first made the United States a global economic superpower and later gave the Confederacy the confidence that it could defeat the Union in the Civil War.

But in a dazzling paradox, this legacy of brutal exploitation also gave rise to what has been called America's greatest artistic achievement. By the early 1900s, New Orleans musicians at second lines and elsewhere were mixing rhythms from Africa with melodies from Europe to create an entirely new type of music: jazz. (It was at a second line that an adolescent Louis Armstrong first played a horn in public.) Jazz quickly became the most popular music on both sides of the Atlantic. Later, it gave rise to rhythm and blues, which led to rock 'n' roll and its many descendant genres, making jazz a fountainhead of 20th century American popular music.

Jazz and second line parades emerged in New Orleans, and only in New Orleans, partly because slavery there began under the French, and the French gave enslaved people Sundays off. Unlike the Anglo-Saxon Protestants who enforced slavery in the rest of the American South, the French in Louisiana were Catholics. At that time, Catholic teachings held that enslaved people, despite their earthly status, were children of God who had souls and spiritual rights and responsibilities just like White people did, including not working on the Sabbath. The French also welcomed the amusements of music and dance, whereas Anglo-Saxons distrusted them as devil's mischief. Anglo-Saxon slaveholders banned drumming by slaves for fear that it would lead to rebellion, whereas French authorities saw its strategic benefit. "When they are singing and dancing, they are not conspiring to rebel," one French commander quipped.

"No place else in the United States is going to let Black people take over the streets for four hours long," Deborah Cotton once said about second line parades in New Orleans. "It's just not gonna happen." If only for a few hours, Black people at a second line parade could feel free—free to express themselves however they wished, regardless of the White world's constraints. "The blues came from slavery," said Gregg Stafford, a prominent New Orleans brass band leader and trumpet player. "Jazz came from freedom."

But demons of death, never far away in New Orleans, haunted that Mother's Day second line parade. Ambulance workers counted twenty people wounded and told Detective Hart to expect three, possibly four, fatalities. Measured by total casualties, it was the biggest mass shooting in the modern history of New Orleans, already one of the nation's deadliest cities, with a murder rate a staggering eight times higher than the national per capita average.

Heavyset, with salt-and-pepper hair, Hart had spent sixteen years as a cop in New Orleans, yet these casualty numbers shocked him and his fellow officers. "We didn't break down and cry, cops don't do that," he later explained. "But I could see on their faces how they felt. Even in New Orleans, typically there will be one or two people shot. In really bad situations, maybe five or six people shot. But twenty? That's unheard of."

The trauma unit doctors were not optimistic that Deborah Cotton would live through the night. The bullet that hit her had pierced her right hip and torn diagonally upward, shredding vital organs before lodging beneath the left side of her rib cage. Late that afternoon, the surgeons emerged from the operating room to inform her loved ones that it didn't look good. She had been shot in what hospital workers nicknamed "the soul hole," because wounds there were usually fatal.

Nevertheless, Deborah Cotton held on long enough to deliver a message that stunned the people of New Orleans.

A surveillance video had surfaced the day after the shooting that offered a bird's-eye view of the attack. It showed a Black man in a white T-shirt standing with his back against the wall of a house, watching as the parade crowd passed from left to right. Suddenly the man pulled a handgun from his pocket, took four strides into the crowd, and began firing at point-blank range. As bodies fell and fled, the man continued firing. After emptying his weapon, he ran off, out of camera range.

TV networks all over the world immediately began airing the video—it was irresistible television. New Orleans TV stations put it in constant rotation. In the glare of such publicity, the authorities soon arrested two suspects: Akein Scott and Shawn Scott, two African American biological brothers aged nineteen and twenty-three. Each brother was charged with twenty counts of attempted murder: one for each of the nineteen gunshot victims and one for a woman grotesquely injured when she was trampled by the fleeing crowd.

In what both Deborah Cotton and the police expressly labeled "a miracle," neither she nor any of the other Mother's Day shooting victims perished immediately. "We had twenty [*sic*] people shot at that parade, and not one of them dies?" said Detective Rob Hurst, Hart's partner at the scene. "If that's not a miracle, you tell me what is."

Hovering near death in the intensive care unit, Deborah Cotton somehow dictated a statement that a close friend delivered on her behalf to a hastily called New Orleans City Council hearing. Over the week since she had been shot, during occasional moments of lucidity between one surgery after another, her friends had briefed her on what happened: the mass shooting, the bird's-eye video, the casualties, the arrests of the alleged gunmen.

Deborah Cotton's City Council statement implored the city and people of New Orleans to stop and think before passing judgment. "These young men have been separated from us by so much trauma," she said, referring to the bleak circumstances facing many young Black men in New Orleans: parents absent or impoverished, abysmal schools, rampant gang and police violence, few job possibilities beyond menial labor or drug dealing. "I have known from the moment the shooting happened that I did not want these young men thrown to the wolves," her statement continued. ". . . Do you know what it takes to be so disconnected in your heart that you walk out into a gathering of hundreds of people who look just like you and begin firing?"

It was Deborah Cotton who told me that I should write this book. *Called* was her exact word.

I managed to connect with Deb a few months after the shooting. She'd been discharged from the hospital by then, but her return to normal life remained uncertain at best. More than one of her vital organs had been severely compromised or outright removed, and the doctors said that she had many more surgeries ahead.

Our first meeting took place over the phone because at the last minute she felt too ill to leave her apartment. We shared our recollections of that fateful afternoon, bonding over the fact that we were both writers and had both been shot, though her injuries were incomparably worse than mine. In a voice timorous yet clear, Deb told me that these days she often felt nauseous, anxious, and sometimes depressed. Yet she evinced not the slightest anger toward the two gunmen who allegedly shot us and seventeen other people at a ritual that, as she well knew from her *Gambit* writings, was sacred to Black history and identity in New Orleans. Instead, Deb reiterated her initial response of mercy and understanding.

"I try to put myself in other people's shoes in life," she told me. "I asked myself, 'What has happened to put those young men in such a dead-hearted place that they would shoot into a crowd of people who looked just like them?'

That's what's so striking to me. They weren't shooting at White men; they weren't shooting at Black women. They were shooting at other Black men."

Drawing on the teachings of African American leaders, from Malcolm X and Martin Luther King Jr. back to W.E.B. Du Bois and Frederick Douglass, Deb felt that one of the most fiendish aspects of White supremacy was how it could lead Black people to devalue themselves. During slavery days in particular, enslaved Black people often were treated as animals more than as human beings. In response, some of them internalized the idea that they were worthless and turned against themselves and other Black people. The alleged Mother's Day gunmen had fired into a crowd of "people who looked just like them," Deb repeated. "There's a level of self-hatred there that is so profound. It's like they're trying to wipe themselves out."

When Deb and I met face-to-face on my next visit to New Orleans, I told her I thought the Mother's Day shooting was a book crying out to be written. The circumstances surrounding the shooting made it more than just one more spasm of wanton violence in a country where mass shootings had become sickeningly common. The fact that the shooting took place at a second line parade seemed painfully symbolic, given that second line parades dated from slavery days, had helped to birth jazz, and remained a beloved source of Black cultural identity and community in New Orleans. I asked Deb whether she'd consider writing such a book after she recovered from her injuries, and I offered to connect her with my literary agent in New York.

Deb, however, wanted no part of that idea. She appreciated the encouragement, she told me, but no thanks: it was bad enough to get shot in the first place, she didn't want to keep reliving the experience by writing a book about it.

Deb did agree, though, that somebody should write a book about the Mother's Day shooting. And that somebody, she said, should be me.

An activist through and through, Deb saw the Mother's Day shooting as a teachable moment that could convey important lessons about the ways racism has shaped life in the United States since the days of slavery. A signature skill of good political organizers is an ability to persuade other people to do things that need doing. Thus Deb pointed out that I had written numerous other nonfiction books, had witnessed the shooting at close range, had even been shot myself. Warming to her theme, she fixed her gaze on me and declared, "Mark, I think you're called to write this book." Her use of the term *called* signaled that Deb, like me, had grown up in the church, where it was common to hear a person say they felt "called" to make this or that major life decision—called by God, the Holy Spirit, or Deb's favorite term, the Most High.

The fact that I was White didn't come up during that first conversation with Deb, nor did I commit to writing the book. As I told Deb, I already had my hands full writing about climate change, a subject I had covered for decades that was becoming increasingly urgent. I had spent much of the 1990s traveling around the world to write a book about humanity's environmental future, then circumnavigated the globe again in 2001 to write a book about why America fascinated and infuriated the rest of the world. By the time I met Deb, I had reported on climate change from twenty-five countries and much of the United States; indeed, it was climate reporting that had first brought me to New Orleans to cover the aftermath of Hurricane Katrina, the first great US casualty of the global warming era. Meanwhile, I had also become a father, and my concern about the future that my daughter and the rest of what I termed "Generation Hot" would inherit compelled me to focus on the climate crisis while it was still possible to avoid the worst.

But I had to admit that, like Deb, I was intensely curious to know what had led someone to shoot her, me, and seventeen other people that day in New Orleans. And I certainly saw the larger dimensions of a shooting that had taken place during an iconic New Orleans ritual that dated back to slavery days and helped bring forth the world-conquering music known as jazz.

When Deb and I talked a second time about doing this book, I broached the issue of me being a White writer, and we talked about it at length. That conversation yielded the first of many enlightenments that I would receive from Deb as she became a dear friend and fellow investigator of what had happened that Mother's Day.

The fact that I was White didn't seem to bother Deb. In her activism and journalism, I would later learn, she had long worked with White and Black people alike. Socially, she was as comfortable with White people as with Black people (though she did date only Black men, she would later confide). As we got to know one another better, Deb learned that I had spoken out about racism throughout my adult life. In my books and journalism, I had written about how racism in the media kept newsrooms White and skewed the resulting journalism, and how people of color and the poor suffer disproportionately from climate-driven extreme weather and other environmental damages. Later, Deb and I came to realize that the anti-apartheid struggle had loomed large in both of our political comings of age. Deb thought it was pretty cool, and confessed to feeling a tiny bit jealous, that I had been arrested with Archbishop Desmond Tutu while protesting apartheid at the South African embassy in Washington, DC.

But Deb's endorsement of a White author writing about race turned out to have even deeper roots. Later, I would be told more than once, usually by White people in US publishing circles, that a White author should not be writing about race in this racially fraught era; that subject was reserved for Black writers, who for too many years had been sidelined by the White-dominated publishing industry. For my part, I absolutely agreed that Black voices had been silenced for too long and needed to be heard, I had made the same argument decades ago in my book about the news business—but I didn't think that meant White writers had to be silent. For her part, Deb outright rejected the view that only Black people should talk about race. Indeed, like many African American activists and intellectuals over the years, she believed that it was White people who *most* needed to talk about race—and not only race but slavery, the original sin at the bottom of today's injustices and pathologies.

"Black people have been talking about it for 400 years, honey," she told me. "It's White people who aren't talking about it." What's more, the activist side of Deb pointed out, White people could talk to—and be *heard* by—other White people in ways Black people simply would not be. "White people listen to White people more than they will listen to Black people," she added. "That's just a fact."

Deb's response to the Mother's Day shooting foreshadowed the Black Lives Matter movement that soon would transform racial consciousness and activism during the Obama-Trump era, but Deb's version of Black Lives Matter came with a twist. She was of course fully aware of the violence Black people had long endured from trigger-happy police and White vigilantes: after all, her activism over the past eight years had focused on reforming the notoriously corrupt, violent, and racist New Orleans Police Department, a mission embraced by the Obama administration, which placed the NOPD under a federal consent decree four months before the Mother's Day shooting. But the evils of systemic racism were much broader than police brutality, Deb believed, their reach more insidious and pervasive.

To Deb, Black lives mattered even if a Black person had done something reprehensible, like shooting into a peaceful crowd at a second line parade. And Black lives mattered even then, she told me, because "racism can kill Black people even when a Black finger pulls the trigger." The gunman seen firing into the crowd in the Mother's Day video "clearly made horrible choices that have ruined his life," she continued. "But he didn't do that in a vacuum. This city and this country created that vacuum."

Deb's message was hard for many people to hear at the time, and perhaps it's still hard to hear today. I eventually spent hundreds of hours interviewing scores of people in New Orleans about the Mother's Day shooting and its aftermath. The overwhelming majority of them, Black and White alike, rejected Deb's plea for mercy and understanding toward the alleged gunmen. "C'mon, man, I'm from the hood, don't give me that shit," Glen David Andrews, a prominent Black musician and a good friend of Deb's, told me. "I ain't no saint, but shooting up a second line ain't about Black and White. It's about right and wrong."

To be clear, most of these people were responding to an incomplete picture of Deb's beliefs. They had heard, or heard about, only the two sound bites the news media had amplified from her City Council statement. My subsequent conversations with Deb made it clear that, in fact, she did not believe that the alleged Mother's Day gunmen should escape punishment. Nor did she believe that racism alone caused the Mother's Day shooting. As much as White America might be to blame for racism as a system, Deb was painfully aware that it was young Black men themselves who were stalking and slaying one another in New Orleans like soldiers in an urban guerrilla war.

In a video recorded weeks before the Mother's Day shooting, Deb said it broke her heart to "live in a city where young Black men hunt and kill each other . . . To see that there is so much death and devastation in the city that I love, and the main perpetrators of that violence are young Black men, it's even more concerning to me."

Deb recognized that the Mother's Day shooting was more representative of the gun violence that typically afflicted African Americans than were the police and vigilante shootings that would spark so much protest in the years ahead. Official data showed that Black people in the United States experienced three times as many deadly police shootings as White people did, a clear indication of racial bias. But Black people also experienced *eighteen times* as many gunshot injuries in general, and most of the gunmen in those cases were Black men. In New Orleans alone, six thousand Black men had been murdered in the thirty-three years prior to the Mother's Day shooting, an average of one murder every two days. "It's Black people killing Black people," Glen David Andrews sang at a gig the day before the Mother's Day shooting. "And that ain't cool."

A decade has passed since the Mother's Day shooting, and the United States that Deb and I inhabited back then has given way to a much more divided and more dangerous place. Days after the Mother's Day shooting, when I first read that a woman named Deborah Cotton had urged mercy and understanding for the two young Black men accused of shooting us, she struck me as a saint. Now, I have come to believe that Deb was also a prophet. The past ten years have overflowed with evidence that race and slavery remain the central, abiding dilemma of the United States— and that Deb was stunningly prescient about the need for Americans to grapple honestly with that dilemma if the nation is ever to escape its grip.

Two months after the Mother's Day shooting, the Black Lives Matter movement sprang to life as killings of unarmed Black people seemed to become a recurring feature of American life. Or, more precisely, as such killings became more widely recognized because, like the Mother's Day shooting, they were captured on video. No cameras were present, however, at arguably the most heinous of these killings. With a symbolism grotesque in its obviousness, the city where the Civil War had begun in 1861 became in 2015 the site of a massacre deliberately intended to spark a race war in the United States. Dylann Roof, an avowed White supremacist, killed nine African Americans at a Bible study class at the Emanuel African Methodist Episcopal Church in Charleston, South Carolina, an iconic gathering place of the modern civil rights movement. When one of Roof's victims, gushing blood, asked why he was shooting them, Roof responded with the same message White supremacists had delivered since the end of the Civil War: "I have to do it. You rape our women, and you are taking over our country. And you have to go."

Eighteen months later, the nation's first Black president was succeeded by Donald Trump, who had risen to political prominence by playing a bizarre variation of the race card—suggesting over and over again, without producing any evidence, that Barack Obama had not been born in the United States. Since the US Constitution requires all presidents to be US-born,

Trump was effectively saying that a Black man was illegally occupying the highest office in the land. Then, in the course of Trump's four years as president, Trump would defend neo-Nazis, demonize people of color, and bring the nation to the brink of civil war by inciting an attack on the US Capitol to try to stay in power after losing the 2020 election.

That an unabashed racist could be elected president of the United States 150 years after the first Civil War was proof positive that the blood of slavery still pulsed through the American body politic. "If we had done the work that we should have done . . . to combat our history of racial inequality, no one could win national office after demonizing people who're Mexican or Muslim," Bryan Stevenson, a civil rights lawyer who established the National Memorial for Peace and Justice to honor America's lynching victims, told the *Guardian* newspaper. "We would be in a place where we would find that unacceptable." Yet as this book went to press in February of 2024, Donald Trump retained the firm allegiance of one-fourth of the US electorate and was the overwhelming front-runner for the Republican 2024 presidential nomination.

Implanted before the very birth of the United States, the twin dilemma of race and slavery sprang from the thundering contradiction between America's lofty ideals—"We hold these truths to be self-evident, that all men are created equal"—and the undeniable reality that White people built the country by enslaving and brutalizing millions of African Americans and slaughtering and stealing land from countless Native Americans. The United States has never resolved this dilemma, despite the rivers of blood shed over it during the Civil War and since. Schoolchildren are taught that the North's victory in the Civil War ended slavery, but that is misleading: slavery did not so much cease as shape-shift. True, to own other human beings was no longer legal. But the formerly enslaved were provided no land or recompense and thus were left with little choice but to keep working, now as sharecroppers or indentured factory workers, for the very people who exploited them before the war. In 1864, as the South's military defeat grew near, a Louisiana plantation owner, William J. Minor, told a fellow Confederate that he hoped the South could rejoin the Union after the war with "things as they were, but perhaps under some other name than slavery"—which is pretty much what happened.

Deborah Cotton believed that until America, especially White America, honestly faces what race and slavery have done and continue to do to this country, America will not be free of its original sin. Like an untended, festering wound, the dilemma will keep bubbling to the surface, manifesting in everything from the blasphemous Mother's Day violence in New Orleans, to the continuing murders of Black people by police and vigilantes, to the threats to democracy posed by Trump and fellow neo-Confederates who openly endorsed waging a second civil war to "make America great again."

Through the particular, one can sometimes glimpse the universal. The Mother's Day shooting, I believe, was one more explosion in the still-unfurling maelstrom that is race in America. For represented in embryonic form in that bloodstained New Orleans intersection were many of the social forces that would convulse the United States during the Obama-Trump era—and that will keep convulsing it until the underlying issues are truly faced and tackled.

Yet the past decade has also shown that many Americans do recognize the legacies of the past and want to make things right. The explosive growth of Black Lives Matter is the obvious example. Demands for justice grew louder throughout Trump's presidency, culminating in the massive protests sparked by the murder of George Floyd by Minneapolis police in May of 2020, when demonstrators took to the streets in all fifty states. The protests were led and populated mainly by Black people, but large numbers of Whites, especially younger Whites, also risked arrest or injury to stand up for justice for Black Americans. Such an outpouring of White support was unprecedented: never in the 155 years since the Civil War's end had large numbers of White Americans put their bodies on the line for Black Americans. (Yes, some Whites did march with civil rights activists in the

1960s, but they were a tiny fraction of the overall White population.) "We have never had so many White allies, willing to stand together for freedom," Harry Belafonte, the singer, activist, and friend of Martin Luther King Jr., wrote on Election Day 2020.

Which side will ultimately prevail in America's long struggle over race and equality is far from clear. Candidate Joe Biden framed the 2020 presidential election as a battle for America's soul, insisting that the American people were better than the nastiness emanating from the White House under Trump. Biden's victory seemed to vindicate his faith in American goodness, but only if one overlooked that the election was a much closer call than news coverage indicated. Biden's seven million vote margin over Trump obscured the fact that the electorate was all but evenly split, with Biden claiming only 3 percent more of the vote than Trump got (51.3 to 48.4 percent). In other words, roughly half of the US electorate thought Trump should remain president for a second term, despite his unapologetic racism and contempt for democracy.

Four years later, as the 2024 election approached, three out of four Republicans still embraced Trump's repeatedly disproven claim that the 2020 election was stolen and its implication that Biden was not the legitimate president. Most Republicans, on Capitol Hill and across the country, also opposed holding Trump accountable for the January 6, 2021, assault on the US Capitol intended to overturn the 2020 election. Trump continued—despite facing four criminal indictments and ninety-one felony charges—to exert absolute control over the Republican base. Militants on the far right were declaring that any attempt to find Trump guilty or send him to prison would spark a new civil war, a prospect they seemed to relish.

In short, the battle for America's soul was far from over.

If the United States does wish to address its twin dilemma of race and slavery, it can find no better place to start than New Orleans. Everything that is needed to cleanse the festering wounds, and to understand why those wounds still need to be cleansed, is here. Older than the nation itself, imprinted with its original sin of slavery but also boasting its most liberating artistic achievement, jazz, New Orleans is living proof that the United States stands in urgent need of racial truth and reconciliation—and that such truth and reconciliation might still be achieved, if more Americans can face uncomfortable truths that have been buried too long.

2

Coming Out the Door

Hanging in the Treme
Watching people sashay
Past my steps
By my porch
In front of my door

—"Treme Song" by John Boutté

Ed Buckner was the president of the Original Big 7 Social Aid and Pleasure Club, which organized the second line parade where the Mother's Day shooting took place. As usual on parade day, Buckner got up at five in the morning to check the weather. The forecast called for a lovely day, beautiful and fair. "They said sunny, no chance of rain," he later told me. "So I lay back down. But the anxiety was working on me, hoping everything would go well that day. So I got back up at seven, checked the weather again. They were still saying sunny, no rain."

Ed Buckner was widely known in the Seventh Ward, thanks to having coached football and basketball for the past twenty-five years at the Willie Hall Playground of the St. Bernard Housing Project. As a kid, he had been a good athlete who gravitated toward leadership positions: quarterback in football, catcher in baseball. Now, at age fifty-four, he was roundish in torso, wore black-framed eyeglasses, and had skin shaded almost as dark as a cast iron skillet. Only when you shook his hand did you realize that he was missing all four fingers on his right hand.

After his second check on the weather, Buckner stepped onto his porch to enjoy the morning quiet. He lived with his wife and children in a squat, tree-shaded house that doubled as the Original Big 7's headquarters; the house fronted on Elysian Fields Avenue, a six-lane thoroughfare that led downtown past the French Quarter to the Mississippi River. The porch looked onto the median strip, a ribbon of land known in New Orleans as the "neutral ground," a reference to olden days, when Canal Street represented a neutral ground between the French settlers who lived downriver and the upriver territory occupied by American newcomers. In the early light of Mother's Day morning, two flowering trees in the middle of the neutral ground radiated a beauty worthy of a street named after the home of Greek gods. "The city had come and mowed the grass like I'd asked, and the oleander bushes were blooming a gorgeous pink," he recalled.

At half past eight, the hamburger and sausage man arrived and began to set up his grill. "He's always the first guy at every second line," Buckner said. "I call him a cultural vendor, because he only vends second lines, he don't vend Mardi Gras. They serve different food at Mardi Gras—popcorn, pizza, candy apples, even Philly cheesesteaks. We don't do that. We have second line food: pork chops, barbecued chicken and ribs, baked chicken, burgers, hot sausage, fried fish, and yacamein—that's a mix of spaghetti, pork, green onions, and broth. Ya don't wanna miss that."

"I was just sitting on my porch, feeling good," Buckner recalled. "Everything looked beautiful and clean. We were all ready to go. It was a beautiful morning. And I still say that today: it was a beautiful morning."

Ed Buckner inherited a love of second lines from his father. From the time Ed was five years old, "My daddy would always bring me with him when he was going to the parade. It was usually him, my uncle Smokey, and my uncle Louis. My dad loved everything about the second line—the Mardi Gras Indians, the kazoo brass bands, he just loved all the culture."

The man Ed referred to as his father, Leonard Johnson, was actually his stepfather; his biological father gave Ed his last name and little else. A country boy from the bayous south of New Orleans, Leonard Johnson moved to the city after returning home from World War II, having served in the Pacific with the US Army. He was an amateur trombonist and a fanatical collector of jazz records: Duke Ellington, Count Basie, Ella Fitzgerald. "I think part of what my daddy loved about second lines was being able to hang out with musicians," Ed said. "He just loved being part of that scene."

The real musician in the family was Ed's Uncle Smokey, one of the most accomplished drummers in New Orleans history. Joseph "Smokey" Johnson spent the 1950s and 1960s playing drums with rock 'n' roll legend and New Orleans native Fats Domino. In 1964, Johnson went to Detroit, where his unusual drum technique was credited as a formative influence on the Motown Sound. Johnson also was a cocomposer of "It Ain't My Fault," a second line standard that was revived, after the 2010 Gulf of Mexico oil spill, by a star-studded pickup band including Mos Def, Trombone Shorty, Lenny Kravitz, and the actor Tim Robbins.

The first second line parade Ed distinctly remembered attending was sponsored by the Money Wasters Social Aid and Pleasure Club, a club Louis Armstrong listed among his favorites back in the day. Ed was seven or eight years old at the time. "They had green and white on, I'll never forget the colors," he recalled. "They had buckets that were like decorations, bowls and castles and three-dimensional stuff, just beautiful, the purity of the art. There was so many people out there with 'em, and the way the people was cheering and dancing and celebrating, you mighta thought they won the lottery. And when you see *them* dancing, *you* start dancing. And you don't even know why. But you second lining now just like them, and that's your culture."

By eleven o'clock on Mother's Day morning, other members of the Original Big 7 were arriving at Ed's house to get ready for the day. A front room bulged with costumes, photos, musical instruments, and club memorabilia in a dizzying array of colors: lime green, sky blue, hot pink, fire engine red, and vivid shades of purple, orange, and silver. A baker's dozen of elaborate headdresses, flanked by matching masks and tunics, hung along two walls, their plumage imparting a gauzy puffiness to the costumes, like swirls of cotton candy. Feathers crowning the rims of the headdresses hinted at the cultural legacy being invoked: Mardi Gras Indians, whose origins can be traced to the era of slavery, when some Native American tribes in Louisiana sheltered runaway slaves. Tacked on a third wall, surrounded by snapshots of club members at past parades, was a poster headlined RED FLAME HUNTERS. It explained that the children's division of the Original Big 7 was led by King Justin "Tugga" Cloud and Queen Tayle "Tutu" Buckner, both fourteen years old; its mission was "to promote and sustain the neighborhood and the cultural heritage of New Orleans through holistic artistic expression."

The musicians showed up closer to the official departure time of 1:00 P.M., hauling their drums and horns up the steps and across the porch into a second front room that served as the ensemble's staging area. As club members fussed with last-minute wardrobe adjustments, the musicians chatted and fingered their instruments. The prudent among them made a final bathroom visit before embarking on the four-hour march up and down the nearby streets.

I made a point of getting there early, excited to experience a second line parade for the second time in my life. I was only spending thirty-six hours in New Orleans on my way back to San Francisco from a speaking engagement in Atlanta. My flight was leaving that afternoon, so I'd only be able to spend an hour at the parade before heading to the airport. I arrived to find hundreds of people gathered in front of a square-framed house at 1825 Elysian Fields Avenue. The crowd, already in a festive mood, spilled across the boulevard onto the neutral ground. The aroma of barbecued meat had me salivating. And then, blasting from inside the house came the buoyant, unmistakable sound of New Orleans horns and drums. The crowd roared its approval.

The kickoff of every second line parade is a process known as "Coming Out The Door." On this day, the first dancers to emerge from the house wore outfits of navy blue and orange. One by one, they burst onto the porch to vigorous applause, each dancer offering a quick preview of the fancy footwork to come. As they descended onto the sidewalk, prancing and preening, the crowd parted before them like the Red Sea before Moses and the Israelites.

The music from inside the house continued, mixing now with ad hoc contributions from the crowd: the eardrum-piercing referees' whistles, the high *thunk-thunk-thunk* of a stick banging an empty bottle. At the end of the dance troupe was an older, distinguished-looking African American gentleman. When he reached the neutral ground, he was helped into a limousine that pulled slowly into the far lane of the boulevard and headed off as the brass band followed.

I started after them until I heard a new roar from the crowd behind me. Now exiting the house was a second group of dancers who were arrayed in pink and white uniforms that carried an especially large number of ribbons, feathers, and other decorations. Peering more closely, I saw that these dancers were children. Ranging in age from six or seven to young teenagers, their expressions alternated between the seriousness they seemed to think maturity required and the joy of celebrating with the grown-ups. As they danced down the front steps and through the crowd, grown-ups whipped out cell phones to snap pictures, squealing with pride and delight.

And still the house rumbled with the thump of drums and enough horns to raze the walls of Jericho. I looked again to the porch. A dancer had climbed onto its ruler-thin railing, where he flashed his feet back and forth like windshield wipers before skipping along the railing as if it were a tightrope. The crowd was going nuts for this guy. He belonged to a final set of dancers who were wearing the most exquisite colors of the day: shirts and trousers of creamy white that were straddled by shoes and hats of tan. Like conquering heroes, the dancers bowed and strutted, whirling and shaking their booties as they descended onto the sidewalk.

Finally, the last of the day's three bands emerged, trombones leading the way, their golden tubes sliding forward and back as the cheeks of the players swelled and emptied like bellows stoking a blast furnace. This was the To Be Continued Brass Band. Following the trombones came the rest of the horns and the percussion section: bass drum, snare drum, cowbell. The musicians looked to be in their twenties and were driving home their opening number with the cheerful panache of confident professionals.

All that, and we'd just gotten started.

Ed Buckner didn't play a musical instrument anymore, but he'd been a star as a kid. Following in his Uncle Smokey's footsteps, he took up the drums in junior high school. "I played the snare, the bass, the timbales, everything," he recalled. "The band at our school was led by Mr. Donald Richardson, and he was a 100 percent disciplinarian. He insisted that we learn how to read music, not just play it. You had to go home, study, and learn that music by heart within one week."

It was excellent training for high school, where Ed was the lead drummer and bandleader at John McDonogh Senior High. Long known for its music program, John McDonogh was a perennial contender in statewide competitions; the training regimen was so demanding that Ed had to give up playing football and baseball. This was in the late 1970s, before guns and crack cocaine flooded the city, a time when marching bands were still the way young people won neighborhood bragging rights and settled conflicts, fighting not with guns or knives but with horns and drum kits. During Ed's last two years at John McDonogh, the band placed second in the statewide competition, while in the competitions among individual instrumentalists, "we had guys coming in first, third, first, fifth—nobody lower than fifth."

Ed's parents were tickled by his musical achievements. His mother's family had lived in Treme for generations, though as a teenager she moved with her grandmother to the St. Bernard Housing Project, where she gave birth to Ed at age eighteen. She worked twenty-seven years for the New Orleans school system, making food for its cafeterias, and never missed a chance to watch Ed perform. "She loved parades," he recalled. "When my band was parading, she used to go three hours early to claim the spot she wanted, right at Canal and Basin Street. She'd be sitting in her lawn chair cheering as we went by every time."

Like many people in New Orleans, Ed Buckner had more than one nickname. To some people, he was "Big Ed." To others, he was "Coach Ed." But in his teenage years, he'd been known as "The Pie Man."

"I been selling pies since I was sixteen years old," he said. He started his business with a friend whose nickname was "Dirty Rice," a reference to a traditional Creole dish made by cooking chicken livers or sausage in a pan with rice, turning the rice brown. "We made little pies, three inches across, and sold them for fifty cents apiece," Ed continued. "Sweet potato was my specialty, but we also made pecan, apple, lemon, and brownies. We had one of those white coolers that roll on four wheels. We'd walk from the St. Bernard project through the Seventh Ward down to Treme, through the Sixth Ward and back to St. Bernard. People'd see me coming and shout, 'Hey, it's the Pie Man!'"

But the young Ed Buckner's life illustrated a rule of thumb often invoked in New Orleans: Don't believe anything you hear, and only half of what you see. On the surface, the teenaged Ed Buckner appeared to be a dedicated, accomplished young man, blessed with entrepreneurial, athletic, and musical talent, leadership abilities, and two devoted parents. Underneath lurked a different story. During the years when he was leading a celebrated high school marching band and running his own small business, Ed Buckner was starting to sell drugs, carry firearms, and make choices that would reduce him to a homeless crack addict and drug dealer whom police would try to imprison for the rest of his life.

"I started selling weed in junior high school," Ed recalled. "I saw that a friend of mine always had money, and he didn't seem to work too hard at it. So I started selling. I had a lot of customers, because I was a leader and people looked up to me."

His parents never knew he sold marijuana. In their eyes, it was bad enough that he smoked it. "Nothing pissed my mother off more than finding out I had been smoking," Ed said. "Lawd, she would get furious. She'd make me run up and down the stairs backward, over and over, and yell at me, 'Bitch, don't you ever smoke weed in my house!'"

Smoking weed was part of Ed's teenage rebellion, his yearning "to be a hippie, at least what I thought was a hippie." Chuckling at the memory, he admitted that he must have made quite a spectacle in mid-1970s New Orleans with his idolization of White rock acts such as Led Zeppelin and Peter Frampton. "I thought *Frampton Comes Alive* was the greatest record ever. I thought the rest of America was cool and my parents were the worst sons of bitches on earth. Of course, I later found out they were the best parents I could have, I just didn't want to listen."

But that realization lay far in the future. First, Ed Buckner had to make lots of mistakes, some of which would nearly kill him.

At age eighteen, tired of his parents' rules, he moved out of their house, determined "to be a man." He found an apartment, paying rent with the proceeds from his marijuana and pie sales. When he was twenty, a friend began snorting cocaine. Ed joined him, and the downward spiral began.

"The more weed I sold, the more money I had," he recalled. "So my friend and I, we started doing coke. Then I had to figure out how to keep it going." He and the friend soon moved from snorting cocaine to freebasing—smoking the highly concentrated, irresistibly entrancing form of coke called crack. The habit quickly became an addiction.

"I went into this period in my twenties when I was in a dead-end spin, just spinning in a circle," he said. He spent days and nights, then more days and nights, in the dull, jumpy haze of the coke addict. For a while, he kept up appearances. He had always loved kids and sports, so he coached football, basketball, and any other sport that needed it, for boys and girls alike. His teams excelled; he won his first citywide football championship when he was twenty-six. But addiction had its fangs in him. He did not show up for practice loaded, never that. But when he wasn't coaching, he was smoking crack, and dealing it to make ends meet.

How did he get away with such a double life?

"I was a sneaky-assed person, Mark. Sneaky! Even when I was loaded, I was still committed to coaching the kids and being there every day. But behind the scenes, I was a drug fiend. My best friends was drug dealers. I would sober up in time to go to practice, but other than that, I was wrapped up in my drugs."

Ed was genuinely devoted to the kids he coached and spent lots of his own money providing for them. "When you coach kids every day, year after year, you have a lasting impact on their lives," he said. "Many of them don't have two parents at home, and they need adult guidance. They also need material things. I was Coach Ed. I put turkey necks on the table when they had nothing to eat. I bought winter coats when they had none. They remember that. Even now, years later, I still have a special relationship with kids I've coached."

The money for the turkey necks and winter coats came from his drug dealing, a form of wealth redistribution Ed thought was only fair. After all, most of his customers were mothers in the Seventh Ward. Although he never sold to the parents of kids he coached, he "felt like some of that drug money should go back to children in the neighborhood who needed it," he said.

As his twenties drew to a close, Ed wanted more in life: a car, a better apartment, nicer clothes. He decided to stop using drugs and get a regular job. He found work as a pressman, operating a machine that stamped labels on burlap bags. The job changed his life forever.

"One day, the machine got stuck," he recalled. "I reached in to drag the bags out, but the burlap got twisted around my hand. When I pulled my hand out of the machine, my fingers were gone. It happened on a Friday. By the next Monday, I was back at football practice with an umbrella to hide my hand from the sun."

At the time of the accident—September 14, 1990—Ed Buckner was three months shy of turning thirty. He was not under the influence of drugs the day of his accident, he insisted, but the trauma of losing his fingers hammered him; he fell back into his old ways with a vengeance. "After I got hurt, I started getting high again," he recalled. "That's what really sent me into my tailspin. From 1990 to 1994 I was using hard, nonstop."

Crack addiction is a heartless, implacable master. Ed knew it was killing him but felt powerless to quit. He lost customers, smoked up all his profits, and committed petty crimes. Perpetually behind on the rent, he got evicted from his apartment.

Ed thought he had hit bottom when he woke up one morning in a hallway in the St. Bernard Housing Project. "A young woman my age, who grew up with me and knew what kind of person I used to be, saw me," he said. "She said, 'Lawd, you sleeping in the hall? You? Unh-uh,' she said. 'Fuck this. I gotta stop getting fucking high.'"

"I'll never forget that morning," Ed continued. "It suddenly hit me: I'm homeless. I got nothing. I'm ashamed to be seen by people I grew up with. I bummed a dollar, got on the bus, and rode as far away from the projects as I could."

The bus took him across town to Jackson Square, the ancient heart of New Orleans and the center of the tourist trade. He didn't know where he was allowed to sit down, and he didn't want to attract police attention, so he walked the streets the whole night and all the next day. He went forty-eight hours without eating until a homeless man taught him how to raid garbage cans for leftover food.

He spent a year and a half homeless. "One weekend, it was getting ready to rain real bad, and I did something I'm still ashamed of to this day," he said. "I started acting crazy so the police would take me to the mental hospital. I said, 'I see people over there, and over there, and they coming to get me.' So they take me to the hospital and I'm sharing a room with this guy. He steps into the bathroom, and I hear him talking about all the different women he's got in there. I take a peek and he's draped toilet paper all over the place, musta been a couple rolls of it, and he's babbling about all these women who aren't there. I run to find a nurse and say, 'This guy in here is crazy, you got to do something.' She look at me and says, 'Get back in there, you crazy too!'"

He laughed when telling the story years later, but there was nothing funny about Ed Buckner's life back then. His older brother got him discharged from the mental hospital, and Ed struggled to find a way back to normalcy. In 1994, he moved into an appallingly dilapidated apartment on North Villere Street that sat half a block away from where the Mother's Day shooting would occur in 2013. The only reason he could afford the place was that it had no front door, no back door, no windows, and no heat.

Ed decided that the only way to get his life back together was to sell drugs again—but this time not to use them, a decision that took immense self-discipline to execute. "Pretty soon, I was making good money," he recalled. "I bought a car and everything." He stayed sober and was diligent about business practices. "I kept changing all the locks on my doors. I made all my sales between five o'clock and ten o'clock in the morning, and I made enough money that nobody had to see me the rest of the day. I wasn't going to slip up or get myself shot."

His neighbors suspected he was dealing, but he spread money around to preempt any complaints. "I would buy gifts on Christmas and other special days to show that I appreciated them taking my BS when people came around there to buy drugs. I would take care of light bills, water bills."

Drug dealing in the Seventh Ward was not for the meek. Police were one risk, robbery another. Junkies tend to be desperate individuals who will trade information in return for a fix or a price break. Word could easily get around that the dude on North Villere was holding lots of coke and probably cash, too.

Ed had owned a sawed-off shotgun and a .357 Magnum pistol since high school, and he had taken lessons in how to shoot them. He didn't look for trouble, but he protected himself and his business. Years later, after the Mother's Day shooting, he expressed contempt for the young man seen on video spraying bullets into the crowd. It was not just the wounding of innocent people that outraged Ed; it was the shooter's violation of the unwritten code of the street.

"If you got a beef with someone, you don't settle it at a second line," Ed sputtered. "If I was coming for you, I'd be coming in the dark, when you were alone. I'd show respect for your family, respect for the neighborhood."

"Have you ever shot someone, Ed?" I asked.

He paused, tilted his head away, and said, "I've pulled my gun out, back in the day."

"Pulling a gun out is one thing," I observed. "Did you ever shoot someone with it?"

Again Ed paused, longer this time. "I'm not going to say," he said. "I pulled my gun out, yes, I did."

Then, one day, Ed Buckner's world came crashing down around him, as he knew one day it might. "The police came in my house," he recalled. "I was lying in bed. I got caught with all the dope and all the money. I was facing sixty years in prison. I was thirty-five years old, so sixty years was basically a life sentence. Luckily, I had some money saved because I knew that that day could come. I hired a good lawyer, and he saved my life."

Ed's lawyer pointed out that the 400 grams of cocaine the police claimed to have recovered at his apartment did not match the amount of cocaine referenced in the lab report presented at trial. Furthermore, the police had done a search and seizure on Ed's apartment only after raiding first one and then another house down the street. The lawyer argued that raiding one house after another undercut the police's claim to have "probable cause" to raid the house belonging to Ed Buckner, as was required by law.

The judge pronounced Ed guilty but imposed a dramatically reduced sentence. Instead of sixty years, Ed Buckner was sentenced to an indeterminate period of "intensive probation." He was required to report to a probation facility at 6:00 P.M. every day and stay there overnight. He was required to hold a job, avoid drugs, and commit no further crimes.

Ed did not have to be told twice; coming within a hair of spending the rest of his life behind bars was enough to make him change his ways. "I changed my life," he said. "I did so well that when the judge reviewed my progress after a year of intensive probation, he excused me from the rest of the probation and set me free. That was in 1997, and I haven't smoked or sold a thing since."

Second line parades helped Ed Buckner return to the straight and narrow and stay there. Dirty Rice, his former partner in the pie business, was one of the cofounders of a Social Aid and Pleasure Club, and he remembered that Ed used to love second lining when he was younger. Now, like a deacon inviting a wayward Christian back to church, Dirty Rice asked Ed if he wanted to get involved with second lines again.

The club Dirty Rice cofounded would later be called "The Original Big 7," but when Ed joined it in 1997 the club was still known by its original name, "7 On The Other Side." It was one of the more obscure names among the city's Social Aid and Pleasure Clubs, which is saying something. The 7 of course hinted at hailing from the Seventh Ward, but what did "On The Other Side" mean—the other side of what?

"I have no *idea* what that meant," Ed later said, laughing. "All I know is that we changed it a few years later to Original Big 7."

With his entrepreneurial skill and organizational experience, Ed soon became the club's business manager. As the official responsible for organizing the club's parades, he would go to City Hall, apply for the necessary permits, and talk with the police and public works department to make sure the parade route did not conflict with construction work or other activities. He also hired the brass bands and handled arrangements with the food and drink vendors. It was work Ed performed so well that he was elected president of the club just before Hurricane Katrina struck on August 29, 2005.

Katrina affected every aspect of life in New Orleans; second lines were no exception. Before the storm, 95 percent of the participants at second line parades were Black and 5 percent White, Ed later estimated. That began to shift a year or two before Katrina, he added, "but it was after the storm when the number of White people at second lines skyrocketed."

The change reflected a larger demographic transition roiling the city. Many Black residents, especially poor and working-class Blacks, did not return to New Orleans after the storm. In many cases, the buildings where they had lived were destroyed or plagued by so much mold and other flood damage as to be uninhabitable. Jobs also disappeared as businesses collapsed. Private insurance payments and government assistance arrived late or not at all. Meanwhile, young White people began pouring into New Orleans from out of town, often for humanitarian purposes; much of the refurbishing of water-damaged buildings after Katrina was undertaken by visiting students and church volunteers. Some of these young people decided to stay, or to return to New Orleans after graduation, drawn by a desire to keep contributing to the city's recovery, to take advantage of the affordable (to them) rents, and to enjoy the endless great music and good times.

More than a few Black locals resented the influx of young Whites and the Whole Foods outlets and yoga studios that sprang up in their wake, but not Ed Buckner. "At one time, White people weren't really welcome at second lines, but after Katrina they became part of protecting our culture," he said. Within two years after Katrina, the proportion of Whites participating in second lines rose from 5 to 35 percent of the crowd, he estimated. "And they not there as motherfucking tourists," he added. "They really parading as locals. That's the way it should be. Just like sports can bring people together, music can bring people together who normally wouldn't be together."

The coach and mentor in Ed did not hesitate to set White people straight when some of them ventured that maybe they shouldn't be attending second lines: after all the grief that Black people had suffered at the hands of White people, these Whites told Ed, perhaps taking part in this iconic African American ritual was an assertion of White privilege they should avoid. Ed didn't agree. "Sometimes my White friends get a little sensitive about this," he said. "But I tell 'em, 'You can't be blamed for what your forefathers did. And you're *not* them, or you wouldn't be hanging out with us.'"

"The White folks moving into these neighborhoods are not their mammas and daddies," Ed added. "They a *force*, and Black people can have them as allies. The young White people I know remind you that not *all* White people are fucked up, just like not all Black people are fucked up. Truth is, most White people and most Black people are *not* fucked up. If we can get people on both sides together, I really think we could get past this racism thing."

As I told Ed, I had my own moments of White doubt while writing this book. As woke consciousness spread through liberal and left-wing circles in the United States, I heard more than once that a White author had no business writing about a politically engaged Black woman or a racially fraught episode like the Mother's Day shooting. How could a White author understand, much less faithfully represent, the feelings, thoughts, and actions of Deborah Cotton and other Black people involved in that shooting, this critique demanded to know. And how dare a White author draw upon this intensely Black story to express his own thoughts about race in America?

I sympathized with much of this critique—I'd expressed variations of it for years in my own writings. I knew full well that because of my white skin, I had benefited from systemic racism all my life. And the larger historical record was unambiguous: Black people had watched for decades as White writers (and White musicians, directors, actors, scholars, and more) got most of the work in their respective fields. Especially galling were instances when White people were employed to tell Black people's stories—as if Black people couldn't tell them perfectly well themselves. Now, here I was, yet another White writer doing exactly that.

Because I took this objection seriously, I checked in about it with various other Black friends and colleagues, in New Orleans and elsewhere, imploring them to be absolutely candid. All of them offered nothing but support, none more so than my friend Giletti.

Giletti lived in San Francisco, drove a cab for a living, used to be a nightclub singer, and had a sly sense of humor. We shared a love of baseball—when he was a kid, he once met Willie Mays and watched as, to his horror, Mays cheated at pool—and we often talked politics. During one of the times when I was trying not to write this book because I felt that the climate story demanded my full attention, Giletti wouldn't hear of it. Like Deb, he firmly believed that fate had chosen me for the job. The idea that my Whiteness disqualified me he thought was silly.

"You were there when it happened, Mark, and you wouldn't have been there if you were racist," Giletti told me. "You've written books all your life. Think about that—a professional writer just happens to be right there at the exact moment the shooting starts. You even got shot yourself. Think about the odds of *that*! You think that's all just a coincidence? Naw, man, you got to write that book."

Deb, as mentioned earlier, actually saw an advantage in having a White writer tell this story: as she said, "White people listen to other White people more than they listen to Black people." Deb's reasoning was echoed by a quote I came across later from Alexandria Ocasio-Cortez, the young Latina activist who shocked the political establishment in 2018 by defeating a veteran middle-of-the-road Democrat for a seat in the US House of Representatives. Sometimes, Ocasio-Cortez said, even well-meaning White people "don't like to talk about race and they say, 'We just want to center the person who's most impacted, so it's not my role to do anything or take a space and speak up.' But we know," Ocasio-Cortez continued, "that when White folks take up space and say the right thing in rooms of other White people, that is the most shifting activity that can happen, more sometimes than any protest."

Everyone who was living in New Orleans during Hurricane Katrina has their own stories about the storm, but not many could say, like Ed Buckner could, that their Katrina story included a Hollywood-style love story. After a few years of dating, Ed and his wife had gotten married the day before the storm. They were still living separately—Ed at his place on North Villere, his wife in the St. Bernard Housing Project, where Ed had grown up. As TV reports warned that the hurricane swirling toward New Orleans was a megastorm, Ed and his wife decided that she and their four children should shelter at St. Bernard. Constructed of steel and brick, the St. Bernard apartments seemed to be safer than Ed's wooden house. But that turned out to be a mistake.

"They weren't that far from the Lakeview and London Avenue canal breaks, so they were under eleven feet of water," Ed recalled. "The whole first floor of the apartment complex was underwater. It was a good thing my wife had a second-floor apartment. They swam down to the courtyard and made their way to my mother's apartment on the third floor, where I lived as a child."

Ed was at his place on North Villere with his best friend of forty years, Melvin Bush. "We started trying to get to St. Bernard project, because we got a radio report that that area was underwater, and we were going to rescue them. But the National Guard had already rescued them by helicopter and taken them to Shreveport [Louisiana's third largest city, located near the Texas border]. So we headed for the Superdome, walking through water that was up to our chests. Sometimes the water got so deep we had to swim. When it got dark, we had to stop and stay overnight in an old YMCA building until morning came. Once we got to the Superdome, we got on the first bus we could, which was going to Houston."

"Melvin was texting and texting, and finally he got a text from my wife saying they were in Shreveport. He told them we was in Houston, where my sister lived. I had a bath, got cleaned up with fresh clothes, and caught a bus for Shreveport. I got there at 9:20 P.M. I knew they were in a certain apartment complex, but taxi drivers didn't want to take me there because it was ghetto. Finally, I found one who would take me for double the fare."

"I didn't know which apartment my family was in, so I'm walking around each courtyard in the complex, shouting my children's names. All of a sudden someone heard my voice, and that was them. That was a romantic, exhilarating feeling, all the things that make a love story."

The reunited family eventually returned to New Orleans and settled into what Ed and his wife described as "our dream house" on Elysian Fields Avenue, the same house from which the Mother's Day second line would depart. Life was looking up. Ed mentored disadvantaged young people, both as a coach at the St. Bernard rec center and through the youth program of the Original Big 7. His children were in school, with the eldest, a boy named Brandon, serving as what Ed called "the blueprint" for how he could help the younger kids find their ways in life. Ed had always favored "sixteen, not twelve, years of schooling" for kids—meaning, graduating from college, not just high school. Brandon attended Southern University in New Orleans, a historically Black school located a ten-minute drive away, near Lake Pontchartrain, where he majored in computer engineering. After years when Ed's drug dealing and addiction had absented him from Brandon's life, he and his son were now close; on his birthday, Brandon said he didn't need presents, he was just glad to have his father back in his life, loving and taking care of him.

And then, one night in 2008, the unspeakable struck. Brandon had gone clubbing with some friends. Ed and his wife went to bed. In the middle of the night, they were awakened by the phone call that is every parent's nightmare. The epidemic of young Black men killing one another that Deb Cotton lamented had now claimed Ed's son Brandon.

"That's the most frightening phone call you can get, that call at three or four o'clock in the morning," Ed told me. "To hear that your child got shot and is lying there dead—it brings out a scream. I can remember the scream, everybody in the house can remember it. The next scream, I'm trying to muffle it, because I don't want to wake up the other kids and let them know something is wrong, so I ran out the door before I screamed again."

"This city has a type of magnet that takes young men and pulls them out of the better things they do and kills 'em," Ed continued. "You don't have to be involved selling drugs, shooting people, none of them things. You can become a victim of the violence just because of the company you keep. There are some clubs that should be rated K for Killer. The club my son got killed at, he wasn't the first kid killed there. There'd been at least fifteen other killings."

How to carry on in the wake of such a devastating tragedy?

"I thank God that I'm spiritually strong," Ed said. "I have a great forgiving heart. I said at the funeral, 'I know my son would want me to go out and kill that young man [who shot him], but I can't do that.' And then three weeks later, that young man was dead. I didn't wish that on that kid, even though he killed my boy. I wished that he could somehow repent in his heart, go to jail, serve his time, and be a testimony to others—don't judge somebody you don't know just because he hanging with people you don't like."

The pain and grief of losing a child never fully disappears. For a while, Ed doubted all that he'd been doing with his life since quitting drugs: "Here I was trying to save all these kids with coaching and second lining, and I can't save my own boy?" Eventually, Ed returned to something like himself, compelled by his responsibilities to his other children and his memories of Brandon. "You still got to raise the other kids, get them to school, put food on the table, there's always something," he said. "You got to get back out there. And I still think about my son every day."

The 2013 Mother's Day second line departed behind schedule, but not egregiously so by New Orleans standards. By 1:15, all three bands and dance troupes were ambling down Elysian Fields Avenue in the direction of the Mississippi River. The procession extended over a space of two to three blocks; the crowd had swelled to about four hundred people. It was a warm but not oppressively hot day, with the sun occasionally obscured by puffy, gray-tipped clouds.

After waiting for the last band to exit the house, I jogged ahead to check out the band that headed the parade. The crowd spread across all three lanes of the boulevard; additional revelers spilled onto the sidewalk and neutral ground. The sidewalk had the advantage of shade; that section of Elysian Fields was graced by a row of massive live oaks. Drawn by the explosion of sound and color, people in the houses we passed stepped onto their porches to watch, cheer, and wave at friends they spotted in the crowd.

Second line parades offer the most authentic musical experience to be found in New Orleans. That's partly because the brass band music played at second lines is the oldest in the city; it's also because second line music is inseparable from dancing, and dancing is the point of New Orleans music. "Certain identifiable qualities set New Orleans music apart . . . [including] an indifference to anything that isn't danceable, a rhythmic displacement that goes back to the history of second lines," writes scholar Jack Sullivan in *New Orleans Remix.*

Second line enthusiasts talk about "being deep in the spirit," especially when they're dancing. There are many different kinds of second line dancing, but the basic approach includes a series of skips and crossover steps that move the dancer forward, occasionally backward, and sometimes in circles. Some of the more intrepid dancers will scale phone poles or rooftops to whirl and twirl, their bodies silhouetted against the sky and sparking applause from the crowd below. And the collective forward motion is vigorous: the pace of a second line is such that the spectator-participants must step smartly or get left behind.

Despite the atmosphere—plenty of beer, liquor, weed, and flirting—a second line parade is no mere exercise in hedonism. "Second lines is like church," Ed said, voicing a view common among Black New Orleanians I came to know. "It's a cultural experience, but it's also a spiritual experience where individuals come together as a community." It is also quite family oriented. Like Ed, many attendees have been second lining since they were kids and now bring their own children to the party.

Second lines bring together, in one incandescent bundle, many of the enchantments that make New Orleans at its best one of the most magical places on earth: incomparable music, delicious food, fine weather, fun-loving people. And no one observing the spectacle can doubt the participants' determination or spirit. This is the beating heart of Black culture in the oldest African American community in North America—a celebration of identity and community that these people, like generations of their ancestors before them, have been practicing on Sunday afternoons for nearly 300 years.

The music and dancing at the front of the Mother's Day second line were exhilarating, but I wanted to give the last set of dancers and musicians one more listen. Walking against the flow of the crowd to the rear of the parade, I observed that the vast majority of participants were Black people clearly having a fine time. There were parents with little kids, teenagers checking cell phones and smoking weed, old friends reconnecting with shouts and teasing. Vendors pulled wheeled coolers through the crowd, calling out in a melodic singsong, "Water one dollar! Water one dollar!"

The band at the back was hitting its stride now, with music that seemed to shoot in all directions at once yet remain focused and bright. The volume of sound was immense, like a sonic boom passing through your body. Just as I decided that this was the band that I wanted to accompany for my few remaining minutes at the parade, I spied the dancer whose windshield wiper moves on the porch I'd noticed earlier. Now that he was closer, I was astonished to see that he was White—the only White I saw among the dancers and band members that day.

Even more astonishing, his face looked familiar. New Orleans, it's said, is a small town masquerading as a big city. I looked again and saw the guy exchange a few words with a woman pushing a toddler in a stroller. The toddler had blond hair, and that's when the penny dropped. I was pretty sure that I had met this guy, with his wife and toddler, a few months ago during a reporting trip to New Orleans. He ran Grow Dat, an urban gardening program that taught adolescents from difficult backgrounds how to grow food and acquire organizational skills that might lead to a better future.

Before I could go say hello, the band burst into the '90s pop song "I Wanna Dance with Somebody." The opening notes seemed to blast a bolt of happy juice through this guy's body. A smile of astonished delight erupted across his face. He leaped into the air like an acrobat, twirled away from his wife and toddler, and began to shimmy down the boulevard. I couldn't remember his name from our interview, but in that moment, I privately nicknamed him Flash Dance.

Leaving the majestic oaks of Elysian Fields Avenue behind, the parade now made a ninety degree turn onto a narrow, treeless one-way street. Black letters on the street sign's white background spelled N. VILLERE.

I figured I could listen to one last song and give a quick hello to Flash Dance before I headed to the airport. I drifted along with the crowd as the band was annihilating "I Wanna Dance with Somebody." I stopped at the first cross street to wait for Flash Dance. As the parade turned onto this narrow side street, the tighter quarters forced the crowd closer together. I stepped off the sidewalk and took a few steps toward the far side of the intersection. As I looked back the way we had come, I saw waving against the sky a rectangular banner of royal blue with ORIGINAL BIG 7 written on it in white. Behind the banner, the top of a tuba bobbed slowly in this direction.

Our section of the parade seemed to be stopping, though. A dark-skinned man dressed in white from head to toe was standing in the middle of the intersection. He wagged his palms up and down, motioning for the band to halt. The musicians, fresh from their triumph on "I Wanna Dance with Somebody," paused on the cusp of entering the intersection. Their instruments fell silent as they awaited instructions from the Black man in angelic white.

"I wanted the little old ladies who lived up and down that block to enjoy some beautiful music on Mother's Day," Ed Buckner later said, explaining why he had the parade pause at that intersection. It was an intersection he knew very well, for he was standing a dozen steps from the house on North Villere Street where he had resided for many years, where he had been a methodical, successful crack dealer, had occasionally pulled out his gun "back in the day," and got busted "with all the dope and all the money" before barely evading life in prison. Thanks in no small part to the spirit of second line parades, that was the life Ed Buckner had left behind a decade ago. Or so he thought.

3

Becoming Deborah "Big Red" Cotton

In New Orleans, at any given moment, life and death change places with each other when you least expect it. . . . You never know what's waiting around the corner that will either thrill you—or level you to the ground.

—Deborah Cotton in her book
Notes from New Orleans

That Mother's Day morning, Deborah Cotton heard an inner voice whisper that maybe she shouldn't go to the second line that Sunday. But inner voices are easy to dismiss, and Deb felt a duty to be there. Covering second line parades was her job, and not long ago, they had saved her life.

Second line parades were not only Deb's journalistic beat; they were her calling. She loved covering them, loved being a part of them, loved documenting them. Deb was proud to be a good time girl, and second lines were usually nothing if not a good time. She once wrote, "Second line parades is like church, like summer vacay, like that first kiss with that first love, like all your favorite grandmomma's dishes on one plate, like your first day of school outfit, like hearing Jill Scott or John Coltrane for the first time . . ."

By Mother's Day 2013, Deborah Cotton's blog for *Gambit* had become a central information repository for all things second line in New Orleans. In a city where hedonism was a shared civic value as well as a lucrative tourist draw, her work was helping to bring the culture of second lining broader attention than it had received in a long time. And as much as she loved fun, Deb was also drawn to second lines for deeper reasons that she felt needed to be celebrated and safeguarded. "As a Black person in the United States, I am conscious of the limitations put upon us because of how we came here, and the White dominant culture not always appreciating or respecting our culture," she once said. "So the fact that we have the opportunity and the right to take over the streets every weekend is phenomenal, with the music and the camaraderie and all the beautiful transactions that happen between people at a second line."

The history and traditions of second line parades connected Deb back through time to the days of Louis Armstrong and beyond—back to the trials of Reconstruction, further back to the brutalities of slavery, and still further back to the cultural and spiritual teachings of her ancient African ancestors.

It was the excitement and spectacle of second line parades that had first enticed a young Armstrong to the possibilities of playing a horn and pleasing a crowd. Most of the second line parades where he performed as an adolescent were funerals. He and the other musicians would trail a casket carried by friends and family members of the deceased as they proceeded to the cemetery. Throughout the journey, the band played dirges—slow, mournful music. But as soon as the body was lowered into the ground and the preacher delivered the final benediction, the musicians flipped the mood, dispensing boisterous, joyful dance music to celebrate not only the departed's release to eternity but the continuing miracle of life for everyone still on earth.

"The band would strike up one of those good old tunes like 'Didn't He Ramble,'" an adult Armstrong recalled, "and all the people would leave their worries behind. Once the band starts, everybody starts swaying from one side of the street to the other, especially those who drop in and follow the [people] who have been to the funeral. These people are known as 'the second line' and they may be anyone passing along the street who wants to hear the music. The spirit hits them, and they follow along to see what's happening."

Even today, most Black people in New Orleans seem to have a nickname—as a boy, Armstrong's was Dipper—and Deb's nickname was Big Red. The name referenced her skin tone, the color of a freshly minted penny, a shade sometimes known in her community as red. Big Red also fit her physique, for Deb was no dainty size four but rather, as she put it, "a comfortably thick sistah." She was favored with a strikingly pretty face, high cheekbones, sparkling eyes, and a wide, easy smile. But her proportions below the neck worked against her during her years of living in Los Angeles.

"You gotta be built like a twig out there for men to want you, have a body like a twelve-year-old Asian boy with plastic tits," she recalled. "I had like two dates in five years. In New Orleans, I'm on the menu 24-7. As soon as I moved here, I couldn't walk out my front door without men hollering at me. Black men here, they love themselves some heavy women."

The Hot 8, one of New Orleans's top brass bands, had a song that shouted the point. One weekend, driving with me in her Jeep Cherokee to a second line parade, Deb cranked up the volume so loud that grinning passengers in the next car over started nodding to the beat. The tune's giddy tempo complemented the bawdy lyric:

> *Big girl, back it up!*
> *Like a U-Haul truck*
> *Back it up and dump it!*
> *Like a U-Haul truck*

"That song cracks me up," she said, her face creasing with laughter. "And those Hot 8 brothers walk the talk. Every one of the guys in that band has a wife or a girlfriend who's a big woman."

Deb had a fairytale childhood but not in a good way. She grew up with a proverbial evil stepmother, a woman who allegedly beat her almost daily. But there was a twist: this evil stepmother was a secret stepmother. From as young an age as she could remember, little Debbie was told by her father and his wife, Sandra, that Sandra was her mother, the woman who gave birth to her in Los Angeles on January 23, 1965. That was a lie. Deborah Dione Cotton was indeed born in Los Angeles on that date, but her biological mother was a different woman, a White woman who also happened to be Jewish.

Not until Debbie reached the age of twelve did she begin to learn the truth. The woman she had called Mama for as long as she could remember, the woman who was married to her father, the woman who allegedly beat her daily, was actually her stepmother. Her father had stolen—"kidnapped" was the word Deb used years later when telling the story—Debbie from her biological mother when Debbie was a toddler.

Deb's father, Hayes Cotton, was a civil engineer who had been born and raised in Mexia, Texas, a tiny town sixty miles south of Dallas. Hayes's father was a high school principal, and Hayes got good enough grades to attend Prairie View A&M, a historically Black college in the north of the state. After graduation, he moved to southern California to work in the aerospace industry, which was growing exponentially in the emerging era of jet travel and space exploration. "This was in the early 1960s, and he was in the first wave of Black engineers who worked in the aerospace industry," Deb later recalled. "Those guys had quite a life. He was well-paid, good-looking, partying all the time, dating White girls. He met my mom, they got together, and they had me."

Exactly why her father took baby Debbie away from her mother—and then deceived Debbie about it for years—cannot be definitively known at this point; Hayes Cotton died before he could be interviewed for this book. But a clue exists in the marriage records of the state of Texas, which note that Hayes Cotton married Sandra Lewan Coleman on August 18, 1966, in Limestone County, the county where Hayes had been born and raised. Thus the wedding took place when Debbie was eighteen months old—and still living in Los Angeles, where Hayes Cotton and Debbie's biological mother, Carolee Reed, had been cooperating to raise their daughter. "Hayes and I separated in early 1966," Reed later recalled. "I knew he got remarried because he brought Sandra to Los Angeles with him later that year, and I would see her when I picked up Debbie or dropped her off at their place."

But sometime in 1968—Reed said she could not remember the precise date because the memory was too painful—Hayes Cotton unilaterally decided to alter the arrangement. Without a word of warning, he and his new wife abruptly left town, taking little Debbie with them.

"One day, I went to pick Debbie up for a visit, and they weren't there," Reed said. "I had no idea where they'd gone. All I had was Hayes's mother's phone number. I called, but she wouldn't help. And that was it for the next sixteen years. My daughter was gone, I had no idea where. I thought I'd never see her again."

Deb's father and his new wife had taken Debbie back to Texas. They settled near Fort Worth, where Hayes helped design the Dallas/Fort Worth International Airport. A few years later, they moved to Oklahoma City, where he worked for the Federal Aviation Administration, teaching courses on airport planning.

Hayes and Sandra consistently told Debbie that Sandra was her mother, but the little girl had questions. "I couldn't understand why there were no pictures of her with me when I was a baby," Deb said. "She'd say the pictures must have gotten lost when we moved houses. That didn't make sense to me."

Harder to understand was why her mother always seemed so angry at Debbie, and why she expressed that anger so violently.

"Do you know that movie, *Mommie Dearest*?" Deb asked. "That was my life with my stepmother. If anything went wrong around the house, she'd beat me. If there was a scratch on the furniture, if a thread was missing from her blouse, or anything was out of place, she would beat me for it. I'd say, 'I didn't do it.' And she'd beat me some more. So I thought, 'Maybe if I say I did it, the beatings will stop.' But they didn't stop, not until Daddy finally got his head out of his ass and divorced her. That was when I was twelve."

It was after the divorce that Debbie began learning the truth. The first revelation came when she and her father were in Mexia visiting relatives. His mother and his aunt lived across the street from one another; grown children and cousins lived nearby. Debbie spent holidays and long stretches of summer vacation in Mexia and grew especially close to her "sister-cousin," Le'Trese, who was two years younger. During one visit, a casual question from Hayes's sister Irma let the proverbial cat out of the bag.

"Irma was a straight shooter who would tell you the truth," Le'Trese recalled. "One day she asked Debbie, 'Are you ever in touch with your mom?' Debbie thought she was asking about Sandra, and she said no, she wasn't. Irma said, 'No, not Sandra, your real mom.' Debbie said, 'What real mom?' Irma said, 'Oh. Uh, you better ask your grandma.'"

Debbie marched across the yard, flung open the front door, and found her grandmother standing at the kitchen sink.

"Why didn't you tell me about my real mother?" Debbie angrily demanded.

The question struck the old lady like a physical blow. Grabbing the sink with both hands to keep from falling, she wailed, "I told Hayes to tell you. I told him."

"Suddenly all the pieces in the puzzle fit," the adult Deb told me. "That's why my mother could never show me pictures of her with me as a baby. Because she wasn't my real mother."

Only years later, after reaching adulthood and undergoing lots of psycho-therapy, did Deb surmise the rest of the mystery of her secret stepmother.

"When my dad kidnapped me and took me to Texas, he knew he couldn't raise me on his own," she said. "He had to work. So, he found his college sweetheart again. But I think she always resented my father for leaving her behind in Texas and marrying another woman out in California. I was living proof of that woman, so she took it out on me."

Young Debbie naturally wanted to know all she could about her real mother, but her father resisted. At first, he said her real mother was Polynesian—supposedly that was why Debbie had straight hair—and he had no idea how to find her all these years later. But such implausible explanations wore thin, and as Debbie grew older, she became increasingly determined to find her mother. She insisted that her father answer her questions. Eventually he admitted that her mother was White, her name was Carolee, he met her while working in California after college, and they split up when Debbie was a baby. He continued to maintain that he had no idea how to contact her.

When Debbie turned eighteen and could legally do as she pleased, she told her father she was going to Los Angeles to look for her mother, whether he liked it or not. Her father tried to stop her, literally standing in the driveway to block her car from leaving, but Deb went anyway. In Los Angeles, she lived temporarily with an older friend of her father's named Carol Ann, who offered to help. Their only clues were Deb's mother's first name and the fact that she was Jewish. Carol Ann talked to a Jewish woman at her job. A man at that woman's synagogue contacted other synagogues in the area, asking if anyone knew a woman named Carolee. When a possible match was found, Carol Ann invited the woman named Carolee to come for a visit.

Sixteen years had passed since a three-year-old Deborah Cotton and her mother had last seen one another, but the physical resemblance was so strong that each knew instantly that they shared blood.

"As I sat there doing my makeup and getting ready, I saw in the mirror's reflection my mother coming in the front door, and her face looked like mine," Deb said years later. "I remembered a woman from when I was little who had long hair like my mom's, but my father told me she was a babysitter. Then when we talked, her voice was like mine, too."

"When she first saw me, Deborah had a look of wonderment on her face," her mother recalled. "She had just come from the gym and was wearing tights, leg warmers, and LA Gear shoes, very eighties. I started laughing and crying at the same time. Carol Ann put a bottle of wine and two glasses on the table and went out for a few hours so that Deborah and I could talk."

Reconnecting with her mother was a transformative experience for Deb Cotton on many levels, and it came at a stage of life—the late teens—when individuals often are seeking their path in life. Deb's deceit-laden childhood made that search especially challenging; she had been wronged in such an intimate way from such a young age. After living with both of her parents the first three years of her life, a period when the foundations of emotional health are formed, she was suddenly ripped away from her mother. That act of emotional violence was then made all the more unsettling by the lies her father told to cover it up. Violence of the physical variety followed as her stepmother routinely beat little Debbie for offenses she did not commit.

Some victims respond to injustice by inflicting it on others; Deb chose a different path. She got counseling, pursued spiritual growth, and came to sympathize with others who faced injustice. "One of the first things I did when I got to Los Angeles was to find a therapist," she said later. "I knew that otherwise I'd never be a healthy adult. I've been in therapy ever since."

Deb also explored the Jewish side of her identity. Her mother was not an Orthodox Jew or even terribly observant. But for Deb, who had been raised in a family of socially conservative Christians, Judaism offered an intriguing new perspective on life's mysteries. She embarked on a spiritual journey—attending synagogue and seders, reading Jewish texts and discussing them with rabbis—that became a permanent part of her life.

Years later, Deb credited her devotion to social justice partly to the Jewish teachings she absorbed after reconnecting with her mother. "There's a Hebrew phrase that I find compelling," she told me. "*Tikkun Olam*. It means, heal the world. Judaism teaches that part of our task as human beings who've been given the gift of life is to heal the world around us, and especially to help the disadvantaged. As a Jew, it is not incumbent upon you to complete the task. But it is incumbent upon you to do your part."

Deborah Cotton loved New Orleans before ever setting foot there, and she never stopped loving it, even after she was shot. As a child she had fantasized about the place; its name alone seemed exotic. Growing up next door in Texas, she repeatedly pleaded with her parents to take her there; they refused. Not until reaching her twenties did she finally visit New Orleans. It was love at first sight.

"I felt like I was being pulled into a dream, so very surreal and familiar, like a memory from another time long ago," she later wrote. "The above ground cemetery tombs, the hot juicy air, the low hanging Spanish moss, the lantern-lit streets, the colorful vintage Creole cottages, the sounds of brass horns, the smell of hot sauce, chicory, and jasmine . . . I knew on that day that I had found 'home.'"

She began visiting New Orleans every year or so, taking respite from her life in Los Angeles, where she worked by turns as a martial arts instructor, a union organizer, and a political consultant. As her twenties gave way to her thirties and her thirties began to accumulate, she was not meeting the man of her dreams and wondered if she'd have better luck back in the South. In California, she fumed, "men jump through doors first, leaving women in their dust, expect you to call and ask *them* for dates, and raise the roof to songs about hoes, bitches, and tricks." Meanwhile, each visit to New Orleans strengthened her affection for the place. In June of 2005, on the cusp of turning forty, she moved there, planning to reinvent herself as a culinary student and freelance writer.

Little did she know that she was arriving three months before Hurricane Katrina would roar out of the Gulf of Mexico and leave New Orleans in ruins. Deb evacuated before the full fury of the storm hit, paying a cab driver three hundred dollars to drive her twelve hours to Houston. From there, she watched in horror as shrieking winds and gigantic waves conspired with shoddy levees to put 80 percent of New Orleans underwater. At least fifteen hundred people died; tens of thousands were displaced; thousands of homes and businesses were destroyed; economic damage was estimated at $200 billion.

Although all parts of New Orleans were damaged, the suffering was most acute among the city's poor, most of whom were African American. Often lacking cars to evacuate, many poor Black people converged on the Superdome and the Convention Center downtown, hoping for shelter and assistance. But government aid was extremely slow in coming. Television viewers the world over saw long lines of poor Black people stretching along the sidewalks, many in obvious distress. One young man cradling a newborn baby demanded of one reporter, "How is a three-week-old baby supposed to survive out here with no milk, no water?"

"Hurricane Katrina laid bare . . . the deep vulnerability of poor Black communities and [made] it painfully clear that race remained a decisive factor in American life," Henry Louis Gates Jr. said in his documentary, *And Still I Rise*. Ava DuVernay, director of the films *Selma* and *13th*, added that the government's "horrific" failure to assist Katrina's victims "revealed the great divide that we know is there and we don't talk about. But for anyone to say it wasn't disregard based on race and class is to be disingenuous about what we all saw."

Deb never wavered in her determination to return to her new hometown. "It is my belief that you don't choose New Orleans—New Orleans chooses you," she wrote of her decision. "Those who have fallen for her . . . know exactly what I mean. Ain't no amount of wind, water, gunfire, potholes, 'ignant' politics, or doomsday predictions can pry your death grip from her. Come hell or high water, you stay—or return."

Once the floodwaters were pumped out and authorities began allowing residents inside the city again, Deb made her way back to post-Katrina New

Orleans. Years before she and I met, I covered the aftermath of Hurricane Katrina as part of my reporting on climate change. The scenery in mile after mile of the city was depressingly consistent: smashed houses with buckled roofs, cars flipped over backward or crushed by fallen trees, mountains of trash and debris awaiting collection, military trucks on patrol. A closer look revealed which houses had been searched: the front wall had a spray-painted circle crisscrossed into four quadrants that listed the number of corpses, which agency conducted the search, and on which date.

Deb resolved to use her talents as a writer and activist to help New Orleans pull itself back together. She began blogging for a national African American website about what daily life in post-Katrina New Orleans was like. Although she had never trained as a reporter, she had a distinctive writing voice—smart, funny, personal, socially conscious but not pretentious—and other outlets soon noticed her work. She began covering local news and politics for nola.com, the website of the city's leading newspaper, the *Times-Picayune*. Her newly adopted nickname, Big Red Cotton, turned out to be an asset.

"I needed that pseudonym because I was writing some pretty incendiary articles," she recalled. "I was tearing into Black politicians who were on the take, diverting recovery funds into their own pockets: William Jefferson, the congressman; Ray Nagin, the mayor. Both of them went to jail later. The reactions I got at the time were, uh, interesting. Some readers thought Big Red Cotton had to be a White man because I was so hard on these Black leaders. But I felt that Black leaders, of all people, should not be abusing the public trust. That money was meant to help people, and people really needed help."

Blogging paid little or nothing, but Deb was able to persevere thanks to a secret income source: The Bank of Daddy. Her father gave Deb large cash infusions throughout her adult life, partly because he felt guilty for having lied to Deb about her real mother, and partly because he thought the financial support would give him leverage over Deb's actions. "Debbie knew that Hayes felt guilty about all the lies," Deb's sister-cousin Le'Trese told me, "and she would use that to her benefit. She'd ask him for money, he'd give her some, and she'd tell me, 'Daddy still feels guilty about lying to me.'"

"After we became adults," Le'Trese continued, "he'd be sending her thousands of dollars at a time because she needed help with her rent or car payments. But along with the money came advice and directives; it was very controlling. So when Debbie could afford it, she would refuse the money. But there weren't a lot of times when she could afford it. Sometimes what she was doing with her life didn't provide a salary, or she would change jobs and there would be a dry period between the first and last paychecks. She was also very wasteful with money. She'd see a new Coach handbag and buy it, even though she already had four of them. 'I treated myself,' she'd say."

Deb's blogging often focused on the discrimination African Americans encountered as they struggled to rebuild their lives. The population of New Orleans had been largely African American from its earliest days as a French colony; prior to Katrina, the US census calculated that Blacks accounted for 67 percent of New Orleans residents—two out of three. After the storm, powerful interests appeared to want to change that. A rebuilding plan recommended that vast swaths of the city be reclassified as parkland; the theory was that parkland could endure future flooding without terrible economic or human losses. Although White as well as Black neighborhoods lay below sea level, the areas proposed for abandonment were predominantly Black: the Ninth Ward, Gentilly, New Orleans East. News coverage of the plan sparked outrage, especially from African American locals. The plan was withdrawn and revised, but not by much. The new plan gave targeted neighborhoods four months to convince the city that they could repopulate themselves; otherwise, Deb reported, "the city would begin a forced buyout program" of people's houses.

Deb was in the room when the authorities unveiled the revised plan for public comment, and her dispatch, reproduced here exactly as she wrote it, captured the fury and fighting spirit of Black New Orleans:

"A huge Black man bellowed out like a sonic boom from the back of the room: 'YOU ARE NOT TAKING MY LAND!! IF YOU COME TRYING TO TAKE MY PROPERTY, YOU'RE GONNA HAVE A BABY IRAQ ON YOUR HANDS! NOBODY WORKED THE JOBS I'VE WORKED, TAKING THE CRAP FROM EMPLOYERS I DIDN'T WANT TO TAKE, TO MAKE MY NOTE EVERY MONTH TO SIT HERE AND HAVE YOU TELL ME I CAN'T REBUILD MY OWN HOME!! THAT'S MY HOUSE AND IF YOU THINKING 'BOUT COMING TO TAKE MY LAND, YOU BETTA COME HEAVY.'"

The revised plan was withdrawn.

Still, daily life in New Orleans remained soul-crushing. The city was like a ghost town, especially at night. Electricity and water were frequently unavailable. So were groceries and other basics. Virtually everyone had lost a home, their possessions, a loved one, or all of the above, or they knew others who had. Residents had been scattered to the winds, taken in by friends or strangers in Baton Rouge, Houston, or other distant places. Many who managed to return were living in toxic trailers supplied by the Federal Emergency Management Agency, an agency whose hapless performance inspired a bitter epithet: "I've been FEMA'd."

The chaos morphed into a general social breakdown that challenged the resilience of virtually everyone in New Orleans. "It was like the Wild, Wild West here," Deb recalled. "Streetlights didn't work, you could go the wrong way down a one-way street, run a red light or stop sign, people were doing whatever the fuck they wanted, and nobody said shit. People were dropping dead from a stroke from the stress of dealing with all this shit, even young people."

About six months after the storm, Deb moved to the Treme neighborhood and was traumatized afresh. From a distance, the new location seemed a dream come true: Treme prided itself on being the oldest African American neighborhood in the United States, and Deb's apartment was just a couple blocks from the French Quarter. But the apartment faced the low-rent Empress Hotel.

"The first night I moved in, I was pulling my things out of the car and there was a police car parked in front of the hotel," Deb said. "There was a drag queen outside the car on the driver's side. He had his head inside the driver's side window and was bent so far over that I could see this hot pink thong up the crack of his ass. There's only one thing he could be doing to that cop. It turned out the Empress Hotel was notorious for prostitution and drug dealing. And the cop in charge of community relations for that area—they're known as the quality-of-life officer, if you can believe that—was a pimp on the side. He ran hookers out of that hotel, and everybody in the neighborhood knew it."

Like others in post-Katrina New Orleans, Deb was overtaken by depression. "I stopped writing," she recalled. "I also stopped talking, stopped answering the phone, and stopped going outside my apartment." The anxiety was strong enough that she developed an ulcer, and doctors said she needed surgery to put her insides right again.

A doctor prescribed antidepressants. They didn't help.

What finally vanquished her emotional funk? What reminded her of why she had loved New Orleans enough to move here? Second line parades.

One day, a hearse rolled past her building, followed by a brass band and a crowd of people swaying beneath black parasols. Out of respect for the dead, she joined the procession for a few blocks. A week later, another second line paraded past her front door. "I tried ignoring the seductive drums and horns," she later wrote, "but before long I was scurrying around looking for flip-flops to throw on and running down the street to catch up, rationalizing that some fresh air and exercise might do me some good."

After Deb attended a couple more second lines, she began to blog about what she experienced there and why it felt so good. "Invariably, the second line begins to take on a dreamscape quality—people stuck in parade traffic jump out and start clapping and dancing instead of honking and cursing," Deb continued. "Young Black men buck-jump wild battle-dance steps with each other atop porches, rooftops, and rickety FEMA trailer steps. Magical Mardi Gras Indians appear looking like giant birds with brilliant white, turquoise, or red feathers, beads and tambourines, chanting and swirling, towering over regular-sized human beings. And the big sweaty Black tuba player is fawned over, flirted with, and appealed to like a rock star."

"This went on every week for months on end," she concluded, "until one day . . . I began to feel alive again. And the haunting images of dead floating bodies faded away."

Before long, Deb realized that second line parades were so central to the culture of New Orleans that they deserved to be their own journalistic beat. She adopted that beat for *Gambit* in part because she viewed second lines as indispensable to restoring the true self of New Orleans. "After Katrina, one of many things I worried about was whether our culture would survive," she recalled. "I made a conscious decision to do what I could to provide public records on the culture of New Orleans." By 2008, she was covering second line parades almost every Sunday and then posting video of the highlights on social media; she eventually accumulated over eight hundred videos of second line parades.

The Social Aid and Pleasure Clubs that organized these parades were the heart of New Orleans's second line culture. They had emerged in the late 19th century, as African Americans banded together to arrange burial services, aid for widows and orphans, life insurance, and other social assistance that White-dominated businesses and government agencies would not provide. Social Aid and Pleasure Clubs also fostered community and racial pride, in part by organizing second line parades. Some parades commemorated the death of a club member, but second lines might also be organized to celebrate a local or national holiday, to mark a religious holy day, or simply to declare a day of pleasure.

One of Deb's innovations was to work with the city's Social Aid and Pleasure Clubs to publicize the name and route of each Sunday's parade in advance. Every week, she posted the name of the club that was sponsoring that Sunday's parade and the route the parade would follow, including where it would stop for restroom and refreshment breaks. Previously, club members knew this information, but precious few others did. If you didn't know a club member, or know someone who did, your only hope of joining a second line was to roam the streets and get lucky.

I got that lucky once. After trying and failing to find a second line parade during previous visits to New Orleans, I literally stumbled upon one the week before Christmas of 2010. I was in town reporting on the Gulf of Mexico oil spill, and my music-loving buddy Tom had flown in from Washington, DC, for the weekend. It was early Sunday afternoon, and we had just stepped out of Sweet Lorraine's Jazz Club on St. Claude Avenue. Eyes blinking in the sudden brightness, I noticed a mass of people gathered a couple blocks down the street. Something seemed to be happening. Tom and I went to investigate, and when we got there, we were told that a second line parade had just departed, heading toward the Lower Ninth Ward.

Although largely ignorant about second lines at that point, I did grasp the import of a second line returning to the neighborhood Hurricane Katrina had made synonymous with death and despair. Like the Pied Piper, the music trilling and pounding from the distant parade beckoned irresistibly. Tom and I followed and within minutes were immersed in one of the most blissful experiences of our lives.

Once we caught up to the parade, my attention gravitated to a troupe of exquisitely attired women dancing ahead of the lead brass band. Dressed in an incandescent mixture of black and white fabrics, the women wore fedoras, high heels, and satin pants and jackets. Above their heads waved

black-and-white feathered signs that announced the name of their Social
Aid and Pleasure Club, THE LOWER 9TH STEPPERS.

The unabashed sexuality on display startled me. A Black man in a
wheelchair was dancing as spiritedly as anyone, spinning his chair around,
doing wheelies and shaking his arms in sync with the beat. Suddenly, a
particularly beautiful dancer turned around to face the man, straddled
his chair and, grinning broadly, thrust her hips back and forth in obvious
copulating motions. To the delight of the crowd, not to mention the man in
the wheelchair, the woman kept at it a good thirty seconds, laughing along
with the man. Amid whistles and shouts from onlookers, she then lifted
herself off and faced front again. But she wasn't finished, oh no. Now she
bent forward and, still grinning, thrust her wagging bottom at the man's
crotch while her fingers spread wide for balance on the pavement below.
The crowd went crazy.

Tom and I were two of the very few White people in attendance, but not
once did we feel less than completely welcome. When a young Black guy
lit up a joint during a pause in the action, he casually passed it to Tom with
a smile and asked, "Where y'all from?" The musicians played an eclectic
mix of selections, switching among traditional New Orleans street songs,
hosannas to the Saints football team, and pop tunes. (A medley of Michael
Jackson songs was a particular crowd-pleaser.) There were also more pointed
numbers. The 1970s pop hit "Back Stabbers" was employed to decry
the shameful treatment of New Orleans by federal and state authorities
in the years since Hurricane Katrina: *They smile in your face/All the time
they want to take your place/The backstabbers!*"

The entire experience—the fabulous music, the sexy dancing, the
complete ease between Whites and Blacks, the spirit of community—was
enchanting. I felt like I had entered a magical land that I never wanted
to leave. Afterward, Tom and I walked back to our bed-and-breakfast in
a daze. We couldn't stop marveling at our good fortune—to stumble by
chance upon such a heavenly adventure! I couldn't wait to do it again.

Even as Deb Cotton was immersing herself in the healing waters of second line parade culture, she was also writing about post-Katrina New Orleans's struggle to return to something like its former self. Deb spoke out strongly when Mayor Ray Nagin's administration and the New Orleans Police Department appeared to discourage second line parades by hiking the price of parade permits. The dispute got especially heated in October 2007, when an NOPD officer arrested some of the city's top brass band musicians during an impromptu second line parade near Deb's apartment in Treme.

"When you live in Treme and hear a brass band at night, its [*sic*] usually a sign that someone important in the community has died, which means that the second line will be an emotionally powerful event," Deb later wrote in *Gambit*. "I immediately threw on my sandals and ran outside to find the parade." She arrived just in time to witness a police car zooming toward a second line comprised of roughly seventy-five people. The police car "screeched to a halt," she wrote, the officer jumped out and "began screaming at the crowd to stop the music."

Leading the parade was Phil Frazier, the tuba player for the renowned Rebirth Brass Band. Frazier explained that the parade was in honor of his brother, Kerwin James, who had just died. The officer insisted that without a permit, the parade had to stop. When the musicians continued to play, Deb wrote, "the officer became furious . . . and began handcuffing musicians." To many in the crowd, this was the ultimate blasphemy—disbanding a second line funeral in Treme, the neighborhood where jazz was born, and even arresting the musicians. Deb dashed home and emailed the officer's boss, whom she knew from her activism with the New Orleans Neighborhood Policing Anti-Crime Council. Other high-profile locals protested as well, and the city backed down. The next day, the police superintendent pledged that, as Deb reported, "no musician would ever be arrested in Orleans Parish for playing his horn."

Deb nevertheless lamented that "the value of culture and tradition is often missed by those lucky enough to be born closest to it. I mean, why come back here and go through the excruciatingly painful and laborious process of rebuilding if not to be able to recapture and preserve our culture and traditions? Otherwise, we all could have all just stayed in Dallas and Atlanta."

Deb gave the officer who lost his composure that night the benefit of a doubt—everyone in post-Katrina New Orleans lost it at one time or another, she figured—but she grew increasingly disturbed by more ominous police misconduct. The NOPD had long been criticized for corruption, racism, and brutality, and its performance during and after Katrina reinforced that reputation. Video footage showed police officers looting stores. Worse were a series of violent interactions with unarmed Black locals that ended with the locals in hospitals or the morgue.

The most notorious incident was the Danziger Bridge shooting. On September 4, 2005, six days after Katrina hit, an African American family was walking across the bridge when four police officers in plain clothes and wielding assault rifles opened fire without warning. Two of the Black civilians were killed; four wounded. The officers then concocted a cover story, falsely claiming that a fellow officer had been shot on the bridge and that additional gunshots had greeted the plainclothes officers when they arrived to assist. Eventually, four of the officers were sentenced to multiyear prison terms; a fifth officer who aided the cover-up was also imprisoned.

A total of twenty NOPD officers were charged with violating the civil rights of civilians in the wake of Katrina, but the actual number of transgressions was almost certainly higher. Writing in *The Nation*, investigative reporter A. C. Thompson documented how some White civilians in the Algiers neighborhood, across the Mississippi from the French Quarter, formed vigilante squads that took undisguised pleasure in shooting at least eleven African Americans after the storm. The NOPD appeared to have investigated none of these murders, Thompson wrote, adding that the NOPD rebuffed without explanation his repeated requests for comment.

Unwarranted violence and corruption on the part of police in New Orleans dated back to slavery days, but the decade leading up to Katrina had been particularly troubled. In 1992, the Justice Department reported that the NOPD received more police brutality complaints than any other force in the country. Nor was the alleged police brutality keeping crime in check. With crack cocaine flooding the streets and spurring gang shoot-outs, New Orleans climbed to the dubious peak as the top murder capital in the United States. In 1994, which saw a record 421 murders, "killing was literally more common than the sun coming up," the *New Orleans Advocate* newspaper observed.

"There were killer cops on the force back then," Deb said, citing the infamous case of officer Len Davis. On October 13, 1994, an FBI wiretap recorded Davis ordering a gangland-style execution of a civilian witness against him. Davis told a local hit man to murder Kim Groves, who had been bold enough to file an accusation of police brutality against Davis after seeing him beat a Black teenager. When the hit man informed Davis that the deadly deed had been completed, Davis exclaimed on the wiretap, "Yeah, yeah, yeah!"

"At that point, New Orleans was arguably the worst police department in the country," Samuel Walker, a professor emeritus at the University of Nebraska Omaha, told the *Advocate*, adding that the NOPD seemed "incapable of reforming itself."

The NOPD's performance during Katrina, at once bumbling and vicious, validated that impression, and the bad behavior continued after the flood-waters receded. "I was keeping an archive after the storm, with one file on crimes that were committed and another file on the NOPD getting in trouble," Deb recalled. "From 2006 to 2008, my file contained fifty-three stories of police officers that were charged with murdering, raping, or robbing a civilian. Fifty-three cases in two years! And those were just the ones we knew about. I was like, 'This police department is unparalleled in the country, and something needs to be done.'"

In November 2008, days before the presidential election, Deb managed to arrange a meeting with Jacques Morial, a New Orleans political insider whose brother Marc had been mayor from 1994 to 2002. "If I were you, this is what I'd do," Deb said Morial told her. "We're about to have a new president, and if it is Barack, we'll have someone who's more sympathetic to imposing a consent decree. As a high-profile blogger, you can help build public support for that consent decree."

"I was like, 'That's brilliant,'" Deb recalled. "'That's why people told me to come and talk to you!'"

After Obama was indeed elected, events unfolded just as Morial had outlined. Obama nominated Eric Holder as attorney general. Holder happened to have been the US deputy attorney general in the 1990s when the Justice Department threatened to impose a consent decree on the NOPD; he was well aware of the NOPD's deplorable record. After a fresh investigation, Holder's Justice Department accused the NOPD of "use of excessive force," "unconstitutional stops, searches and arrests," and "racial profiling." In January 2013, the Justice Department, the NOPD, and the city of New Orleans signed a federal consent decree. It obliged the NOPD to "fundamentally change the way it polices" and cooperate with an independent Monitor officer who would serve as the federal government's "eyes and ears" to ensure that the mandated reforms were implemented.

Deb Cotton was among the criminal justice advocates who praised the consent decree as a good first step, but soon she was publicly calling out what she saw as racist behavior on the part of Ronal Serpas, who'd been appointed NOPD superintendent in 2010. "Of all the boneheaded moves Serpas made," she said, "one of the worst was to show up at the scene of a murder and recite the arrest record of the victim. This person, whose dead body was lying there under a sheet, was arrested for x, y, and z, he'd say to the cameras. Not convicted, arrested. But an arrest record is not a guilty record!"

Deb chose a highly visible setting to go after Serpas: a City Council budget hearing, when reporters and opinion leaders were likely to be present. "They allow the public to give three-minute comments," she recalled. "When my turn came, I said, 'This police department is the most depraved police department in the United States. It's so bad that it's under a federal consent decree. It's the only department that has someone on death row [Len Davis] for murdering a civilian. So anyone who is arrested by this police department, you have to look with some skepticism at those charges. You, superintendent Serpas, have the nerve to act as if you are trying on the one hand to build relationships of trust with the community, but on the other hand you are scandalizing this same community by standing over a warm dead body and reciting arrest charges that were filed by a police department that not only has been caught racially profiling young Black men but has been responsible for murdering, robbing, and raping civilians.'"

"I let him have it," Deb later told me, relishing the memory. "I remember watching the back of his neck turning red and the audience applauding."

Second line parades not only rescued Deb from depression, they also answered her wish for romance. She had decided before leaving Los Angeles that she was ready to settle down, and she knew just what kind of man she wanted. First and foremost, she explained in one of her columns, her man had to be Black. "And I don't mean a little Black," she wrote. "I want him 12:45 A.M. Black." He also had to be on the large side and enamored of her own plus-size figure—her "winter-time body." She even had a name for this dark complexioned, big bellied, cuddly bear of a man: James.

She eventually found her James in the person of Edward "Juicy" Jackson. And as if decreed by fate, what brought them together was a second line parade. Giving fate an extra twist, the second line in question took place on Mother's Day, three years to the day before the parade where Deb would be shot.

Deb and Juicy met at the 2010 edition of the Original Big 7 Social Aid and Pleasure Club's second line parade. After four hours of parading up and down the streets of the Seventh Ward, the festivities concluded on St. Bernard Avenue just after 5:00 P.M. Mouthwatering smoke puffed from the massive barbecue grills where husband and wife teams were cooking ribs, chicken, and pork chops. Behind card tables laden with cheap liquor, mixers, beer, and soda pop, vendors sold beverages at rock-bottom prices. The crowd was beginning to disperse, though many of the revelers, as if wishing to prolong the afternoon's high, continued to mill about in the middle of the avenue, chatting and sharing farewells.

"I was heading back to my ride when I saw her up ahead in the crowd," Juicy recalled about meeting Deb. "I recognized her face from other second lines. She's a beautiful woman, you know. I decided I wanted to talk to her."

He wasn't named James, but Juicy fit Deb's vision of her ideal man in other respects. He was a big man, over six feet two, with an ample belly. His skin was nearly as black as the charcoal that grilled the pork chops that he loved to eat. He wore his hair short and favored long white T-shirts that extended to mid-thigh.

And he was a musician. He played trombone in To Be Continued, one of the bands that had just finished performing. TBC, as its fans called it, got its start playing for tips at the corner of Bourbon and Canal streets in 2006, after New Orleans had recovered enough from Hurricane Katrina for tourists to return. The band had opened for the Grammy Award–winning hip-hop group the Roots and was on its way to becoming one of the top brass bands in New Orleans.

Juicy had a musician's confidence with women, reinforced by lessons he picked up from his grandfather. "My grandfather was a pimp, and I lived with him sometimes growing up," Juicy told me. "He had lots of bitches around. So I know bitches." Juicy's confidence was all the more remarkable considering his age difference with Deb. Deb looked much younger but in fact was forty-five; Juicy looked much older but was actually a mere twenty-two.

As befitted his generation, Juicy didn't ask for Deb's phone number when they chatted after the second line. "I knew I could hit her up later on Facebook, and that's what I did," he said. He was instantly smitten, it seems. Later that night, his Facebook page carried the announcement that he was "In a relationship with Deborah Cotton."

Juicy began spending more and more time at Deb's apartment in Treme, watching sports on TV while she tapped out a writing project on the computer. Deb got to know the rest of the TBC band as well, hanging out with them and videoing their performances. She had a regular paycheck now as the communications director for the New Orleans Coalition on Open Governance, a nonprofit organization dedicated to improving public policy by increasing public participation and transparency. Her apartment was a tiny one bedroom converted from a former attic—the sleeping area had been a crawl space—but it had a sweet back porch that opened toward Congo Square, a hundred yards from where jazz was born on long ago Sunday afternoons. Life felt pretty good. "I've got a TRULY amazing man;" she wrote in a Facebook post, "really good job(s); I live in the city I love with neighbors I adore. . . . Lord THANK YOU! I look at the world around me and I know it didn't have to be this way."

Yet a shadow hung over Deb and Juicy's romance from the start. For in the same hour as their first conversation at the second line, a domestic dispute on the other side of town turned violent and a TBC band member was shot dead.

Brandon Franklin, twenty-two years old, was the tenor saxophone player for TBC. He had skipped that day's second line to do a favor for a former girlfriend. She and he were separated, but they had a four-year-old son together and were on friendly terms. She now lived with another man, Ronald Simms, with whom she had a second son. Recently, she and Simms had been having problems, and she ordered him to leave their home. She asked Brandon to come over and change the locks.

According to court records, Ronald Simms returned to the house to retrieve his belongings at the same time that Brandon Franklin was there to change the locks. The two men exchanged words. Tempers flared. Franklin pushed Simms, taunting, "That gun you got on ya, I'm a make you use it today." Simms left but soon returned, with a friend, to demand more of his belongings. Another argument ensued. Simms pulled a Glock semiautomatic pistol from his waistband and pumped thirteen bullets into Franklin while the mother and her two little boys cowered in another room.

Juicy and the rest of the TBC were devastated by their bandmate's violent death. "For the next two months, it was like they were all suffering post-traumatic syndrome," Deb said. "They'd be crying and drugged out all day. Soon as they'd wake up, they'd start smoking weed and just smoke all day, not doing anything but moping around and self-medicating."

On May 12, 2013, three years after Brandon's death, the To Be Continued Brass Band was again scheduled to play the Mother's Day second line parade of the Original Big 7 club. By all rights, Mother's Day should have been a happy day for Deb and Juicy, the day their love first sparked to life after the Original Big 7 parade in 2010. Instead, Mother's Day called forth memories of death.

"Juicy and I never talked very much about the day we met," Deb said. "I've been around men enough to know that they don't feel the need to share every feeling the way women do, even feelings as raw and strong as a friend getting shot to death. So I never pressed him on it. If he wanted to talk, I was there for him. But I didn't bring it up."

For his part, Juicy opposed TBC's decision to play the Mother's Day 2013 second line. "I never wanted to do that gig," he recalled. "The rest of the band had to talk me into it. We decide things by majority vote, and I got outvoted. Ask them, they'll tell you. I never had a good experience at that second line. It was not well organized. It wasn't fun. There was nothing good happened there, not ever!"

"What about you meeting Deb?" I asked. "Didn't that happen at the Original Big 7's second line?"

"So what? That was the day my bandmate got shot to death. That wasn't no kinda good day."

Embarrassed by my foolish suggestion, I then made things worse by asking Juicy where Brandon had been shot.

"What does that matter?" he replied scornfully. "You get shot thirteen times, it don't matter where. You could be shot in your toe, you get shot thirteen times, you gonna be dead."

The night before Mother's Day 2013, Juicy stayed at Deb's place as usual. They did not talk about the next day's second line, nor the fact that TBC would be performing. Nor did they discuss whether Deb would video the parade. They just chilled.

When Deb awoke the next morning, Juicy was nowhere to be seen. It was only nine o'clock, the parade didn't begin until 1:00 P.M., but Juicy was up and gone.

Deb was left alone with her thoughts. It was then that the inner voice began whispering about staying home that day. "I had a heavy heart, and I didn't feel like going," she recalled. "The truth was, I didn't really care for that particular second line. It fell on the anniversary of when Brandon was killed, and when another good friend of mine also had died. So I kind of didn't wanna go that day."

But Deb's sense of responsibility overrode her misgivings. "I pushed through my grief and decided to go after all," she said.

Running late, Deborah Cotton got dressed, grabbed her camera, and climbed into her Jeep. Soon she was crossing St. Bernard Avenue on her way to the Original Big 7's second line parade. It was one o'clock on Mother's Day afternoon, and the music was about to begin.

4

Like Shooting Up a Church

Now it don't matter if you don't have a father . . .
It don't matter if you have a cracked-out mother . . .
It's not okay to go shoot up a second line.
—"Bury the Hatchet," adapted lyrics
by Glen David Andrews

A kid on a trampoline was bouncing high above a vacant lot on the corner as Ed Buckner halted the To Be Continued brass band on the cusp of the intersection of Frenchmen and North Villere streets. Deb had caught up with the band now, and she halted alongside Juicy and the other musicians. The kid bouncing on the trampoline caught Deb's and Juicy's eyes at the same time, Deb recalled, and they smiled at each other. And then, pandemonium.

"We were starting a song by the Hot 8," Joe Maize later said, "just the first four notes: *baum, boum, bum bah-ba*. Then we hear, *pop, pop, pop pop pop*." Maize thought someone in the crowd had jumped up and smacked a stop sign with the palm of their hand. "People be doing that all the time when we play a second line," he said. "As musicians, we turn toward the sound," he added, panning his head to the right to illustrate. "But this wasn't nobody banging no sign. This was a motherfucker pointing a gun and firing every which way."

As the crowd scattered, Deb Cotton suddenly found herself with an unobstructed view of the shooter. She saw him in profile, to her right, about ten feet away, and her brain started playing tricks on her. As she stared, the shooter's face morphed into the face of her beloved nephew, Austin, to whom she had been a second mother during a family crisis years earlier.

"I was looking at the shooter, but there was Austin: same hip-hop clothing, same body motion," she later said. "Then I saw the shooter's face, then Austin's face again. It was Austin with a gun, Austin second lining, Austin shooting. It was like the shooter and my nephew were the same person."

"I stood frozen, watching him shoot," she recalled. "He was kind of spraying his gun wildly, and he had a strange smile on his face, like a sneer. Then my rational mind took over and I thought, 'I better run.'"

But Deb waited too late to run, and she paid a grievous price. It turned out there was a second shooter targeting that intersection and, unlike the first's, his gun was pointed at Deb.

"I felt the bullet hit my right hip," she told me later. "It felt like I'd been pelted by a rock. But I grew up in the country, and I knew what it felt like to be pelted by a rock. I told myself, 'That's not what this is.'"

She fell to the pavement, pretty sure that she was dying.

"I said to myself, 'This is it. I'm gonna leave. It's happening.' I have a friend, Wanda, who is a practitioner of Yoruba [a religion enslaved Africans brought with them to the New World that believes in human destiny and transcendence]. She had called me, like a month before the shooting, and was very dire. She said, 'I've been wrestling for a week now whether to share this with you, but my priest said I have to.' It'd come through in some of her readings that I was in danger, the spirit of death was around me and I had to do serious spiritual work. When I hit the pavement, I thought: 'Wanda was right!'"

As if from far, far away, Deb heard the voice of Chris Conwell, who played cowbell for the To Be Continued band.

"Cotton, you shot?" he asked.

"I'm shot," she managed to reply.

"During the first ninety seconds, I was trying to figure out if I was dying or not," she later said. "I was saying to myself, 'Wow, it doesn't hurt that much to get shot.' But that changed pretty quickly. I felt a burning ache more than a sharp pain, a dull, aching, growing pain that was blossoming in my stomach."

"So, I began surveying my life. I thought, 'I've traveled the world, I've done work that made a difference, I've experienced most of the things I wanted. I didn't get married, but I can go without that.' Once I'd ticked off the list, I thought, 'Okay, I'm ready.'"

"But then, it didn't seem to be happening. I wriggled my toes and they still worked, so I figured I wasn't paralyzed. After ninety seconds, I thought, 'I guess I'm gonna survive.'"

That is not, however, what the emergency medical technicians thought. As they loaded her into an ambulance, Deb Cotton was lucid enough to tell one of them, "I really need a Percocet." Then everything went dark.

When the gunfire began, I was standing on the far side of the intersection from where Deb and the TBC band had halted following Ed Buckner's command to pause. I heard a *zip, zip, zip* coming from not far behind my left shoulder, but I didn't recognize the sound. It wasn't loud enough to be firecrackers, and gunshots simply didn't occur to me. Twenty years earlier, as a reporter covering famine and civil war in South Sudan, I had occasionally heard the distant boom of artillery or the clatter of small arms fire. But gunfire here in the United States, up close, at a Mother's Day parade? It didn't compute. Only after the people around me started pushing past me and diving to the ground did my brain finally catch up and tell my legs to move.

I took two, maybe three, running strides toward the far side of the intersection and threw myself onto the cobblestone street. There was a brief interlude, no more than five seconds, when all was quiet. Then it seemed as if everyone in and around the intersection suddenly began shouting at once, a ragged chorus of fear, pain, and grief.

Still prone on the street, I looked to my left. In the middle of the now empty intersection, I saw the dancer I'd nicknamed Flash Dance. He was alone, crouching as if ready to spring, his eyes like lasers searching for his wife and son.

I pushed myself up to a seated position. There was blood on my hands. It seemed to be coming from a cut that split open the heel of my left hand. I also noticed blood on my right leg, trickling in a straight line from below my knee to my ankle. I felt no pain. I thought I must have cut myself on a piece of glass or sharp stone when I threw myself down on the pavement. The screaming around me continued, the sounds of frantic, frightened humans. As I sat, dazed, I began to realize what had happened. It looked like the casualties would be many and severe.

A woman with blond hair approached and asked if I was alright. She identified herself as Lauren McGaughy, a reporter with the *Times-Picayune*. She had already tweeted a bulletin on the shootings and called her newsroom to alert colleagues. I told her that I was a reporter, too, and I gave her some brief background on me. She gave me her cell number, handed me a bottle of water, and walked off to continue reporting.

A Black guy carrying a video camera appeared and asked if he could take my picture. He said he filed for the Getty photo agency. I told him I was a freelancer for *Vanity Fair* and *The Nation*, and we agreed to tape a video report. Speaking straight to camera, I stated the basics: there had been a mass shooting at a second line parade here in New Orleans on Mother's Day. At least a dozen shots were fired into a crowd at Frenchmen and North Villere streets. No word yet on the motive, the perpetrator, or the severity of casualties, but it appeared that many people had been wounded, some seriously.

I looked across the intersection at the guy lying face down where I had been standing just seconds before. The circle of blood near his shoulder was larger now, but his eyes were open, and a man and a woman were bent beside him, giving him aid. The thin, wounded woman with wild, frightened eyes was now nestled against the building behind me. She looked to be in bad shape, clutching her midsection. Two women were comforting her even as they screamed for somebody to come help, quick.

Now came the sound of sirens, and moments later the first contingent of ambulances pulled up. I waved away the first EMTs who approached me, urging them to help victims who really needed it. I tried to count how many ambulances came and went, but the scene was too chaotic to be sure.

Then I heard a male voice above me ask, "Are you alright?"

A middle-aged White guy with a friendly smile was peering down at me. He was missing two front teeth and wearing a blue bandana with white speckles. A woman beside him looked on with a concerned expression.

"Yeah, I'm okay," I replied. "I wasn't shot. Just a little cut up."

I tried to push myself up to standing, but they wouldn't let me.

"Don't get up," the guy said. "The ambulances are on their way."

"I don't need an ambulance," I said. "Actually, I need to get to the airport. I've got to catch a flight home."

Clearly my brain wasn't working properly, but the Good Samaritans couldn't have been nicer about it. "Don't you worry about that," the man said. Noticing the blood on my leg, he asked, "What's that on your leg? Does it hurt?"

"Nah, I'm fine," I said. "I must have cut myself on some glass when I dove to the ground. I'm really fine."

"Well, tell you what," he said. "How about we wrap that up until the ambulance guys can take a look?" Disregarding my protests, he removed the bandana from his head and gently wrapped it around my wound.

"You take care now," he said with another smile before he and his companion headed down the street.

When a second round of ambulances arrived, an EMT with short, dark hair and a youthful manner knelt in front of me and asked where I was hurt. I said I hadn't been shot, just cut up a little. He wasn't buying it. He leaned in to take a closer look.

"Oh, yeah, you were shot," he said in a matter-of-fact though not unkind tone.

"I was?"

"Yeah, I can see the bullet right there," he said. He pointed to a small lump a few inches below my right knee, two inches from a star-shaped entry wound. "See, the bullet hit you here," he said, pointing to the entry wound, "and it traveled under your skin to there."

"Really?" I asked, astonished. "It doesn't hurt."

"Oh, it will," he replied in the same matter-of-fact tone. "That's just the adrenaline."

Realizing at last that I wasn't thinking straight, I asked the EMT, "Am I in shock?"

"No, you're not in shock. But we need to get you to the hospital."

Moments later, I was lifted into the back of an ambulance and told to wait. I took a seat on a bench that ran the length of the compartment. Seconds later, technicians lifted into the ambulance a gurney that carried a woman with white hair, an oval face, and a deeply pained look in her eyes.

Trying to take her mind off her obvious suffering, I introduced myself and asked her name. She said that she was Sister Ann, a Catholic lay worker. She was sixty-eight, was White, and had been living in New Orleans for just a few months. She supervised a Catholic youth program that brought kids from across the country to help refurbish houses still in disrepair eight years after Hurricane Katrina. Today, she and a young colleague had decided to celebrate Mother's Day by attending their first-ever second line parade. Now she was experiencing what she called the worst pain of her life.

"Do you remember what happened?" I asked.

"I'm not sure," she said. "One minute I was enjoying the parade, next to the band. Suddenly, people started running. Two big men fell on top of me, and my arm got broken."

That was a gentle way of putting it. In fact, the inertia of the two fleeing men had slammed Sister Ann down onto the pavement with such force that her elbow shattered. White bone now extruded through her skin. I couldn't imagine the pain she must be feeling.

As the ambulance sped across town, siren blaring, I held this dear woman's hand and told her that everything was going to be okay. I'm not sure either one of us believed it.

New Orleans Police detective Chris Hart had just finished grilling steaks for a Mother's Day picnic with his fiancée and his parents when his cell phone rang. Caller ID showed that it was his boss, Christopher Goodly, commander of the Fifth Police District.

"You heard the news?" Goodly asked.

"No," Hart replied.

"We got twenty people shot."

Hart thought twenty people had been shot throughout the city. "And I'm blown away," he later said. "That's a massive number of people shot, even in New Orleans."

But Hart had misunderstood.

"No, Chris," Goodly said. "We got twenty people shot in the 1400 block of Frenchmen."

"I'll be there in fifteen minutes," Hart replied.

The detective grabbed his gun and radio and zoomed to the Seventh Ward. What he found there was "surreal," he later told me. He had traveled in Croatia in his twenties, during the wars of the 1990s, where he witnessed the aftermath of atrocities that "made me rethink how I looked at life." The scene at Frenchmen and North Villere streets, where there were "still people on the street, bleeding," brought the dark memories rushing back.

"Most of us have never seen someone die," Hart explained. "But in the first couple of months on the street as a cop, you see a person who is not yet dead but while life is leaving them. It's hard for all of us. It taps into our own mortality."

Even before reaching the scene, Hart realized that this was going to be what he and his colleagues called a "heater."

"A heater," he explained, "is a high-profile case where the media, the public, the elected officials all want answers. It's the kind of case that shocks people. They want to know what happened, why it happened, and they want to know it quick. I had worked one heater case before this one, when a guy got shot and killed at Jazz Fest one year. But that was one guy who got shot. This was, like, twenty."

Television stations in New Orleans wasted no time proving Hart right—and alerting the world that something big had just happened in New Orleans. Because Lauren McGaughy of the *Times-Picayune* happened to be near the shooting and instantly tweeted about it, television trucks with satellite dishes on their roofs soon rolled up. The camera crews didn't wait for reporters to arrive before sending live images to their stations. The New Orleans stations in turn shared those live feeds with their network partners—CNN, ABC, CBS, Fox, et al.—and the networks shared them with their overseas counterparts.

Which is how Hart and his colleagues began receiving phone calls from all over the world. There was the buddy in Afghanistan who was watching Hart on Al Jazeera in real time, even describing the clothes Hart was wearing. Another NOPD colleague called from Chicago. "This buddy of mine was Polish," Hart recalled. "He tells me he and his family are watching me on Polish TV that very moment, and he asked, 'Chris, why are you on Polish TV? This is weird. What is going *on* in New Orleans?'"

Detective Rob Hurst, Hart's aide on the Mother's Day shooting investigation, got a phone call from even farther away. A family friend in Australia called Hurst's cell and said, "Rob, we're seeing news about a mass shooting in New Orleans. Is everything okay?"

For people outside New Orleans, the thought that first leaped to mind about the Mother's Day shooting was terrorism. The "war on terror" that President George W. Bush had declared after the September 11, 2001, attacks was still underway. After eight years of fighting, US troops had left Iraq in 2011, but they remained in Afghanistan. A month before the Mother's Day shooting, two bombs at the Boston Marathon had killed three people and injured 264 others, seventeen of whom lost limbs. The perpetrators, two brothers of Chechen background, planted the bombs as retaliation for the US wars in Afghanistan and Iraq, the younger brother said. And terrorism of a different sort had struck four months before the Boston Marathon bombing, when a lone gunman shot and killed twenty-six people, including twenty children between the ages of six and seven, at Sandy Hook Elementary School in Connecticut. The Sandy Hook massacre made for "the saddest and angriest" moment of his presidency, Barack Obama later said.

The earliest TV news reports about the New Orleans Mother's Day shooting specified that there was no word yet on whether the attack was related to terrorism. Within hours, the Department of Justice issued a statement saying that they had "no evidence" indicating that terrorism was a motive. By the next day, the federal government was definitively saying, "This was not a terrorism incident."

Ed Buckner strongly disagreed. In an interview with a New Orleans TV station, Buckner maintained that the shooting was indeed "a terrorist act. You don't need to wear a turban on your head to be a terrorist. Whoever did this is a terrorist. They were attacking innocent people and the culture of African American people in New Orleans. That's terrorism."

It wasn't easy to shock residents of New Orleans about gun violence—after all, the city had averaged a shooting a day for decades—but the record number of victims at the Mother's Day shooting, combined with the targeting of the beloved ritual of a second line parade, managed to do it.

"Who would imagine that somebody would come to a second line, this beautiful celebration, and start shooting?" John Boutté, one of the city's most renowned singers, told me. Years before, a second line parade had inspired Boutté to compose one of the all-time classic New Orleans songs, "Down in the Treme," the theme song for the HBO series *Treme*. The song came to him, Boutté said, when "I was sitting on my porch having my morning coffee. I heard a bass drum coming, and down the street I saw a second line funeral leaving St. Augustine's Church. They stopped right in front of my door and played. I wrote the song then and there, music and lyrics, in about fifteen minutes. I knew right away it was good."

As Ed Buckner and other second line enthusiasts often said, second lines were like church for Black people in New Orleans, so Boutté spoke for many when he said the Mother's Day shooting "equated to bringing a gun to church and starting to shoot people. It's just hateful. Who would do something like that?"

Who, indeed? Mass shootings had increased to epidemic proportions in the United States over the past decade or so. No other country on earth had experienced anything like it. But then, no other country had anything like the number of guns per capita that the United States did—more than one gun for every man, woman, and child. Mass shootings, defined as four or more killings in a single incident (not counting the possible death of the shooter), were actually responsible for barely 1 percent of total gun-related deaths—the majority of deaths were suicides—but the large number of victims in a mass shooting attracted more news coverage and public attention. And the epidemic shows no sign of abating: the United States suffered more mass shootings in 2023 than in any previous year—thirty-eight, breaking the previous record of thirty-six, set in 2022.

Why any mass shooter does what he does (and it is almost always a *he* who does it) is challenging for outsiders to determine. Before the video of the Mother's Day shooting surfaced, someone aware of the cultural and historical significance of second line parades might plausibly have suspected that a White supremacist had targeted the parade to make a political point, like Dylann Roof would do two years later when he shot nine Black church members to death with the express hope of igniting a race war. Other mass shootings appeared to be motivated by nothing more or less than a desire to kill as many people as possible. In the first hours after the Mother's Day shooting, both interpretations seemed possible. The number of wounded was in double digits, and they weren't shot in a workplace, shopping complex, bar, or club—the locations where most mass shootings in the US take place—but rather at a beloved ritual that amounted to an outdoor church service for Black people.

At the time, only the shooters themselves knew who was behind the Mother's Day assault. The surveillance video of the attack had not surfaced yet, and Chris Hart and his fellow detectives were just beginning to gather clues. A handful of people in the intersection, including Deb Cotton, Joe Maize, and some of the TBC band members, had seen the face of one gunman. But the band had fled the scene like everyone else, and Deb was on the way to University Medical Center.

After the ambulance screeched to a halt at the emergency entrance, the gurney carrying Deb was rushed inside toward the trauma unit. In a corridor, responding to instinct, Deb's body attempted to rise and pull the oxygen tubes from her nose. The nurses accompanying the gurney pinned her arms back down. More sedation was applied, the gurney was wheeled into the operating room, and surgeons commenced trying to save Deborah Cotton's life.

Bullet holes can be deceiving. On the surface of the skin, they can look small, even discreet, a smudged circle no bigger across than a dime. But underneath, that same gunshot can billow like an inflated balloon and blast through tissue, bone, organs, blood vessels, and anything else in its path. The bullet that struck Deb entered through her right hip, leaving only a small mark on the skin. It then traversed her abdomen diagonally upward before lodging on the opposite side of her torso, beneath the left side of her rib cage. Along the way, the bullet ripped through most of the vital organs in her abdomen.

Hence the "soul hole" term bestowed by surgeons. The soul hole is not a specific place but a metaphorical reference to how a gunshot wound in the gut is often fatal. The organs occupying the abdomen are called vital for good reason: they process food and water, extracting the glucose and proteins the body needs and eliminating the rest as waste. Without those functions, a body cannot survive for long. There was a second danger as well. Bacteria and microbes due to be eliminated as waste normally remain encased within the intestines and other organs until expelled as urine and feces. The bullet that hit Deb Cotton shredded that protective casing, flooding her abdomen with microscopic particles that could unleash deadly infections.

The first afternoon in the hospital seemed to last "a long time," Linda Usdin, Deb's close friend, later said. "I remember the doctor was coming out to the waiting room at various points and saying, 'We don't know. This is really bad. We don't know how bad yet. It depends on whether we have to take out her duodenum, that's the soul of the body. We hope not.' That's when I knew how bad it was, when they were saying, 'We don't know whether she's going to make it, she got hit in a really bad place.'"

I was taken to a different hospital, Tulane Medical Center, still feeling no pain but wondering what the hell happened. The physician who treated me, Dr. Prateek Adhikari, was calm, friendly, and by no means surprised by the Mother's Day shooting. A clean-cut guy in his thirties, Adhikari had grown up in New Orleans and knew that deadly street violence had a long history there. As a trauma unit specialist, he had treated many victims of that violence. He and his colleagues had noticed a shift in recent years, he told me, as shooters took advantage of special events like second line parades to punish enemies, regardless of the collateral damage that might result.

"It seems like family holidays are when we see some of these mass casualties," Adhikari said. "People who may have left the neighborhood come back for second lines and holidays like Thanksgiving or Mardi Gras. The shooters know where those individuals will be and when, and they don't care if other people are in the way."

After bandaging me up, Dr. Adhikari said I'd been lucky. The bullet that lodged in my right calf "didn't hit any bones, arteries, or nerves, so you're going to be fine. We're not even going to remove it. The safest thing is to leave it where it is." I must have looked surprised because he smiled. "That may sound odd, but if surgery isn't necessary, it's best to avoid it," he said. "We'll bandage you up and eventually your body will expel the bullet on its own." I wondered how that expelling of the bullet would work exactly, but I didn't argue.

My friend David, who ran the B&B where I stayed in New Orleans, gave me a ride home from the hospital. Bandages swaddling my left hand and right calf, and leaning on David so as not to put much weight on my injured leg, I was walking out of the hospital when a woman with dark hair called to me. She was Sister Ann's younger colleague. She was glad to learn that my injuries were minor, and I was relieved to learn that Sister Ann was expected to make a full recovery. "She's in surgery," the young woman told me, "but the doctors say she should be fine." David drove me back to the B&B, we had a quiet supper, and I fell into a deep sleep.

Meanwhile, the members of the Original Big 7 Social Aid and Pleasure Club gathered on the front porch of Ed Buckner's house to grapple with the day's events. Among those present was Flash Dance, whose real name was Leo Gorman. Later, Gorman told me that when he first heard the gunfire, he assumed that someone had set off firecrackers. "Then I saw people running and suddenly everyone was down on the ground," he recalled. "And I go, 'Oh, NO! I know what this is. Not this! Not here! Not now!'"

Until then, Gorman had been having the time of his life, dancing to that Whitney Houston song with his ten-year-old nephew, Shiloh. Recruited by

Ed Buckner explicitly for his dancing skills, Gorman had been a member of the Original Big 7 for a couple years. Shiloh had moved from Portland to New Orleans a year ago with his parents. The ten-year-old had attended previous second lines, but today was his first time dancing as a club member like his Uncle Leo.

"At first I thought it was, like, a drill or something," Shiloh told me. "Then I saw my aunt Nikki [Leo's wife] ahead of me, and she was going like this," waving his hands, palms down, toward the floor. "I didn't know what she meant. Then she grabbed my shirt and started pulling me up the street and we hid behind this white truck. I saw bullets hitting the house behind where we were hiding. That's when I knew what was happening."

Not long after the shooting, Shiloh's parents moved their family back to Portland, but his Uncle Leo said that "not for one second" did he think about leaving. When the club members convened on Ed Buckner's porch that evening, Gorman, as the only White person, made a point of staying quiet and listening to his compatriots process the day. "It was weird and terrible but also important for us to be together," Gorman told me. "I remember there was this numbness. On one hand, people were saying, 'This is SO fucked up, this is SO wrong.' On the other hand, there was a feeling of, 'Yeah, but it's been happening so often and so long in New Orleans that you can't help but build up a numbness to it.'"

"That shooting was, to me, the juxtaposition of beauty and destruction that is the essence of New Orleans," Gorman told me. "New Orleans steals your heart, and then it breaks it."

5

"The Blues Came from Slavery, Jazz Came from Freedom"

"The single most uncontroversial thing one can say about the institution of slavery vis-a'-vis contemporary time, is that it haunts us all."

—Toni Morrison

I was scared, yeah?"

Joe Maize was recalling his moments in the line of fire at the Mother's Day shooting. As a journalist who has spent much of my career outside the United States, I've heard my native tongue spoken in scores of different accents from many parts of the world. I can think of only three people who spoke English with an accent as pronounced as Joe Maize's. When Joe said "yeah," he split the word into two syllables, like "yeah-uh." He also stressed the second syllable and raised its pitch, as if asking, "Do you understand me?" I did understand Joe, most of the time, but I had to listen very closely and sometimes just guess.

Joe was standing two, maybe three, steps from Deb Cotton when the bullets started flying. Joe had known Deb's boyfriend since high school; he and Juicy met in the marching band at George Washington Carver High, where they founded the TBC band. In the decade since, the TBC had played scores of second lines, building a reputation as perhaps the best brass band of its generation. Joe was twenty-six now, a husband and a father. The TBC was successful enough that he supported his family largely from his music, supplemented by a part-time job with a fire safety company.

Like Deb, Joe and the other band members found themselves with a close-up view of the Mother's Day shooter when the crowd suddenly scattered from the gunfire. Also like Deb, they saw the shooter in profile, as he fired again and again into a knot of people in the middle of the intersection, steps ahead of the band. But Joe and the other band members did not watch the shooter for long.

"He saw us looking at him," Joe said of the shooter. "He's like, 'Y'all looking at me? *Don't* be looking at me!'"

The TBC band members didn't have to be told twice. Most of them had grown up in the Ninth Ward, and they knew plenty of people who'd been shot. Indeed, their bandmate Brandon had been shot dead three years ago on this very day, May 12.

"Somebody shouted, 'Everybody down,'" Joe remembered. Each of the musicians "took two steps to the left and fell to the ground."

Joe and I didn't meet until months after the Mother's Day shooting; I introduced myself after the TBC's performance at a separate second line parade. The parade was over, but remnants of the crowd were still milling about on a backstreet near the intersection of Canal and South Broad streets. Three policemen in sky-blue uniforms were exchanging pleasantries with revelers, but their eyes stayed on the crowd, watching for signs of trouble. Joe was buying two white wine miniatures from a street vendor when I approached.

"How you doing?" I said. "You guys are the To Be Continued band, aren't you?"

"Yeah-uh," said Joe as he twisted the top off the first white wine miniature. He was tall, strikingly handsome, with dark skin and a high forehead.

"Weren't you the band at that second line where all those people got shot? On Mother's Day?"

"Yeah-uh."

"Were you in the band that day?"

"Yeah-uh," he repeated, taking a long pull of wine.

"Well, I was one of the people who was shot that day."

Joe's eyes widened and his eyebrows arched. "For real?" he asked.

"For real," I replied. Lifting my pants leg, I showed him where the bullet was still embedded under my skin.

"And you back here today?" Joe said, his voice rising. He shifted his grip on the wine, reached forward with his right hand, and clasped mine forcefully. Looking deep into my eyes, he declared in a piercing tone, "Well, you a *real nigger*."

Unnerved by the n-word, I didn't know how to respond. I kept gripping his hand and ventured a half-smile. "Okay," I said. "What does that mean exactly?"

"It means you real," Joe said, his eyes fierce. "You take that kind of suffering and you back again? You the real thing, man. You a real nigger. You one brave motherfucker."

"Not really," I protested. "Actually, I'm a writer. I'm writing a book about that shooting. Could I ask you some questions?"

"Sure, man."

Before I could get out my next sentence, Joe spotted a short, stocky guy standing two steps away. "Hey," he said, grabbing his pal by the shoulder and spinning him around to face me. "This guy got shot at that Mother's Day second line. And he back here today. Can you believe that shit? He a real nigger."

The second guy was named Chris, and he played trumpet for TBC. He shook my hand energetically. "He right, he right!" he affirmed. "You a real nigger!"

I asked if we could sit somewhere and talk, but Joe and Chris said they needed to get to their next gig. I offered to drive them, and they seemed glad to accept. Leaving the dwindling crowd behind, we had walked a couple blocks toward my rental car when a motorcycle suddenly growled to a halt behind us.

The motorcyclist stepped off his bike and pulled the helmet from his head. He was in his mid-twenties, with short dreadlocks and medium brown skin. Joe and Chris greeted him fondly and introduced him to me.

"Hey, he got shot too," Chris and Joe told me at the same moment, pointing to their friend and laughing at the coincidence.

As the motorcyclist and I shook hands, I suddenly noticed his neck. It appeared to throb with a grotesque scar, a protuberance like nothing I had ever seen except in refugee camps in South Sudan. Extending from just below his right ear down to his collarbone were a series of bulging lumps, as if a string of golf balls had been implanted beneath the skin. It looked painful, bizarre, and scary all at once, but the motorcyclist didn't seem the slightest bit self-conscious. He simply smiled and asked where I had been shot, as if that were the polite thing to do in New Orleans. Not wanting to contrast my pitiful flesh wound with his monstrous injury, I pretended not to hear the question.

"How did that happen?" I asked, my horror plain to see.

Again the motorcyclist smiled calmly. "I got shot in the back, but the bullet came out the front and ruptured my aorta," he replied.

Ruptured his aorta! The aorta is only the main artery in the human body. How could anyone survive such a wound?

"Why did someone shoot you like that?" I asked, incredulous.

The motorcyclist started to reply, but Chris broke in with a nervous grin. "Uh, maybe better not say."

The motorcyclist unwound a shoulder bag from around his neck and asked, "What you guys need?"

"I'll take a fifty," Joe said.

"I'll do thirty," chirped Chris.

The motorcyclist opened his bag, counted out five tiny plastic bags, and dropped them in Joe's hand. Joe pulled a mess of crumpled bills from his pocket, counted out fifty bucks, and handed them over. Chris paid thirty bucks for three more bags. The three men exchanged warm farewells, promising to connect again soon. The motorcyclist nodded at me politely and zoomed off.

As we walked on, Joe confessed to feeling exhausted. Not only had he and the TBC spent the last four hours walking miles through the streets of New Orleans while giving a high energy performance, they had also played a late gig the night before on Frenchmen Street. Joe had gotten only four hours of sleep. The Frenchmen Street gig was lucrative but had an unpleasant side. "The guy owns that club is an asshole," Joe told me. "During a break, one of our band members walked up the bar. The owner told him to get the hell out of his club, this area's only for the band. Our guy says, 'I'm in the band.' The owner says, 'I don't care who you are, get the hell outta my club.'" Shaking his head at the absurdity, Joe said, "I was glad to take that White man's money, but some people are racist."

Sounding a bit punch-drunk, Joe again marveled that I had come back to a second line parade after getting shot at one on Mother's Day.

"Man, you must have clanking balls," he said.

"I really don't, trust me," I said. "I'm just trying to figure out what happened that day. What do you think that shooting was about?"

"Who knows?" said Joe. "Shit like that happen in New Orleans. You and I can walk outside your house and suddenly you not be here no more."

"Is it because there are so many guns around?" I asked.

"It ain't just guns that's dangerous round here," he said. "What you got to understand about life in New Orleans is, all this can be gone like *that*!" His arms swept wide to encompass the surrounding streets and buildings. "Since Katrina, that's what we live with, yeah-uh? I lived in New Orleans for eighteen years and Katrina swept away *everything*. I grew up in the St. Bernard projects. But my mother *worked*, and paid the rent—on *time*," he emphasized, as if to dispel a horde of stereotypes. "After Katrina, they tore down those projects and wouldn't let us go home."

"This been going on *forever* in New Orleans," Joe continued. "In the early days it was yellow fever. In slavery times, it was violence from the overseer or patrols. Nowadays, it's gunshots. Everything can be gone like *that*," he said, snapping his fingers. "So the way we look at it, we gonna live *today*. Because tomorrow, we might not be here."

We piled into my rental car, Joe in front with me and Chris in the back. They didn't have the address of their next gig, so they decided to go to Chris's place and wait for word from the rest of the band. Joe directed me toward the freeway, and soon we were climbing an arcing entrance ramp. Behind us, the silhouette of downtown loomed against a sunset of clouds streaked with yellows, pinks, and grays.

"When you guys are performing at a second line, is that what you're thinking?" I asked. "Let's enjoy today, because we may not have tomorrow?"

"Not really," Joe said, "but it's always a real spiritual experience. You know, second lines is where we come from. It's what we was doing when they first brought us here, even *before* they brought us here. Most Black people don't know a lot about our history, but when you're in a second line, you *feel* your history. It's coming out in the moves you dance and the way you play your horn."

"Second lines," Joe continued, and then paused. "I don't know, it's hard to explain. It's like a bright, bright, colorful feeling. Every Sunday feels like your birthday, and there's nothing but goodness. You can feel your ancestors around you, and you thinking, 'Where does this come from?' Sometimes we marching and a certain energy passes through the band. We look at each other and say, 'You feel that?'"

Soon we reached Chris's place, but Joe wasn't finished talking. Second lines called forth lots of themes for him: joy and transcendence, loss and grief, the past, present, and future. In that moment, he struck me as the spirit of second lines incarnate.

"The old cats were always saying to us, 'Y'all need to learn to play the traditional music,'" Joe said. "So we learned that stuff, and they was right.

Now I realize I *am* the tradition they talking about. Check me out on Facebook. My Facebook name is 'Joe I Am the Tradition Maize.'"

"It's like this here," he said, before climbing out of the car. "There was slavery. There was history. And now there's me."

"There are three forms of American popular music: jazz, blues, and gospel, and they all come out of the slave experience," Deacon John Moore, one of New Orleans's musical giants, told me during a separate visit to New Orleans. "When the slaves were planting tomatoes and picking cotton, the heat was so unbearable that they sang while they worked to make the work go a little bit easier. One guy was like the lead singer. He started the chant, then he and the rest of them did call-and-response. That was the start of the blues. The first two lines are almost identical, and the third line is a commentary on those first two. That's the basic structure of blues."

Deacon John oversimplified in saying that there are only three forms of popular American music—what about country music and the Great American Songbook?—but the three forms he listed as outgrowths of the slave experience certainly have been influential, especially if one counts the many descendants of those three forms, such as rock 'n' roll and hip-hop. Born in 1941, Deacon John had played all kinds of music during his decades as one of the most beloved and successful musicians in New Orleans. He was not well known nationally, but he had performed at the White House and was the only musician to have played at every New Orleans Jazz and Heritage Festival since the event was launched in 1970. Part of what limited his career outside of New Orleans, he suspected, was his skin tone, which was light enough to pass for White.

"I never had the kind of notoriety some of my contemporaries did, like Fats Domino, Irma Thomas, Allen Toussaint," he told me. "I think it has a little to do with the way I look. Most of the artists that go to festivals representing New Orleans music look like Fats or Irma; they have dark skin. I can't think of hardly any that look like me, a high yellow Negro. I'm a product of miscegenation, and miscegenation is unpredictable, baby!" he added with a cackling laugh. "I have one brother who is black as black, and another brother who looks like an Irishman."

As a boy, John Moore was forbidden to attend second lines—his mother was a strict Catholic who condemned such spectacles as "low class"—so the first second line parade he attended was the mass funeral after Louis Armstrong died in 1971. Second line parades, he explained, "come from a tradition of how they bury the dead in Africa. It's not written down. It got passed down from generation to generation through the oral tradition of the slaves: 'this is how we bury people.' You know, art cannot be silenced. Music is intangible. It comes through. You can't grab it and say, 'I'm gonna stop that music!'"

We were sitting in the music room of his house, a Creole cottage on a side street in the Uptown neighborhood. Crammed with guitars, drums, music stands, and piles of sheet music, the room was testimony to decades of performances that had given him a secure enough livelihood to raise seven children. But life as a working musician was never easy. Tacked on one wall, beneath a photo of Deacon John on stage embracing Barack Obama, was a handwritten quote attributed (inaccurately, but no matter) to Hunter S. Thompson. The music business, it said, "is a cruel and shallow money trench, a long plastic hallway where thieves and pimps run free and good men die like dogs for no reason. There is also a negative side."

"Blues is the parent of jazz," Deacon John continued. "If you can't play blues, you can't play jazz. Jazz came with adding syncopation to the blues, syncopation that originated in Africa but sometimes came by way of the Caribbean. When they sent slaves to America, a lot of the slaves went first to the Caribbean. So in New Orleans, you had African music get mixed with Caribbean music, which was syncopated slightly differently. The mixing happened when slaves from different tribes met in Congo Square to practice their culture."

Grabbing a guitar, he unleashed a dazzling burst of notes. "Bo Diddley's syncopation comes straight out of Africa," he said, "you hear?" Switching to a different syncopation, he played another string of notes before adding, "But Professor Longhair [the legendary New Orleans piano player] used a Mambo rhythm. That's Caribbean syncopation."

This mixing of rhythms led to the "collective improvisation" that animates New Orleans music. "Everybody is playing something a little different, but together it sounds good," Deacon John said, grinning. "It's the same as when people are dancing at a second line. They're all doing different movements, responding to the music. If you didn't grow up with that kind of syncopation, you wonder, 'How do they do that? How do they move their feet like that?' But the five-year-olds see the elders doing it, and they copy that and add a little something to it. That's how it's passed down through the generations."

If improvisation was a defining aspect of New Orleans music, it had also been a defining aspect of the transatlantic slave trade, including during the notorious ocean crossing known as the Middle Passage. The horrors of those voyages—when enslaved Africans were packed head to toe below decks amid festering pools of vomit and excrement—are well documented. Less known is that some of the enslaved were granted brief respites from that hell and brought up on deck, where they were unshackled and ordered to drum, sing, and dance. An etching dated to the 1840s and published by the National Geographic Society depicts three Africans clapping hands and kicking feet as they trace a circle on deck beneath the watchful eyes of White sailors, one of whom grasps a bullwhip. The captains of slave ships "were not really concerned about the health and well-being of their captives," *National Geographic* explained, but rather about protecting their cargo's economic value: "Dancing was seen as a form of exercise, which helped to preserve and maintain the captives' health during the tedious voyage."

Improvisation was imperative partly because most slaves belonged to different tribes in Africa and did not know one another's languages, much less their songs and dances. Improvisation continued after the slaves reached land and were distributed to plantations, where each slave contributed songs and dances from their cultural memory while trying to follow the songs and dances of others. Scholars say that the roots of today's grammatically imperfect but beautifully expressive African American English can be traced to this early improvisation and the need of enslaved Africans to communicate with their enslavers as well as with other slaves. "Each slaving expedition brought together by force captives from one or more linguistic and cultural community; by the time such captives were transported and sold, they normally entered slave groups in the New World that were very heterogeneous in ancestral culture and in language," wrote anthropologist Sidney W. Mintz. "Thus, New World slavery created, among other things, a kind of Babel, within which the slaves had to discover how to understand, and how to be understood—in short, how to communicate."

Improvisation went on to characterize not only second line parades but also the jazz music they helped bring forth. "If you were a slave, you *had* to learn how to improvise," the trumpeter and New Orleans native Wynton Marsalis has said. "You came on the land, you couldn't speak the language. You had all kind of foods you weren't used to eating. You had another whole system to deal with. If you couldn't improvise, you were going to be in a world of trouble." In a second line parade, Marsalis added, "The musicians are improvising, and the dancers are improvising, and they [also] doing something that they *been* doing a long time. So they have the feeling that not only is this moment something that never happened, it's a moment that's always happened."

Jazz theorists have argued that improvisation within a group is also a defining feature of democracy. "Democracy is about the freedom to create and to participate as an individual with the group," said Dr. Michael White, a clarinetist and professor at Xavier University in New Orleans. "In a band, one instrumental voice responds to the roles of melody and harmony with the other members of the band." White added, "Jazz can teach us about history. We learn where we come from and how we can become better people if we understand our ancestors."

The improvisational essence of jazz and second line culture was also a natural fit for Deborah Cotton. From the time she was kidnapped as a toddler and torn away from her biological mother, Deb had been improvising, even if she wasn't yet old enough to understand the word. She had to navigate, first, a path between the lies her father and stepmother were telling her and what she sensed to be the truth. As a teenager, she had to find a way to integrate her suddenly discovered Jewishness with her lifelong identity as a Christian. Throughout adulthood, she was improvising a relationship between her White identity and her Black identity, trying to take the best from both without losing track of who she was deep down inside. New Orleans was an ideal spot for such improvisation, given its wondrous mix of peoples, music, cultures, and cuisines. No wonder she loved the place.

As noted earlier in this book, one reason jazz was created in New Orleans, and only in New Orleans, is that the type of slavery initially practiced in Louisiana—French and Catholic—was different from the slavery administered in the rest of the American South. To be clear, this is not to say that slavery in Louisiana was a pleasant institution. Just read the recollections of former slaves who were interviewed in the 1930s as part of the Federal Writers' Project and published in books such as *Chained to the Land*. Some of them were enslaved in Louisiana, where they were forced to work from sunrise to sunset and beyond; were lashed with bullwhips until blood streamed down their bodies; were raped; were allotted pitifully insufficient food, water, and clothing; and were forbidden to learn to read or write. Not every slave owner or overseer was a vicious sadist, but plenty of them were. Conditions overall were so miserable that runaways were common, even though runaway slaves, if caught, received particularly brutal punishment.

Slave revolts began almost as soon as enslavement commenced in Louisiana, in 1722, and despite savage retaliation they continued until the Civil War. The first uprising on record occurred in 1731. Authorities crushed it after an incautious remark by a female slave alerted them to the plot. Eight suspected ringleaders were executed, their severed heads impaled on pikes along the Mississippi River to warn other slaves against revolting. The same gruesome deterrent was employed after subsequent rebellions, including the German Coast Uprising in 1811, the largest slave revolt in US history and the first time that federal troops were used to suppress a slave insurrection.

Slavery was deeply entrenched in New Orleans by the time the United States took over the city with the Louisiana Purchase of 1803, but it was slavery as administered first by the French and later by the Spanish. French and Spanish slavery was by no means gentle, but the French permitted practices that Anglo-Saxon slavers in the rest of the South never countenanced, notably allowing enslaved people to make music and practice their own spiritual beliefs. Nor did the French and Spanish reflexively condemn sexual relationships outside of marriage, as the Anglo-Saxons did. To be sure, White men in both systems raped enslaved women. The Anglo-Saxons simply lied about it, while French and Spanish slavers were inclined to acknowledge paternity. Indeed, upon their deaths French and Spanish slavers sometimes freed their mixed-race children, along with the children's mothers and even bequeathed them property, thus engendering in New Orleans a sizable population of "free persons of color."

The acceptance of having a second woman on the side, and a Black woman at that, transformed both the reality and perception of race in New Orleans. Individuals of mixed race were an accepted fact of life from the settlement's earliest days. So when White people encountered people of color, they could not assume they were enslaved. By 1830, one of every seven inhabitants of New Orleans was a free person of color, and free women of color owned a substantial amount of property, thanks to inheritances from their White sexual partners. Black, White, and mixed-race people lived jumbled together, without the strict demarcations slavery imposed elsewhere.

Deb thought that this history of racially fluid relationships helped foster a social ease between White and Black people that could still be observed in present-day New Orleans. "Black and White people are more comfortable with each other here," she told me. "It probably goes back to the different kind of slavery we had in New Orleans. Slaves here didn't have their African identity totally stripped from them, so they were able to maintain a greater sense of self, individually and collectively. Even though they were obviously going through a terrible, terrible experience, they continued practicing the cultural and spiritual beliefs they brought with them from Africa, and they passed those practices down to their children and grandchildren. Black people could see themselves as still human and connected to a past worthy of respect. Maybe that gave them an inner strength and sense of community that Black people in other cities of the United States didn't have."

Just how different slavery in New Orleans and its environs was from the rest of the South was elaborated in the *Code Noir*, the Black Code, established in 1724. In deference to Catholic theology, the Code Noir specified that slaves not only had the right to a day without work on the Sabbath and holidays, they also had a right to a Catholic education, marriage, and baptism. Slave owners were required to furnish slaves with a stipulated amount of food, clothing, and medical care, and slaves could be confiscated if those stipulations were disobeyed. Perhaps the greatest difference was the relative protection of slave families that the Code Noir enshrined. In the rest of the South, enslaved husbands, wives, and children were routinely sold to different enslavers, never to see one another again. Under Louisiana's Code Noir, the separation of slave families was forbidden.

To be sure, slaves were still brutalized under the Code Noir, but French slavery did not annihilate the entire personhood of enslaved people by depriving them of all leisure, family life, and human agency. On one hand, slave owners were allowed to strike slaves, including with metal rods, and confine them in shackles, while a slave who dared to strike back faced the death penalty. Enslaved people could, however, buy their freedom and hire themselves out as day laborers to make the money to do so. One way that slaves made money was by selling fruits, vegetables, meat, and fish they raised or caught, with the buying and selling often transpiring on their day off, at the Sunday assemblies where drumming, singing, and dancing were also allowed.

The earliest recorded instance of large numbers of slaves in New Orleans joining together to make music occurred in 1726, four years after the first shipment of enslaved Africans arrived. A man named Le Page du Pratz was the overseer of the Company of the Indies, which managed the colony of Louisiana for the French crown. Newly arrived in New Orleans, at that point a collection of primitive docks and a few rudimentary plantations nestled along the Mississippi River, Le Page was shocked one Sunday afternoon to come across, in his words, "at least 400 Blacks" gathered together, drumming and dancing. The gathering took place on the west bank of the river, across the Mississippi from today's French Quarter, in what is now the neighborhood of Algiers. Slaves were doing the same thing on nearby plantations, according to Le Page.

This first episode of African music and dance in New Orleans did not take place at Congo Square, the fabled spot later credited as the birthplace of jazz. But historians believe that not too many more years passed before Congo Square became a location where slaves came together on Sundays to enjoy "their half day of half freedom," in the apt phrase of Freddi Williams Evans, the author of *Congo Square: African Roots in New Orleans*.

Congo Square was an open field behind the rectangular cluster of streets that later became known as the French Quarter. By 1731, the French Quarter had assumed much the same layout it bears today. A central *place*, today's Jackson Square, faced the river. Streets as straight as a ruler extended four blocks upriver, four blocks downriver, and four blocks inland. Earthen levees separated the settlement from the Mississippi and its potential floods. Stretching along the back of the quarter was a fortified wall; on the other side of the wall was Congo Square, or, as the French called it, *Place Congo*. (Nowadays, Congo Square is part of Louis Armstrong Park, which features statues of Armstrong and other jazz giants, including Sidney Bechet. Embedded in the concrete patio in front of Armstrong's statue is a placard reading, HIS TRUMPET AND HEART BROUGHT EVERLASTING JOY TO THE WORLD, EMBODYING JAZZ AS *The Pulse of Life*).

On and off for the rest of the 1700s and the first half of the 1800s—almost until the outbreak of the Civil War—slaves and free people of color gathered on Sunday afternoons at Congo Square to make music, socialize, buy and sell goods, and preserve a sense of community and collective identity. There are no photographs of these gatherings, but observers described them in journals, letters, and published dispatches. The most famous description came from Benjamin Henry Latrobe, the architect who designed the US Capitol in Washington, DC, whose drawing skills enabled him to produce vivid sketches of the dancers and musical instruments he witnessed in Congo Square.

Writing in 1819, Latrobe recorded his astonishment at seeing five or six hundred Black people, unsupervised by Whites, gathered on the town's commons for uninterrupted hours of music, dancing, commerce, and visiting. "The music consisted of two drums and a stringed instrument," he wrote. "An old man sat astride of a cylindrical drum about a foot in diameter and beat it with incredible quickness with the edge of his hand and fingers. The other drum was an open staved thing held between the knees and beaten in the same manner. They made an incredible noise."

The crowd formed into circular groups for dancing, and from Latrobe's sketches, it appears the calinda was the dance of choice, with the bamboula also a favorite. Both dances originated in Africa. The sketches show two women holding handkerchiefs in the air as they danced, a gesture still seen at second line parades today. Separately, Latrobe witnessed two "Negro funerals" that were unlike any he had seen in the rest of the United States. Two hundred men and women "all dressed in pure white," he wrote, marched in a procession that sounds strikingly like second line funerals today.

Latrobe's observations highlight a distinguishing fact about slavery in New Orleans: enslaved people were able to make music largely on their own terms, a privilege forbidden to slaves in the rest of the South. Authorities in New Orleans did limit where and when slaves could make music, and at times they tried to suppress the practice entirely. Within such limits, however, enslaved people were free to express themselves as they chose—to sing in their own languages, to say what they wanted to say, to recall and create music for their own pleasure, to dance the dances they remembered or that elders taught them from their previous lives in Africa. In short, the cultural connection to their homeland and history was not severed. "Only in Place Congo in New Orleans was the African tradition able to continue in the open," scholar Dena Epstein has written.

This could hardly have been more different from the rest of the South, where slaves also sang and danced but under restraints that fettered their spirits. These slaves might or might not be allowed a day off on Sunday, but certainly they were not granted the freedom to express themselves that enslaved people in New Orleans had. Generally, enslaved people in the rest of the South sang openly only while laboring in the fields, or trudging along with shackles around their ankles, or in other postures of servitude.

Frederick Douglass, who was born into slavery but escaped it as a young man, later wrote, "I have often been utterly astonished, since I came to the north, to find persons who could speak of the singing, among slaves, as evidence of their contentment and happiness. It is impossible to conceive of a greater mistake." Often, slaves sang because they were ordered to sing, Douglass explained, for "A silent slave is not liked by masters or overseers. 'Make a noise,' make a noise,' . . . are the words usually addressed to the slaves when there is silence among them." The aim of such orders was not entertainment but surveillance. Slaves working in a field might be obscured from view by vegetation, but if they sang, the overseer knew where they were, making escape harder.

Slaves also sang to convey news to fellow slaves. In this sense singing functioned as a messenger service that operated right under the noses of slave owners and traders. A White traveler in Maryland once heard a shackled group of slaves sing about a neighboring slave who was on his way to Georgia:

> *William Rino sold Henry Silvers*
> *Hilo! Hilo!*
> *Sold him to the Georgy trader*
> *Hilo! Hilo!*
> *His wife she cried, the children bawled*
> *Hilo! Hilo!*
> *Sold him to the Georgy trader*
> *Hilo! Hilo!*

Slaves elsewhere in the South had to convene in secret to express themselves as fully as slaves in New Orleans did. Because many slaveholders either forbade slaves to attend church or allowed them to hear only preachers who said God wanted slaves to obey their enslavers, slaves would organize their own prayer meetings. Sometimes known as night sings, these meetings almost always took place under cover of darkness to evade masters and overseers. "The evidence indicates that [night sings] were usually held once a week on most plantations and that often slaves from several plantations would attend," scholar George P. Rawick writes in *From Sundown to Sunup*, his book about slave activities in the hours when they were not officially at work: "Men and women would crowd into an earthen-floored hut to sing, to pray, to shout and get 'happy.' Often they would do a slow circle dance, each individual's hand on the next person's shoulder."

The shoulder circle dance hints at another reason why slaves sang and danced: because they were Africans, or only a generation or two removed. In Africa, song and dance have been central to daily life from time immemorial. This was certainly the case in the 1700s and 1800s, when captured Africans were being shipped to the New World by the millions, and it remains true today, especially in the rural areas.

In my journalistic career I've been fortunate to travel for extended periods in many parts of Africa, including the Senegambia region of Western Africa, from whence came many of the enslaved people who populated New Orleans. The circle shoulder dance described above is all but identical to dances I've witnessed among rural Africans. I've also observed village market days of the sort described by visitors to Congo Square, as well as night sings. While covering the civil war and famine in Sudan in the 1990s, I drifted off to sleep one night listening to singing that emanated from a refugee camp a couple hundred yards away. Infants and elders had been dying from hunger and disease in that camp for weeks on end by then, but one would never guess that from the strong, calm voices wafting across the parched savannah.

Those Africans were singing amid their sorrows for the same reason, one imagines, that slaves in New Orleans and the rest of the South sang: to ease the pain. They were asking help from God, giving voice to their misery, expressing solidarity with one another, seeking strength to carry on. Singing and dancing were not merely a way to have much-needed entertainment; they were a means of coping with the circumstances of enslaved people's lives. Singing and dancing can foster joy, as in the slaves' efforts to "get happy" and temporarily leave behind the burdens of life. Singing and dancing can also release grief and provide comfort in the face of sorrow, even the ultimate sorrow of death.

"Music chases the devil away," was how Deb Cotton's grandmother would phrase it a century later; it can "transform wrong into right." To say that making music was a bright spot in the lives of enslaved people in New Orleans is not to sugarcoat that they were plainly oppressed and suffered unspeakably. It simply means that they had access to a wondrous source of comfort and strength amid their dreadful tribulations. And they went on to develop this wondrous source of comfort and strength, passing it down from generation to generation, until it evolved into jazz. Like a many splendored butterfly that emerges from a homely caterpillar, jazz began in ugliness, but it ascended to glory, as the descendants of enslaved people secured for the United States a permanent place in the history of human artistic achievement.

It's been a dilemma for ruling classes throughout history: what balance between repression and tolerance will most effectively induce the masses to obey? Too much repression and the downtrodden might decide they have nothing to lose and rise up; too much tolerance and they might also sense an opportunity to rebel, perhaps with greater odds of success. The colonial authorities and plantation owners in Louisiana went back and forth, favoring repression at certain times and tolerance at others. Hovering over their deliberations always was the knowledge that the enslaved exponentially outnumbered them and a failure to find the correct balance between repression and tolerance might be the last mistake the authorities ever made.

"Slaveholders were endlessly on edge over the cultural life of their slaves," Lawrence N. Powell wrote in his history of New Orleans, *The Accidental City*. "They never knew when to tolerate or suppress it. . . . They ended up doing both." When Spanish authorities proposed replacing the French Code Noir with a new set of slavery rules called La Cedula in 1789, the proposal was rejected after slaveholders objected. Among the new restrictions the Cedula would impose, slaves would no longer have Sundays off or be allowed to visit other plantations for festivals. One slaveholder countered that such rules were bound to provoke slaves in dangerous ways, fretting, "Would they not grow desperate when hearing the sounds of distant music without being able to join the festival?" When a rebellion nevertheless erupted near New Orleans in 1795, it was crushed with methods "as bloody as ever witnessed in the plantation districts of North America to that point in time," wrote Powell. Once again, the heads of the suspected ringleaders of the revolt were severed and displayed on posts along the Mississippi to warn against further resistance.

In response to the rebellion, a new element emerged with direct relevance to modern violence against African Americans: squads of White vigilantes, known as *Fronde,* joined uniformed soldiers to suppress the uprising. A recently updated slave code had empowered *all* White people to arrest any Black person found without an identity pass. "It was a license to bully," Powell observed, adding, "From here, it was a relatively straight line to the emergence of the notorious slave patrol system, in which special militias comprising slaveowners and nonowners alike swept the neighborhoods for runaways." Extending that straight line into the future brings us to the Ku Klux Klan, the White League, and other vigilante groups that terrorized African Americans with nighttime raids well into the 20th century.

Back and forth between tolerance and repression the pendulum swung: sometimes, slaves in New Orleans were allowed to gather on Sundays for music and dance; at other times, they weren't. The German Coast slave uprising of 1811—when an estimated two to five hundred slaves with axes and other farm implements massacred enslavers twelve miles upriver from New Orleans before marching on the city and being overpowered by federal troops—triggered a lurch toward repression. Slave uprisings nevertheless continued. The rebellion Nat Turner led in Virginia in 1831 particularly terrified Whites near and far, and increasing agitation by abolitionists further unsettled slavery proponents. The situation in New Orleans, always a less straightlaced place than the rest of the South, remained fluid. Sunday gatherings of enslaved and free Black people at Congo Square continued through at least 1845, when the authorities restricted such gatherings to the summer months. In 1858, with the North and the South increasingly at odds and some in the South urging secession, a final swing of the pendulum further favored repression: a New Orleans city ordinance prohibited all persons of color from assembling for *any* purpose without White supervision. Music and dancing by African Americans at Congo Square ceased. It would take a civil war to reinstate it.

"The blues came from slavery, jazz came from freedom," New Orleans brass band leader and second line champion Gregg Stafford had told me. "When slaves were singing in the fields, they bent their notes," Stafford explained, demonstrating the point by unleashing a long, soulful moan that slid from one tone to the next. "They did that in Africa. If you listen to people from Africa today, they hum like that. The blues was a product of all those long, dark nights of women being raped, men being beaten, and there was nothing they could do but moan and mourn."

"When they had the opportunity to have church, they brought that note bending with them," Stafford continued. "Church was where they could feel some comfort. They sang to feel better. That bending of notes went into gospel music later, and jazz, too."

Wiry, intense, with squinted eyes that carefully watched what was going on around him, Stafford looked much younger than his sixty-two years. A former leader of the iconic Young Tuxedo Brass Band, he had toured nationally—playing at the White House in 1978 for Jimmy Carter—and internationally, spending so much time in Scandinavia that he made "Helsinki" part of his email address. In the family tree of New Orleans musicians, he was one generation removed from Louis Armstrong. Stafford's link to the master was Danny Barker, a banjo and guitar player who performed with Armstrong and other giants—Jelly Roll Morton, Cab Calloway, Dizzy Gillespie, Charlie Parker—from the 1920s through the 1960s. Like Deacon John, Barker never became nationally famous. But he holds an enduring place in New Orleans musical history, for he almost singlehandedly kept brass band music from dying out in the modern era.

After Barker quit touring and moved back to New Orleans, he founded a brass band program for youth at the Fairview Baptist Church in the Seventh Ward in 1971. There he tutored Stafford, clarinetist Dr. Michael White, drummer Herlin Riley, and many of the other musicians who spearheaded the revival of brass bands in New Orleans during the 1970s. Barker made sure to instruct his young charges in not only the theory and technique of brass band music but also its cultural and historical significance—its true history, not the one imparted by the institutions of White America. As young Black men in the 1960s, Stafford recalled, he and others mentored by Barker initially "thought the banjo was an Uncle Tom instrument that was only played in minstrel shows. We didn't want anything to do with it. Danny taught us that the banjo came out of Africa, and we should be proud of that."

Like Deacon John, Stafford traced the evolution of second line parade music in three stages, starting with blues in the field, followed by gospel in the church, and then jazz in the streets. Formal histories often date the emergence of blues music to the decades between the end of the Civil War in 1865 and the turn of the century in 1900, but this chronology is not definitive; scholars seem to have settled on those dates because no written evidence of the blues from earlier years has been found. But lack of written evidence is not proof the blues didn't exist before the Civil War. Enslaved Africans had brought call-and-response singing and bending of notes with them when they arrived in the New World more than a century and a half earlier. The music they made while working in the fields or among themselves at night may not have had instrumental accompaniment, and it certainly wasn't written down in the conventional sense of the term, but it is not the presence of sheet music that defines the blues. Those early vocal expressions in the fields certainly qualified as the blues in form and spirit—the precursor to the music that Robert Johnson, Muddy Waters, B. B. King, and other giants would make famous.

Just as parents create and live on within the child, the blues gave rise to gospel and jazz and then lived on within them. Gospel arose first, when the field hollers and work songs of the blues mingled with the hymns and other sacred music enslaved people heard in White churches. Blacks, whether slave or free, were rarely allowed inside White churches, but often they attended separate services that relied on the same music and teachings. They adopted White music but made it sound different, not only by singing a hymn with bent notes but also by adding foot-stomping and handclapping that most White churchgoers—and some Blacks as well—considered blasphemous.

Only in New Orleans did this musical evolution of blues into gospel extend into a third stage to become jazz. One reason it did is that African Americans in New Orleans had their own Sunday gatherings, where they could push the music in directions they themselves chose, rather than Whites choosing for them. Whether in Congo Square or at the corner saloon, Blacks in New Orleans could inflect blues and gospel with more of their African heritage, which made it livelier, for two principal reasons. In Africa, music was inseparable from dancing; it was supposed to move one's body. Music in Africa also did not assume the separation between performer and audience that prevailed in America; music in Africa was more a collective pursuit in which musicians and onlookers created a shared experience, much as brass bands and crowds at second line parades still do today.

"Jazz is a music; jazz is a language," wrote Jason Berry in his history of New Orleans, *City of a Million Dreams*. "From African American pews and parades came an ensemble style, 'playing the melody with a beat,' writes Bill Russell, 'sung by the various instruments with a beautiful, vocal-like warmth . . . [and] moderate, relaxed tempos to which people dance or march, even in a hot climate.'"

The period between the Civil War's end in 1865 and roughly 1900 was when New Orleans musicians felt their way from blues toward jazz. The moaning and bending of notes that was the hallmark of blues had initially been expressed vocally, but when African Americans got hold of musical instruments, "they pushed that moan through a horn," said Stafford, adding with vehemence, "Which was completely new. You didn't hear that in Bach's music. You didn't hear that in Shostakovich's"—he all but spat the name—"music. It came from the plantations. Jazz came out of the hearts and souls of Black people who were trying to express themselves, not as slaves but as free people."

The jazz heard in second line parades, Michael White said in the documentary based on Jason Berry's *City of a Million Dreams,* "goes all the way back to the core of Africa. For someone coming up in the United States, dealing with American racism, trying to find your place in this life and society and the world, that's the real value of the second line parade—why people follow four, five, six hours on end: because you can be transformed into another world that really sets you free."

Both jazz and second line parades, then, were inseparable from slavery. But as I explored the history of slavery while researching this book, I was amazed and, frankly, embarrassed to discover all that I did not know about slavery. As a young man, I had attended an elite university, where I took courses on US history and even West African history. After graduating, I worked at a research institute in Washington, DC, where I was fortunate to be mentored by leaders in the US civil rights and anti-apartheid movements and to take part in many demonstrations for racial justice. Yet my ignorance about slavery remained profound: there was *so* much I didn't know. Perhaps worse, so much of what I thought I knew turned out to be misleading or outright wrong.

Take the notion, long taught to American schoolchildren, that the Civil War ended slavery. That was true in a narrow, legalistic sense: after the Civil War, White people could no longer legally own Black people. But as a practical matter, slavery continued, simply under different names and legal forms.

As Douglas A. Blackmon documented in his searing book, *Slavery by Another Name*, in the decades immediately after the Civil War tens of thousands of Black men were arrested throughout the South for no valid reason and forced to work in mines and factories under abominable conditions for years, often until death. It was "a system in which armies of free men, guilty of no crimes and entitled by law to freedom, were compelled to labor without compensation, were repeatedly bought and sold, and were forced to do the bidding of White masters through the regular application of extraordinary coercion," Blackmon wrote. De facto slavery continued well into the 20th century, as thousands of Black people were lynched, while "Jim Crow" segregation and discrimination deprived Blacks of the vote, decent schools, wages comparable to Whites', and much more. When the modern civil rights movement demanded an end to such injustices, some White supremacists were as incredulous as they were outraged. "We killed two-month-old Indian babies to take this country, and now they want us to give it to the niggers," one Mississippi man complained to reporters in 1962.

So, if it took nearly fifty years after the Civil War for musicians in New Orleans to evolve the blues into jazz, it may be because slavery did not cease after the Civil War as much as it shape-shifted. Within one year of the war's end, every state in the former Confederacy had passed laws prohibiting Black people from voting. For their part, many Whites in the South simply refused to accept the outcome of the war and worked to reimpose Black servitude.

"The best we can do is keep 'em as near a state of bondage as possible," a Louisiana plantation owner said after the Civil War. Which is pretty much what happened. Despite their previous decades of unpaid labor, and a Union Army general's promise of "40 acres and a mule," newly emancipated slaves were granted no land of their own. As a practical matter, therefore, they had little choice but to continue laboring—now as sharecroppers or indentured factory workers—for the very White people who had exploited them before the war. Thus doomed to perpetual poverty, African Americans were then abandoned by the North in what has been called the Great Betrayal of 1877, when the federal government withdrew its troops from the South. With the end of Reconstruction, Black people across the South were left to fend for themselves against a fresh onslaught of terror aimed at "keeping the niggers in their place," in the words of Nathan Bedford Forrest, the former Confederate general who founded the Ku Klux Klan.

In a striking parallel to how Donald Trump and his White supremacist outlook took hold within the Republican Party during Barack Obama's presidency, the White supremacists of this earlier era got away with their aggressions partly because not enough other White people opposed them. It was no secret that Southern White elites, despite having been militarily defeated, wanted to perpetuate their hold over African Americans, as author Bruce Levine has detailed in *The Fall of the House of Dixie*. Louisiana plantation owner William J. Minor, for example, said that the South should aim to rejoin the Union with "things as they were, but perhaps under some other name than slavery."

A few brave voices in Washington warned against such trickery. "If we want a lasting peace . . . we must take away the platform on which slavery stands—the great landed estates of the armed rebels of the South," future president James A. Garfield, then a congressman from Ohio, told colleagues on Capitol Hill. Former slaves also saw through their oppressors' designs. "Gib us our own land, and we take care of ourselves, but widout land de ole massas can hire us or starved us, as dey please," one former slave told a Union officer in the dialect ascribed to him. But by early 1864, Levin wrote, "the federal government had already returned to their original owners two of every three of the Mississippi Valley plantations that it had previously seized."

The end of Reconstruction gave rise to the Jim Crow era, when legally free Black people were subjugated, intimidated, and brutalized by a White minority. In the oft-quoted words of W.E.B. Du Bois, "The slave went free; stood a brief moment in the sun; then moved back again toward slavery."

As the protections of federal laws and troops receded, large numbers of Black people moved from rural areas to New Orleans, unwittingly setting the stage for the emergence of jazz. With White supremacists now free to terrorize at will, Blacks across the South migrated to cities between 1880 and 1910. The cities were far from idyllic for Black people, but Blacks perhaps calculated, in Du Bois's words, that "huddling together" promised them greater safety and economic opportunity. The migration of rural Blacks to New Orleans "created a huge mass of patronage for the new music, an essential element of any artistic flowering," Thomas Brothers suggested in *Louis Armstrong's New Orleans*. The new music took shape in a variety of places—second line parades and funerals, but also nightclubs, dance halls, and storefront churches of the Sanctified faith, where worshippers gave voice to impassioned praying and singing shunned by "respectable" Black churches. All classes and nationalities were represented in these places, recalled Jelly Roll Morton: "There weren't any discrimination of any kind."

These were also the decades when Social Aid and Pleasure Clubs arose in New Orleans, as both sources of social services and popular entertainment and centers of civic action. In 1890, when activists challenged the segregation of New Orleans streetcars, the person of color chosen to board a "White" train was Daniel Desdunes, a top local musician. Desdunes played in the Onward Brass Band, whose members later included Joe "King" Oliver, Louis Armstrong's mentor. Shortly afterward, the activists' second challenge to streetcar segregation led to the landmark US Supreme Court case *Plessy v. Ferguson*, in which the Court articulated a doctrine of "separate but equal" that extended segregation throughout the United States.

Louis Armstrong grew up poor, the son of a single mother named Mayann who appears to have arrived in New Orleans in the late 1890s as part of the "huddling in place" described by Du Bois. But even a poor boy could enjoy the sights and sounds of second line parades. "To watch those clubs parade was an irresistible and absolutely unique experience," Armstrong later recalled. "All the [club] members wore full dress uniforms and with those beautiful silk ribbons streaming from their shoulders they were a magnificent sight. At the head of the parade rode the aides, in full dress suits and mounted on fine horses with ribbons around their heads. The brass band followed, shouting a hot swing march as everyone jumped for joy. . . . I had spent my life in New Orleans, but every time one of those clubs paraded I would second line them all day long."

As the US economy industrialized and shifted to war production upon entering World War I in 1917, jazz spread from New Orleans to become the most popular music in the country. Armstrong and other jazzmen had plenty of work, but White supremacy remained entrenched, by no means only in the South. Black musicians routinely received insults from White audiences, even as they played the music those Whites loved. "Without fail," Danny Barker later recalled, he and his bandmates would hear White audience members say things like, "'Dem coons sho' can play.' And if it wasn't that it was niggers, darkies, Zulus, piccaninnies, Africans, monkeys, gorillas, Ubangies (I learned years later what an Ubangi was—the African tribe that wears a disc in the lips)."

Racism did provide Black musicians occasional moments of humor, though. Barker recalled a tour that took his band through a small town in Florida in 1926. During a break between sets, the sheriff told the band, "I don't want to see or catch any of you niggers with any of these White men's nigger wimmen, and if I do, it's going to be some dead Louisiana niggers shipped back to Louisiana." After a pause, the bass player spoke up:

"Mr. Sheriff, could, er, uh, you show us or point out these White gentlemen's lady friends to us?" The sheriff, recalled Barker, replied "very curtly: 'I ain't showing you niggers nuthin', but I'll tell you this: *all* them nigger women you see out there belong to them White men.'"

Forty years later, as Gregg Stafford came of age in 1960s New Orleans, racism remained a menacing presence. Indeed, racism helped nudge Stafford into his musical career. As a kid, he wanted nothing more than to be a navy pilot, and a teacher at his high school gave him the books needed to master the entrance exam. After weeks of diligent study, Stafford was confident of success. He took the exam at the Belle Chasse Naval Station in New Orleans, the only Black person in the room. When he handed in his paper, he was sure he had scored a perfect one hundred, but the instructor, he recalled, "said all of us failed. He looked at me and said, 'You're the only one who almost passed.' I looked him straight in the eye and said, 'I know I passed that test.' He just grinned, like it was our private joke."

Stafford began playing music that same year and joined Danny Barker's program at Fairview Baptist Church in 1971. His instrument was the trumpet. Barker became like a father to him, and Stafford made tremendous progress: at the age of twenty-one, he was accepted into the Young Tuxedo Brass Band, the modern-day descendant of the band Louis Armstrong did his last New Orleans gig with before leaving for Chicago and stardom in 1922. The 1960s and early 1970s was an era of Black consciousness and pride; Stafford's immersion into the Social Aid and Pleasure Club tradition inspired his emerging worldview. "Black people knew they didn't have anything," he told me. "They were facing the evils of segregation and discrimination every day. Members of Social Aid and Pleasure Clubs couldn't *wait* to come out on Sundays and dance at second lines. I saw that. I *did* that."

Stafford went on to a very successful musical career, but the old attitudes remained as demeaning as those Barker endured sixty years earlier. Stafford and his band, including fellow Fairview Baptist alum Dr. Michael White, did a gig in the late 1980s in Hattiesburg, a small city in neighboring Mississippi. Upon arrival, they encountered a fellow musician who was booked to play the piano bar at the same convention. She was White, blond, easy on the eyes. She and Stafford got to talking in the bar before their respective gigs and, he recalled, "it was apparent she likes me."

The White woman and Stafford stepped over to the piano to chat further, but an old White guy at the bar decided he needed to join the conversation. From ten feet away, he started hurling questions at Stafford, asking if he and his band could play this or that song.

"I remember I was irritated," Stafford said. "He was obviously trying to break up the little conclave this woman and I were having. But I stayed steady and just said, 'No, I never heard of that song.' I resumed talking with her and he interrupted again, asking if we can play some other song. I told him we didn't know that song, either. Then he said, 'Well, what kind of a nigger *are* you?'"

My mouth literally fell open when Stafford told me this, and he said the blond woman at the piano had the same reaction.

"Everything got real quiet," he continued. "Michael and the rest of the band were all looking at me, waiting to see what I would do. I took a breath, looked that White man straight in the eye and said, 'I'm the kind of nigger who knows that there are still a bunch of ignorant ass old White motherfuckers like you out there. And I'm the kind of nigger who's not gonna let you provoke me into doing something stupid so you can call the cops.'"

In 1993, Stafford cofounded the Black Men of Labor Social Aid and Pleasure Club, a name he and the other cofounders chose to make a point. "We wanted to repudiate all the shit that's said about Black men in New Orleans not wanting to work, not caring about their families," he said. Stafford had worked twenty-four years as an elementary school teacher in the New Orleans public school system. "The men in our club worked; we took care of our families," he continued. "Some of us were professionals; some worked blue-collar jobs. But *all* of us worked, and we wanted that to be recognized and respected."

The Black Men of Labor went further, arguing that the ideology some Black men embraced that celebrated guns, drug dealing, and sexual irresponsibility was a form of self-hatred, just as Deb Cotton would suggest years later about the Mother's Day gunmen. The club's manifesto declared, "The Black Men of Labor Love the Culture and Traditions of New Orleans: Conversely, the Black Men of Labor Deplore Violence, Crime and Self-Hatred. When you hear and see it coming down the street, a traditional New Orleans Second-Line Parade is a social trumpet echoing loud and clear a message that, as Black men and women, we are fully present and still here in spite of racial discrimination and the vicissitudes of life." The manifesto continued, "The Black Men of Labor and the New Orleanians who parade with us will not be intimidated or fearful of those unfortunate souls who seek a life of drug dealing, murder, and crime. The Black Men of Labor do not condone violence of any kind—shooting and murders have no place in the dance rituals we perform on the streets of New Orleans."

Because of their reverence for second line history, Stafford and the Black Men of Labor were sticklers for a traditional presentation of second line music, dance, and outfits. For their parade in 2016, for example, club members dressed in resplendent light blue suits with white piping, gleaming two-toned shoes, and the black bowler hats that Social Aid and Pleasure Club members began wearing a century ago. Stafford's signature performance was a dance routine that began when he removed the bowler from his head, turned it upside down, and placed it back atop his head. He then somehow balanced it there as he strode forward a few paces, back a few paces, forward and back, all while his arms swept stiffly forward and backward like a toy soldier's. Throughout all this, he clenched an unlit cigar between his teeth, again as club members of old did. The crowd went wild, whooping, whistling, and clapping as if the Lord himself had suddenly materialized among them.

How Stafford managed to keep a bowler hat, with its rounded crown, balanced atop his head while he strode back and forth to the thumping rhythms of a brass band was a secret he did not divulge. "It's not easy," is all he would say. He continued to perform the act year after year because his community expected it. "One year, we were getting ready to start the parade and a very elderly Black man walking with a cane approached me," he recalled. "He said he'd traveled all the way across town, took three buses, because he wanted to see that dance of mine. Then he lifted his cane, poked it at me and said"—here Stafford affected a deep, grizzled voice—"'Now don't you go shortin' me! Don't go shortin' me!'"

Like his mentor Danny Barker, Stafford felt a duty to pass along the meaning and spirit of traditional jazz music and second line parades to new generations of musicians and spectators who could keep African American dignity and achievement alive. "If Black history was taught in the schools of New Orleans the way other history is taught, Black children would have the self-confidence of knowing where they came from and the great things they can do with their lives," Stafford said. "We were the creators of this music, jazz. If we don't keep the tradition alive, before long we'll be hearing that British people created this music, like with rock 'n' roll. And Black people will believe it because we won't know any better."

Joe "I Am the Tradition" Maize was part of the next generation Stafford was talking about, and Joe appeared to be of two minds about the music's future. "You got a hundred brass bands that are younger than us now," he told me. "Walk down Bourbon Street and you'll see ten bands playing on the street for tips, and more on Frenchman. All the high schools have real good band programs, and middle school children are starting, too."

On the other hand, the broader society in New Orleans showed a distressing lack of knowledge about second lines, Joe said, and he included his fellow African Americans in that criticism. "A lot of Black people think that second line parades is umbrellas and handkerchiefs, just the stereotype of second lines," he complained. "They don't understand that it come from Congo Square, we were enslaved by the French, but the French let us do this every Sunday, and we still doing it now. You can go to Congo Square and read all about it on the signs there, but our own people don't know it."

"How is that possible?" I asked. "How can any Black person in New Orleans not know the truth about second lines?"

"You wouldn't believe," Maize replied. "People 'round us, they basically want to watch football."

"Do they see you as Uncle Toms because you parade in second lines?"

"We see *them* as Uncle Toms," Joe huffed. "Because they don't know where our culture come from, where *they* come from. This is what we was doing when they brought us here. It comes from before we *were* slaves. But we're not taught that in school, not even in music classes. They teach us how to read music and play your instrument. Nothing about the history or culture of it."

"What about the guys who shot us at that Mother's Day second line? Do you think they knew about second lines?"

"They mind fucked," he said. "They don't care about nothing but themselves. They was having a beef with someone, and whoever they had to take down, they don't care as long as they get their target."

"But why at a second line?" I pressed. "It seems like blasphemy for anyone to shoot up a second line parade. But for African Americans to shoot up a ritual that helped their people through slavery and segregation, that's beyond blasphemy. That's tragedy."

"They probably had no knowledge of second lines or anything we doing," Joe said. "If it was taught to them, if they had a little knowledge, they wouldn't a did it there."

6

The Unblinking Eye

When I first got the blues
They brought me over on a ship
Men were standing over me
And a lot more with a whip
And everybody wanna know
Why I sing the blues
  —"Why I Sing the Blues" by B. B. King

I awoke the morning after the Mother's Day shooting to find an email
from a CNN producer asking if I felt well enough to come on the air
to discuss what had happened. Physically, I felt surprisingly well—no
real pain. Emotionally, not so much. Early news reports said that the
shooting had sent twenty people to the hospital, including a local writer
named Deborah Cotton. The *Times-Picayune* article mentioning me as
one of the victims had gone out over the Associated Press wire service
to hundreds of newsrooms around the world, which explained other
emails I got that morning from colleagues in Europe and New York
asking if I was okay.

I agreed to do the CNN show, which meant I first had to break the news that I'd been shot to my mother—I didn't want her to learn about it from television.

I wasn't sure how Mom would take it. She grew up during the Depression, the first child of hard-working, God-fearing tenant farmers in southwest Minnesota. She was not the emotional type, but that steadiness had once helped to save my life. Years earlier, while traveling around the world to do the reporting for my book about the environmental future, I fell seriously ill after spending four months in Africa, much of it in famine-stricken areas where deadly diseases were common. I collapsed in a Bangkok hotel room, the victim of a severe gastrointestinal infection. Upon hearing the news, my mother was alarmed but kept her head. Working from halfway around the world, she helped me obtain first-rate local medical care. On another occasion, however, when a mega earthquake struck San Francisco shortly after I moved there, Mom called me immediately to demand, with a tremulous voice, "When are you coming home?"

The day before the second line shooting, I had called Mom to wish her a happy Mother's Day, so she knew that I was in New Orleans. I punched her number into my cell phone, and she picked up on the second ring.

"Hi, Mom. How ya doing?"

"Hi honey, just fine. Sitting here doing the crossword puzzle."

"Good, good. How was the rest of your Mother's Day?"

"Fine. We had a nice brunch. Are you still in New Orleans?"

"Yeah. Did you hear about the big shooting here yesterday?"

"No, what shooting?"

"Someone shot into the crowd at a second line street parade. Twenty people ended up in the hospital."

"That's terrible."

"Yeah. I'm going on CNN in an hour to talk about it."

"Okay, I'll turn on the TV."

"Good, good. Actually, Mom, the reason I'll be on CNN is that I was at the parade where the shooting happened. But I'm okay."

"You are?"

"Yeah, I was lucky. Actually, I was standing right there and I saw the shooting happen. But I'm fine."

Mom didn't say anything.

"So don't worry, okay Mom? But Mom? I have to tell you, and I'm really fine, but I was one of the people who got shot. Just a flesh wound in the leg. The hospital didn't even keep me overnight. That's why I'm going on TV, because I'm totally fine. Okay?"

There was a long silence. I was afraid Mom was too upset to speak. Suddenly, she broke the silence.

"Actually, Mark, I'm surprised that you haven't been shot before."

"What?" I wondered if I'd heard her right.

"I'm surprised that you haven't been shot before," she repeated.

"What do you mean by that?"

"Well, considering what you've been doing with your life, I'm just surprised that you haven't been shot before now."

Now I was the one who was speechless. What I'd been doing with my life? I guess she meant my years of reporting overseas.

"Okay, Mom," I finally said. "Well, I'm really fine. I better get to the studio."

"Okay, honey. Good luck on the show."

Only after I arrived at CNN's New Orleans studio did a producer inform me that the police had just released a video of the Mother's Day shooting, and CNN was going to air it during my interview. I wasn't sure how I felt about that, but there was no time to argue. I was already seated on the set, my earpiece in place. The camera's red light came on, and we were live around the world.

The video released by the police was one minute and twenty-six seconds long. It offered an aerial view of the shooting, with the camera looking down on the crowd from a close enough distance that a viewer could make out the color of individual marchers' skin and clothes. As I watched it live on the CNN set, the video went by so quickly that I found it difficult to recognize some details, but later viewings brought more clarity, as did newspaper articles that divided the video into a series of eight still images.*

In the first of the eight images, the main gunman was circled in red ink for ease of identification, but he would have been easy to spot in any case given his location. He was Black, with dark skin and short hair. Wearing a white T-shirt and dark pants, he was standing with his back against the house that occupied the near corner of Frenchmen and North Villere. His head was turned to the left, away from the camera, as he watched the parade pass from left to right. Although the image was grainy, women and small children were plainly visible in the crowd. If one followed the gunman's gaze toward the intersection's near corner, one could see the pale yellow fedora I was wearing, though the rest of me was obscured by people milling about between the gunman and me. Deb and the TBC brass band were not visible; the camera's field of vision did not extend far enough leftward to reveal them halting in place on the cusp of the intersection.

In the next image, a second individual, a Black male, was striding from the opposite side of Frenchmen Street toward the shooter. He was shorter and wore a dashiki shirt, not a common look in New Orleans. There was an air of familiarity in his approach to the shooter, and once he was a step away from him, the second guy appeared to address words to the shooter. The shooter listened but kept his eyes on the passing crowd. The guy in the dashiki walked away quickly, back across Frenchmen Street. After three steps, he looked back at the shooter. An observer would be forgiven for thinking that the second guy was a lookout man who had alerted the shooter that his target was coming into range.

---

*   Here are links: https://www.youtube.com/watch?v=wo1nXFfgs5M/ and http://www
.dailymail.co.uk/news/article-2323525/BREAKING-NEWS-Twelve-people-shot-New
-Orleans-Mother-Day-parade.html/.)

No sooner had the guy in the dashiki disappeared among the crowd than the shooter made his move. Drawing himself up to full height, he took a decisive stride toward the crowd. As he was taking a second step, his right hand reached into his pants pocket. Meanwhile, my fedora indicated that I was moving from the corner toward the middle of the intersection.

As the shooter took a third step, he pulled a handgun from his pocket. After a fourth step, he lunged into the crowd, coming close enough to grab people by their shirts. He pointed the gun further into the intersection, which was now thick with pedestrians. My fedora showed I had now drifted directly into his line of fire.

With his right arm extended, the shooter began firing. The muzzle of his gun emitted little starbursts of light as the bullets exited. In the first split second, almost no one reacted. The one exception was a man immediately to the gunman's right who was rocked sideways by the force of the bullets discharging eighteen inches from his face. He fell to the pavement. The gunman kept advancing, firing as he stepped off the sidewalk onto the street. His left arm flew up to balance his aim as his forearm splayed outward at an unnatural angle.

In the next photo, the crowd was in flight. A young, slender African American girl, perhaps ten years old, dressed all in white, raced offscreen to the right, her pumping arms and legs a blur of motion. Behind her, the intersection was emptying fast. "It was like a wave," numerous people in the crowd would later tell me, recalling how the crowd swept outward as if it were a single organism.

Embarrassingly slow to react, I was now directly in front of the gunman, with no one left between us shielding me. As he unleashed his final shots, he seemed to be aiming right at me. The photo showed my body twisting to the right as I threw myself onto the pavement.

The shooter lowered his gun, glanced over his right shoulder to the far side of Frenchmen Street, and turned to run. He headed away from the intersection, back up Frenchmen Street, still holding the gun. Only the right side of his face was visible, and the downward angle of the camera made it impossible to discern his features.

There was no sound to the video, but as in an old silent movie, the action got the point across. The gunman was Black; he had been lying in wait; he had fired point-blank into a crowd of people who were overwhelmingly Black and included women pushing baby strollers; and he had fled on foot. And the video made clear one more thing: the gunman had no idea that everything he just did was captured on camera.

Of all the coincidences embedded in the Mother's Day shooting, and there were many, none was more consequential than the emergence of the Unblinking Eye—the video camera that recorded the shooting as it happened. The Unblinking Eye would have no place in this story except for a last-minute change in the parade route, a coincidence itself. When Ed Buckner initially discussed his proposed route with city officials, they agreed that the parade would leave from his house, proceed down Elysian Fields toward the Mississippi, and turn right onto North Robertson Street. The morning of the parade, however, the police told Buckner that that route had to be adjusted. Construction work on North Robertson had left a large hole in the pavement; revelers might trip and be injured. Instead, the police directed Buckner to turn the parade right one block later, onto North Villere Street, where, unbeknownst to all, the Unblinking Eye kept watch.

The Unblinking Eye was perched in its usual spot that Mother's Day morning, doing its usual job, gazing ceaselessly down on the intersection of Frenchmen and North Villere streets. The eye was tiny, smaller than a child's fingernail, and like many tiny things, it often went unnoticed. But peering out of a private surveillance camera, the Unblinking Eye noticed everything. And it kept a record, twenty-four hours a day, methodically stamping its images with the corresponding date and time.

Nestled beneath the second-floor eaves of the corner house the gunman had been leaning against before firing his weapon, the Unblinking Eye had been installed a year earlier by the house's owner, Leroy Williams. Mr. Williams took that precaution after a fire broke out in the building next door and almost burned down his house. "They was doing drugs in there," Mr. Leroy, as he was known on the street, later told me.

Mr. Leroy grew up in that house when it belonged to his mother, but he no longer lived there. After retiring, he moved to the country, about an hour and a half's drive northwest of New Orleans. Now his adult daughter lived in the house with her family. To keep an eye on the property, Mr. Leroy installed a surveillance camera whose unending stream of images he could monitor from his new home far from the city.

The Mother's Day shooting was not the first violent crime that had taken place in front of the house. "Oh my, no," Mr. Leroy told me. "There's been a number of shootings there, going back to the 1980s, even a murder. Drugs are part of it, and young men today are not the same as when we come up. They don't care who they shoot or who else might get hurt. It's shameful they shot up a second line on Mother's Day. You come from a mother! How can you shoot innocent people, even women and children, on Mother's Day?"

Mr. Leroy's camera played a pivotal role in the Mother's Day shooting, especially its aftermath. If the Original Big 7's parade route had not changed at the last minute to pass beneath the Unblinking Eye, there would have been no visual record of what happened that Mother's Day. Without that visual record, it would have been much more difficult, perhaps impossible, to determine who the shooters were. Finding, arresting, and prosecuting the shooters would have been even harder. In other words, the perpetrators of the biggest mass shooting in modern New Orleans history might well have gotten away with it.

Most New Orleans gunmen did. "If you kill a Black man in New Orleans, the clearance rates for those shootings—meaning, the police know who did it—are in the 40 percent range," Peter Scharf, a crime expert at Louisiana State University's School of Public Health, told me. That meant, Scharf added, that the shooters responsible for the majority of the murders in New Orleans "are still out there on the streets."

Within twenty-four hours of the Mother's Day shooting, though, the detectives had the Unblinking Eye's visual record of the shooting in hand, and that changed everything. Chris Hart noticed the Unblinking Eye shortly after reaching the crime scene. "We're trained to look for stuff like that," he explained. After retrieving the Eye's equipment and data from inside the house, NOPD's "geek squad," as Hart called them, labored overnight to produce the video that would be broadcast the next day on CNN and other TV networks around the world.

TV journalists had swarmed the Mother's Day shooting story as soon as it happened, and now, a day later, they did so again. After all, the Unblinking Eye's video, despite the human carnage it revealed, was riveting television. Viewers could watch a shoot-'em-up in real time, peering down on the scene like gods in heaven, marveling at what fools these mortals be.

The Mother's Day shooting was far from the first or last time that stark visual images had illuminated racially charged realities in the United States. Personal videos, TV reports, feature films, documentaries, photographs, and drawings had been transforming people's thoughts and feelings about race in America for centuries. "Almost as color defines vision itself, race shapes the cultural eye—what we do and do not notice, the reach of empathy and the alignment of response," historian Taylor Branch wrote in *Parting the Waters*, volume one of his magisterial biography of Martin Luther King Jr. Cameras transform the abstractions of race into concrete images that can move popular opinion and spur government action, for good or ill.

One of the most consequential examples began unfolding a year after the Mother's Day shooting, when cell phone videos documented incident after incident where unarmed African Americans, usually men, died at the hands of police. When these images were shared with the public, they fundamentally changed the public conversation about race, crime, and police in the United States, energized the budding Black Lives Matter movement and leading some police departments to reexamine their practices and promise improvements. Black people had complained for years that police mistreated them; White society generally dismissed such complaints as special pleading or paranoia. Now, the cell phone revolution had furnished a tool with which Black people could prove their accusations, and the rise of the internet meant that they no longer had to rely on the mainstream media to share the news. Black people could post videos online and rely on social media to spread the word.

This scenario played out after the choking death of Eric Garner by police in New York in 2014; the fatal shooting of twelve-year-old Tamir Rice by police in Cleveland, also in 2014; the de facto execution of Walter Scott in South Carolina by a police officer who shot him in the back while Scott was running away in 2015; the shooting of Philando Castile in St. Paul, Minnesota, when he tried to hand his driver's license to a police officer in 2016; and many more. Two of the most consequential incidents took place in 2020, when cameras captured the slaying of Ahmaud Arbery, a twenty-five-year-old African American man shot by two White men while Arbery was jogging in suburban Georgia, and the murder of George Floyd, the forty-six-year-old Black man whose death at the hands of Minneapolis police ignited unprecedented protests across the United States.

These incidents became international news stories and helped spark reform because the images were raw and undeniable. "Black and Brown people have been making these complaints for years, but they fell on deaf ears because no one wanted to believe some officers would act that way," said Dr. Cedric Alexander, the president of the National Organization of

Black Law Enforcement Executives. Now, Alexander continued, cell phone videos and social media distribution of them enabled people to see that, "Wow, they really did shoot this guy in the back."

Earlier images had likewise been instrumental in changing popular attitudes and public policy about race. In the 1780s, abolitionists in Great Britain scored their first breakthrough in mobilizing popular opinion against slavery by utilizing the photography of their day—a detailed diagram of a slave ship's innards—to show the public what the slave trade truly looked like. The diagram depicted the *Brooks*, a cargo ship that transported enslaved Africans across the Atlantic to the British-claimed colony of Jamaica. When fully loaded, the *Brooks* sometimes carried as many as 740 enslaved men, women, and children. The drawing provided a top-down view of the ship's hold, where stick figures representing the enslaved were stacked head to toe and shoulder to shoulder, like sardines in a can. "In an era before photography, the *Brooks* diagram 'seemed to make an instantaneous impression of horror upon all who saw it,'" observed an activist quoted in Adam Hochschild's history of the British abolition movement, *Bury the Chains*. "The diagram began appearing in newspapers, magazines, books and pamphlets; realizing what a powerful new weapon it had, [activists] also promptly printed up more than seven thousand copies as posters, which were hung on the walls of homes and pubs throughout the country."

"Iconic images have power because they allow us to see what previously we could barely imagine," Hochschild explained. The same held true during the civil rights struggle in the United States in the 1960s, when visual images became weapons in the battle for public opinion and the political influence it delivered. Photographs of young Negroes sitting at "Whites Only" lunch counters and of Governor George Wallace standing in a doorway to block admission of Black students at the University of Alabama, TV coverage of water hoses blasting Black demonstrators down the street like tumbleweeds, and of Martin Luther King Jr. delivering his "I Have A Dream" speech at the Lincoln Memorial—these and other images had the effect of pressuring public officials to take action. John Lewis, the civil rights leader who marched with King and later served more than thirty years in Congress, once observed that, "Without television, the civil rights movement would have been like a bird without wings."

Taylor Branch recounted in *Pillar of Fire*, the second volume in his history of the King years, that on March 28, 1963, a CBS News TV crew filmed a crowd of angry Whites heckling a line of a hundred Negroes assembled outside a courthouse in Mississippi to register to vote. As some of the Whites yelled, "Sic 'em," police officers unleashed attack dogs. Still photographers captured the moment, and when one of the photos was printed the next day in the nation's most powerful newspaper, the image triggered a response from the highest office in the land. "President Kennedy saw a photograph of a German shepherd biting [an African American who happened to be a preacher] in the next morning's *New York Times* and sent word that [US assistant attorney general] Burke Marshall should do something about it."

The power of visual images was a double-edged sword, though, that at times denigrated Black people and rationalized their mistreatment. An infamous early example was *The Birth of a Nation*, the 1915 silent film that, fifty years after the Civil War, lionized the Confederacy as a noble cause. Brilliantly shot and arranged by director D. W. Griffith, the film portrayed slavery as an honorable institution, Black men as incurable rapists, the federal government and military as tyrannical occupiers, and the Ku Klux Klan as heroic resisters of Northern oppression. President Woodrow Wilson, after ordering a screening of *The Birth of a Nation* in the White House, exclaimed, "It's like writing history with lightning. And my only regret is that it is all terribly true." Buoyed by that endorsement, *The Birth of a Nation* had enormous political effect, reviving the Klan, which had all but died out since its founding immediately after the Civil War. Within a decade of the film's release, the Klan claimed four to six million dues-paying members across the United States and wielded significant political power in Texas, Oregon, Indiana, and more, electing governors and passing new laws.

The 1939 Hollywood blockbuster *Gone with the Wind* was even more influential, shaping Americans' perceptions of slavery, the Civil War, and Black people for generations to come. *Gone with the Wind* embedded in the national consciousness an understanding of slavery in which slow-witted Blacks were grateful for their servitude, the Confederacy's defeat was a terrible tragedy, and Reconstruction was an imposition of spiteful Northern dominance over Southern gentility. For decades, *Gone with the Wind* remained the most financially successful film in US history (adjusted for inflation), because Hollywood kept rereleasing it, each time attracting legions of fresh admirers. Like *The Wizard of Oz* (also released in 1939), *Gone with the Wind* was ingrained in popular culture and mass consciousness with enduring effects on the nation's political and social interactions.

Visual representations of racial matters began to improve with the civil rights gains of the 1960s, but fairness and accuracy remained distant goals more than achievements. The TV series *Roots*, first broadcast in 1977, was the first mass audience representation of slavery that did not soft-pedal the violence and degradation inflicted on enslaved Africans. In another shift, *Roots* portrayed enslaved people as complex, fully human beings whose humanity was constrained but not wholly defined by their circumstances. *Roots* attracted huge audiences, sparked news coverage and public discussion, won numerous awards, and exerted lasting influence on how Black and White Americans viewed the nation's past. Further altering public beliefs about race was the arrival of Bill Cosby and Oprah Winfrey as megastars headlining, respectively, the first situation comedy featuring a middle-class Black family and the most successful national talk show headed by a Black woman in US history.

Stereotypes continued to flourish, however, reinforced in the 1980s by President Ronald Reagan's demeaning racist caricatures and the uncritical news coverage they received. Reagan never tired of telling the story of a supposed "welfare queen," a Black woman who disdained working because her welfare check was sufficient to satisfy her craving for vodka. When asked by reporters, Reagan could never supply the woman's name or other corroborating information, but that didn't stop him from repeating the story over and over to his supporters' delight.

Reagan further intensified racist stereotyping when his administration revived the "War on Drugs" initiated a decade earlier by Richard Nixon. Joined by First Lady Nancy Reagan, who famously advised young people to "just say no" to drugs, Reagan insisted that drug use was a national scourge that drove increased crime. Again, the evidence was weak or non-existent, but evidence was not the point. Years later, Nixon's domestic policy adviser John Ehrlichman revealed that the true motivation for the "War on Drugs" was to destroy Nixon's political adversaries by smearing them as violent drug fiends. "The Nixon White House," Ehrlichman told writer Dan Baum in a 1994 interview published in *Harper's*, "had two enemies: the antiwar left and Black people. You understand what I'm saying? We knew we couldn't make it illegal to be either against the war or Black, but by getting the public to associate hippies with marijuana and Blacks with heroin, and then criminalizing both heavily, we could disrupt those communities. We could arrest their leaders, raid their homes, break up their meetings, and vilify them night after night on the evening news. Did we know we were lying about the drugs? Of course we did."

By the 1990s, the drug used to vilify Black people was no longer heroin but crack cocaine, and the mainstream media played its role with vigor, breathlessly broadcasting one report after another about the crack epidemic ravaging Black neighborhoods. There was enough truth to the contention to make it plausible: crack was indeed invading Black neighborhoods, and the human toll—in ruined lives and overdose deaths, not to mention increased gun violence as dealers fought over customers and suppliers—was all too real, as Ed Buckner could attest. In truth, though, White people used cocaine just as much as Blacks did; Whites simply tended to use powered cocaine rather than the cheaper, more destructive crack cocaine sold in Black communities. And when Whites were caught, they were punished much less severely. As images of young Black men being arrested appeared over and over on the nation's television screens, the not-so-subtle message was that Blacks were uniquely susceptible to crack's allure and uniquely responsible for its ruinous impacts.

The scapegoating of African Americans around the crack epidemic contrasted sharply with how White people were portrayed twenty years later when many of them fell prey to opioids. "Crack use was stigmatized, and Black women in particular were demonized for abandoning their children," Andrea Queeley, a professor of anthropology and African diaspora studies at Florida International University, told me. "Crack addiction was not talked about as a disease but as a moral failing of the Black community. Compare that to how opioid addicts are represented today—not as junkies but as victims who got addicted after physicians prescribed opioids to relieve their pain. I'm not saying that's not the right way to treat them; it is. But let's not forget how differently the crack epidemic was discussed."

Even as racial stereotyping was putting unprecedented numbers of Black and Brown people behind bars in the early 1990s, an amateur videotape surfaced that cast a starkly different light on the realities of race in America: the video of four Los Angeles police officers brutally beating Black motorist Rodney King. The video showed the officers dragging King from behind the wheel of his car, hurling him to the pavement, and beating and kicking him over and over and over until his body stopped moving. In a precursor to the cell phone videos that would document police brutality twenty years later, the video of the Rodney King beating was shown repeatedly on local, national, and international television, sparking spirited public discussion and calls for reform. After the police officers were charged with using "excessive force," their trial made headlines worldwide.

The Rodney King video ranks among the most socially resonant images of race ever circulated, and among the millions of people it transformed was a twenty-six-year-old Deborah Cotton. Deb was living in Los Angeles in 1991, happily reconnected with her mom, taking college classes, and trying to figure out her path in life. Through her synagogue, she had gotten a job as a receptionist at an investment firm operated by Orthodox Jews. "They were delighted to learn that I was Jewish and they were instrumental in helping me explore my Jewish identity," Deb later recalled. "They would suggest I attend this or that event, and of course they wanted me to date a nice Jewish boy. Then, the day after the Rodney King verdict was announced, it all changed."

After a jury of ten Whites, one Latino, and one Asian acquitted the four White police officers on April 29, 1992, Los Angeles erupted in violent protest. African Americans were outraged, and their neighborhoods suffered much of the destruction: over the following six days, an estimated 53 people died, 2,383 were injured, and nearly $1 billion in financial damages were inflicted. The uprising, and her coworkers' reaction to it, also triggered what Deb later called "my racial awakening."

"I was on edge the day of the verdict, the whole city was," she told me. "I couldn't believe that anyone could see that video and think that it was acceptable behavior. On the news the next morning, they said fires were starting in parts of the city, but I went to work as usual. Everyone in the office was listening to the radio or watching television. I was seated at my desk out front like always when these two ladies in the back shouted, 'They're blowing up the Ten,' the freeway that runs through downtown LA. Suddenly, everyone in the office came running up to my desk, hysterical, and started shouting at me, 'What are they gonna do? What are they gonna do?'"

"In that moment, I suddenly realized, 'Oh, I'm not Jewish anymore—I'm one of *them*,'" Deb continued. "These sweet Jewish ladies who'd welcomed me to seders and tried to set me up with their nephews, their real feelings were coming out now. In their eyes, I was Black, and I would always be Black. It was a life-changing moment. It was like when you get a chiropractic adjustment, and everything clicks into place. Suddenly I saw the world with a new focus."

"I had grown up with kind of a conservative view of race," Deb continued. "My father used to say stuff like, 'Black people should stop blaming the White man and pull themselves up by their bootstraps.' That experience after the Rodney King verdict changed my life's trajectory. I stopped taking screenwriting classes at UCLA and went to work as an organizer for the Service Employees International Union. I got more political. I went to San Francisco State and got a bachelor's degree in Black Studies. In a way, that Rodney King experience put me on the path that took me to New Orleans and the social justice work I've done ever since."

Chris Hart and the other police officers investigating the Mother's Day shooting were overjoyed when they watched the Unblinking Eye video. It provided unmistakable images of a gunman before, during, and after the attack, including his exchange with the apparent lookout man, whom the detectives dubbed Dashiki Guy. "Holy shit," Hart declared. "We got the shooter!"

The video also underscored the "miracle," as detectives Hart and Hurst called it, that no one died that day. That miracle had a practical explanation, however, according to Hurst: "Look at that video and you can see that the shooter is not well trained or proficient with the weapon he was using. It takes practice to shoot well, and these guys don't practice. And they're using ammunition that isn't really meant to kill. It's practice ammunition—round-nosed projectiles, rather than hollow point. They don't use hollow point because it's expensive. Twenty hollow point bullets cost about $17, while you can buy fifty round-nosed for $12."

Something still didn't fit, though, and it led the detectives to surmise that there must have been a second shooter. "The camera only captured the near side of Frenchmen," Hart said, "but we had people shot on Villere back toward Elysian Fields. The shooter in the video had his gun pointed down Frenchmen, which made it physically impossible for him to have hit people on Villere. That told us there had to be a second shooter, probably on the opposite side of Frenchmen from the first."

The police immediately released the video to the news media, partly to reassure the public that the Mother's Day shooting was not a terrorist attack and partly to encourage people to call in tips that might help solve the crime. Sure enough, within hours Dashiki Guy appeared in Hart's office. He was a high school student who had been brought in by his mother, who feared for his life. "The mother saw the video on the news and understood the gravity of the situation," Hart said. "She was very cooperative, brought the dashiki shirt, too. She was very afraid of what would happen to her son with the video out there. She was more afraid of the shooters trying to eliminate him as a witness than of anything the police might do."

Dashiki Guy told the police that he knew the name of the shooter seen in the video, but he emphatically denied being any kind of lookout man. The authorities believed his story, partly because, as one diplomatically explained, he "did not seem sophisticated enough to concoct a cover story." According to Hart, "The story he laid out was that he was at the second line and saw Akein Scott there. He and Akein had played ball together at Hunter's Field; he knew Akein by his nickname, Keemie. He hadn't seen him in a couple years and walked over to say hi. He said Akein had a look on his face that made the kid feel scared. Apparently Akein told him, 'You best get up outta here; something bad's gonna happen.' The kid told us, 'I thought he was gonna do me something.' So he walked away and looked back to make sure Akein wasn't following him."

The police checked out Dashiki Guy's story by showing him a "six pack"—a lineup of six photographs of potential suspects. The NOPD's files contained a mug shot of Akein Scott because he had been arrested three months previously for illegal possession of a firearm; he was released after posting bail of $15,000. Dashiki Guy looked at the six pack and pointed to Akein Scott's face. "That's Keemie," he said.

By the end of Monday afternoon, Hart and his team were confident that Akein Scott was the shooter in the video. They assembled a separate six-pack for a second eyewitness, who also identified him. Grateful for Dashiki Guy's testimony, the police agreed to help his mother spirit the young man out of town to stay with relatives far from New Orleans. (Detectives Hart and Hurst declined to tell me the young man's name, whereabouts, or contact information, explaining that his safety required confidentiality.)

By Monday evening, Akein Scott's face as shown in his previous mug shot was staring out from TV screens across New Orleans and beyond. Within seventy-two hours, Akein and Shawn Scott would be taken into custody and charged with twenty counts of attempted murder.

The Unblinking Eye video and the media coverage of the Scott brothers' arrests enabled Deb Cotton's loved ones to bring her gently up to date, once she returned to consciousness, on what had transpired since she passed out in the ambulance on the drive to the hospital. The surgeons and other members of the team at University Hospital had worked a miracle on Deb's ravaged body. To stave off infections, they initiated a routine: they would open her abdomen, suction out infectious materials, do what repairs they could on the injured organs, and close her up again. They repeated the procedure numerous times in the days following the shooting, fighting a multifront medical battle with many possibilities for failure and zero guarantee of success. A second key procedure was "The Whipple," an exceedingly complex operation in which surgeons remove the head of the pancreas and attach the rest of the pancreas to the small intestine. The surgeons also removed Deb's right kidney and two-thirds of her stomach.

"It was like a roller coaster," Deb's friend Stacy Head said about those days. "The doctors would say, 'We've got a certain amount of time she needs to get through for us to know she's going to survive procedure X. Then there is a certain amount of additional time she needs to get through to know she's going to survive procedure Y.' Those were the times when it was super scary."

Deb's mother arrived from California amid the fight to save her daughter's life. "I got there a couple of days after the shooting," Carolee Reed recalled. "I would go to the hospital and just sit there all day. I was allowed into Deb's room to see her four times a day, for thirty minutes each time." Compounding the unpleasantness, Reed was obliged to provide updates to Deb's father. She had not spoken to Hayes Cotton for decades, not since he had kidnapped little Debbie away from her. Now he was calling her constantly, frantic with worry and, according to her, oblivious to why she might not welcome reconnecting with him. "One day, after I left the hospital, I went down to the French Quarter for a change of pace. I had coffee at Café Du Monde and took a walk along the river, just crying my eyes out."

A milestone was passed not long after Deb's mother arrived: the ventilator was removed, and Deb began breathing on her own. She also began to regain consciousness. She could hear and understand the words of the medical personnel and the loved ones keeping a round-the-clock vigil at the hospital. Before the week was out, she was able to converse for short periods.

Her inner circle shared basic information about what happened: there had been a mass shooting at the Mother's Day second line; Deb was one of nineteen people who'd been shot; somehow, no one had died; TV news had played a video of the shooting that showed a Black man firing into the crowd at point-blank range; police had arrested two young Black men for the crime. It was a lot to absorb, especially for someone whose body had been battered by a gunshot and multiple surgeries and whose brain was fuzzed by powerful painkillers and other drugs. But Deborah Cotton was still alive.

Susan Guidry, who chaired the Criminal Justice Committee of the New Orleans City Council, seized on the Mother's Day shooting to focus fresh scrutiny on the city's approach to gun violence. Mitch Landrieu, the mayor, was championing a strategy that combined aggressive pursuit of suspected criminals with outreach efforts to connect young Black men with education and employment opportunities through a program dubbed NOLA For Life. Two days after the shooting, Guidry announced that she had asked the Landrieu administration "to give a full overview" of its programs at a meeting of her committee to evaluate whether the program was "achieving its purposes."

Afterward, no one in Deb's inner circle could say who came up with the idea of Deb giving a statement to that City Council session. The available evidence suggests that it was Deb herself. That's how Linda Usdin recalls it, and Usdin's recollection carries special weight, because she was the one Deb asked to help draft and deliver the statement. "Deb was in really bad shape at that time, in a lot of pain and going in and out of making sense," Usdin told me. "I don't remember for certain whether it was she who wanted to make that statement or whether someone asked her, but I think it was Deb. I do remember her asking me if I would help her."

No one who knew Deb would be surprised that she wanted to testify. Deb had been outspoken since she was a little girl, said her sister-cousin, Le'Trese. "Debbie was strong willed and kind of idealistic," Le'Trese said. "She had a clear picture in her mind of what was right and wrong and how people should be treated, and she would always say what she thought." The activist in Deb also would have recognized the value of using the City Council platform to speak out about issues she had spent much of her adult life addressing, particularly the challenges facing Black men. There was also, it must be said, a Queen Bee side to Deb's personality that would welcome the public recognition. "Deb was always doing PR for herself, and when we first heard she'd been shot, some of us thought, 'She's going to make this all about herself,'" said Lisa Palumbo, once a close friend who subsequently had a falling out with Deb. "When we found out how seriously she'd been hurt, I thought, 'Oh my god, she's really in trouble.'"

The Criminal Justice Committee meeting took place on May 22, ten days after the Mother's Day shooting. At that point, Deb was much too ill to leave the intensive care unit, much less the hospital. It's a truism among hospital personnel that someone who undergoes major surgery feels like they have been hit by a bus; Deb had been enduring a major surgery roughly every other day for the past ten days. She was taking all kinds of medications, including potent painkillers. She was very weak, often asleep, at times irrational. "She had a lot of pain, and the doctors didn't know if it was from the shooting, the surgeries, or the infections she had," Head recalled. "Her lucidity would come and go. Some days she'd be clear, others not."

To draft the statement, Usdin would sit beside Deb's bed and wait for the right moment to take notes. "She would be completely coherent for three or four sentences and then go off into these outer space, drug-induced meanderings," Usdin recalled. "I took down everything she said, edited out the parts where she went off into la-la land, and strung together what I thought she wanted to say."

Arriving straight from the hospital, Usdin took a seat in the gallery of the City Council's chamber. The first hour was devoted to official statements about the NOLA For Life program, including by police chief Ronal Serpas, followed by questions from Guidry. Then came the public comment period, when citizens were allowed two minutes each to speak. As was customary, the proceedings were video recorded for live streaming and archival viewing.

Usdin spoke on Deb's behalf for nearly three minutes, though most people in New Orleans heard only the two sound bites the media later reported. "I'm sorry there aren't more people here, because the statement I'm reading is from Deb Cotton," she began, addressing roughly twenty members of the public, council member Guidry, and a scattering of City Council staff. Wearing a long-sleeved white top and a chunky green necklace that Deb had gifted her, Usdin stood at a lectern, facing the semicircular bank of council members' seats, and continued. "I just was at the hospital, and [Deb] worked very hard to give this statement."

"A little over a week ago I was shot," the statement began, "along with nineteen other people, at the Mother's Day second line. Everyone survived varying degrees of injury. I'm still in the ICU. I have at least two more months of possible hospital stay."

Next came the media's first sound bite: "I have known from the moment the shooting happened that I did not want these young men thrown to the wolves, and that we have been given yet another opportunity to demonstrate a different way of treating our humanity." As if to explain this line of reasoning, the statement continued with these words: "Those young men, and other young men like them, did not end up at twenty years old saying, 'I'm going to go out and shoot twenty people today.'" Then came what would become the media's second sound bite: "Do you know what it takes to be so disconnected in your heart that you can walk out into a gathering of thousands of people who look just like you and begin shooting? They have been separated from us by so much trauma."

After this sympathetic portrayal of the accused, Deb donned her activist's cap, pivoting to the question of next steps: "Now, where do we go?" The remainder of her statement was almost wonky in its focus on policy, demonstrating that Deborah Cotton was no mere idealist but an experienced advocate with detailed knowledge of the relevant issues. "We have, over the last two and a half years, brought to town and invested in reports and programs created by the best experts in the fields of public safety and criminal justice," her statement continued. "We have programs that have been identified that have made great strides but not been given a full-blown chance to succeed. We spend money on other programs that aren't proven and communities don't know how to access."

Deb then turned to prescriptions for change. "Every young man at risk should know about available programs of proven success that can help him," Deb argued. "We need to know the twelve-plus best practices for reforming our system already identified by criminal justice experts over the last two and a half years and to hear that the [Landrieu] administration has a reinvigorated commitment to integrate these changes into policies." Calling for fresh thinking and constructive action, the statement concluded: "To continue to run the opposite way in a crisis is counterproductive and makes no sense. We need more answers and leadership from all involved."

No one can fault the news judgment of the journalists who chose the two sound bites that summarized Deb's statement for the general public. Here was testimony from the most gravely injured victim in the Mother's Day shooting, an African American writer and racial justice activist who was also one of the city's foremost champions of second line parade culture. Instead of condemning the two Black men accused of desecrating that culture, Deborah Cotton urged mercy and understanding and, more than that, solutions. Mercy and understanding were not enough; deliberate corrective action was needed. This was not the reaction one usually heard to gun violence in New Orleans, least of all from one of its victims.

Back in San Francisco, when I read those quotes in the online edition of the *Times-Picayune*, I almost couldn't believe my eyes. At that point, the only thing I knew about Deborah Cotton was that she was the person who'd been the most seriously injured in the Mother's Day shooting. I felt an instant kinship with her as a fellow victim and a fellow journalist. I reflected on the fact that if the hand of fate had twitched slightly differently, our roles could have been reversed: it could have been me who was shot in the soul hole and she who escaped with a mere flesh wound. Part of me felt awed by Deb's courage in the face of what had to be extraordinary physical suffering. Another part of me felt inspired and a bit intimidated by her call for mercy and understanding toward the accused gunmen.

I had been raised a serious Christian—my family and I attended church almost every Sunday, I read the Bible cover to cover five times for Sunday school contests, I attended Lutheran schools from kindergarten through high school—and, although I later left the church, I never stopped trying to live up to the teachings of Jesus, including his call to "forgive those who trespass against us." But this Deborah Cotton woman was advocating a level of forgiveness that unsettled me; it seemed saintlike in its insistence that every human being deserved compassion and help, no matter how much pain and grief they had inflicted on others. Forgiveness in the abstract was one thing; forgiveness for a person who shot and nearly killed you was something else.

Was Deborah Cotton right that these two young Black men deserved our understanding and mercy? Why did she feel that way? If the accused gunmen turned out to be guilty, what did she think should happen to them? And what about justice for everyone else—not just the other gunshot victims, but also the people who loved second line parades but now might be too afraid to attend them, not to mention the general population of New Orleans, a city that had endured rampant gun violence for so long?

Sitting at my desk in San Francisco, I realized there was only one way I could answer such questions: I had to meet Deborah Cotton.

7

"Mama, I Don't Wanna Die"

I saw cotton and I saw black
Tall white mansions and little shacks
Southern Man, when will you pay them back?
—"Southern Man" by Neil Young

More than once in the days and weeks after the Mother's Day shooting, Deb Cotton felt like she wanted to die. "There were times, especially when I was still in the hospital, when I wanted to give up," she later told me. "I was in so much pain, I wasn't allowed to eat decent food, it was unpleasant in every way, and I was tired of fighting. I remember at one point I wasn't sure I could make it, and I asked if someone would please promise to take care of my cat after I was gone."

"The only thing that kept me going," she added, "were the close friends who formed my support group." Her devoted inner circle included Linda Usdin, Stacy Head, Karen Gadbois, Ed McGinnis, Meg Lousteau, Annie LaRock, and Kevin Allman, her editor at *Gambit*. "They took care of everything," Deb added, "signing medical and legal papers, dealing with doctors and nurses, paying my bills, raising money for my expenses, everything. They were so great. They just wouldn't let me die."

Single dad duties in San Francisco meant that three months would pass after the shooting before I was able to return to New Orleans. Deb proved impossible to reach during that visit, and she wasn't feeling much better when I returned a month later. But she and I had connected via email in the interim, and she welcomed the idea of meeting in person. We set a date, time, and place. But half an hour beforehand, she emailed to say she wasn't feeling well and couldn't make it. I called her cell, hoping to leave a message. To my surprise, she picked up.

"Hello," said a weak voice.

"Hi, it's Mark Hertsgaard. Is this Deborah Cotton?"

"Yes. Hi, Mark."

"Hello. I'm sorry to disturb you, I was just going to leave a message. I only wanted to say I hope you feel better soon."

"Thanks. I'm sorry I can't make it today."

"Don't worry about that. How are you feeling?"

"I'm feeling very depressed, to be honest," she said. "The nausea is pretty constant, and I'm dealing with anxiety, even panic attacks."

I didn't want to impose when Deb was feeling so poorly, but I couldn't help repeating what I'd written in my first email to her—that I'd been awed by her City Council statement's call for understanding and forgiveness toward the young men accused of shooting us. I quoted verbatim her suggestion that everyone think about "how disconnected from your heart you have to be to walk out into a gathering of hundreds of people who look exactly like you and begin firing." I told her I hoped that someday she and I could have a long talk so I could understand how she found the grace and strength to be so generous.

"It never occurred to me to feel hostile toward those young men," Deb replied. "I grew up middle class, I had resources, but I've walked the projects and I know what people there are facing. They're working two or three low-wage jobs if they've even got a job. Or they're doing some kind of hustle to try to make ends meet. They feed their kids cereal with water, not milk, because that's all they can afford. A lot of them are illiterate because they never got a real education. They get hassled by police. There are guns and drug dealers all around. It's not an easy life."

"And they get angry about all that," Deb added. "They see on television that other people have nice things. They see that society doesn't respect them and doesn't care to give them an opportunity in life. They figure, 'You don't respect me, why should I respect you?'"

After we hung up, I went online and learned that a few months before the Mother's Day shooting, Deb had been interviewed for a public service video about the endless gun violence in New Orleans. Shot in black and white, the video showed her speaking in a friendly but somber tone about the catastrophe unfolding in her adopted city.

"I've lived here six years, and I would have to sit back and count the number of people I know—either as friends or people I'm connected to through my work, or neighbors, or people I just know from eyeball—who have been killed. That's unnatural." Unnatural and, Deb continued, unnecessary. This problem "can be addressed," she said. "We are just not rising to the occasion. That's what's heartbreaking about it. . . . The over-arching problem is the lack of education and employment opportunities for young people, especially young Black men, and the history of oppres-sion and political corruption that has taken resources and opportunities meant for some of the most vulnerable, at-risk people in our community and diverted [them] to self-serving people in leadership. So we're seeing the result of that here."

Deb had made these same points in an interview published in *The Lens*, a local news site, a month after the Mother's Day shooting. Always the activist, she argued that "we can change what's happening out on the streets. We have the resources to deal with this problem. . . . Money can be strategically invested to save and rehabilitate many of these young men. All of them? No. But this is a small town, not a sprawling metropolis like Los Angeles, where I come from. Take the whole population of Black males between, say, thirteen and thirty, the target demographic. Pull out the ones at risk, the troublemakers, and you're looking at what, 1,500 kids? We know who these people are. Assign every one of them a case manager, and start getting them everything they need," from literacy and general education to job training and employment opportunities. "I'm no Pollyanna," she added. "I'm not saying this is so easy, why didn't someone just do it already. But, yes, I'm saying that solutions are not as hard as we're making them out to be."

Deborah Cotton had come a long way from the young innocent who was shocked into racial consciousness by the police beating of Rodney King over twenty years before. Stunned by the unwitting racism of the White coworkers in Los Angeles who suddenly revealed that they saw her as Black first and Jewish second, she had embarked on a new trajectory, educating herself at San Francisco State University about race and racism and becoming a labor activist with the Service Employees International Union, where she organized women of color to fight for better working conditions.

During these years, Deb also deepened her spirituality. Just as reuniting with her mother led her to embrace Judaism alongside the Christianity she had absorbed as a child, now she was investigating expressions of African-based spirituality. Her favorite was capoeira, a melding of dance, prayer, and self-defense that Black women in Brazil had created. Deb ended up leading capoeira classes, an activity she continued when she moved back to Los Angeles after earning her bachelor's degree in 1998. Melding her spiritual beliefs with her long-standing commitment to "heal the world," as her Jewish tradition taught, she offered after-school classes in capoeira to youngsters in South Central Los Angeles, one of the country's most impoverished and violence-ridden neighborhoods.

By the time Linda Usdin delivered her City Council statement, Deb had developed a unified theory and practice of social change that centered on race as a fundamental influence on how the world worked. Deb had been brought up believing that race did not matter very much and that Black people should concentrate on bettering themselves. Her post–Rodney King journey of discovery convinced her that in fact race mattered a lot, explained a lot, and needed to be addressed if her ideals of equality and fairness were to be realized.

The Mother's Day shooting, Deb believed, could not be judged apart from its social and historical context. In the case of the accused gunmen, that context included the many ways that race had shaped the possibilities for Black people in the United States going back to the days of slavery, especially Black people unlucky enough to be born into the poverty, violence, drug dealing, and lack of opportunity so common in New Orleans and other US cities. Unleashing a hail of bullets into a second line parade, terrorizing and wounding people who looked just like them, was an abominable act. But seen within the larger realities of the suspects' lives, it was an act whose perpetrators, in Deb's view, were to be pitied more than shunned.

"Those boys, I feel sorry for them," Deb told me. "When I was their age, I was trying to scheme how to get money to go to Europe. I was dreaming about what career I was going to choose. There was a whole world of opportunity waiting for me. They didn't see any of that."

I soon learned that many people in New Orleans, Black and White alike, did not share Deb's views. Virtually all of the dozens of people I spoke with expressed sympathy for what Deb had gone through. Most were baffled at best, however, by her City Council statement. Some scoffed that her views were political and racial correctness run amok—that she was urging forgiveness simply because the alleged gunmen were Black. Every one of the Black locals I interviewed affirmed that racism was a pervasive, destructive force in their hometown, but more than a couple of them took exception to the notion that the injustices of racism excused shooting anyone, much less other Black people at a second line parade. After all, if such crimes were the result of social ills—the lack of a decent education, jobs, economic opportunity, and so forth—then virtually all young African American men facing those obstacles should end up as drug dealing gunslingers. But all young African American men decidedly did not end up as drug dealing gunslingers, and it insulted their lives to obscure that fact.

Joe Maize of the TBC band, for example, was by no means blind to the realities of racism in America. "Going to jail is something nearly all of us experience at some point, it don't matter what you do or don't do," he told me. "I went into a store once when I was seventeen. Police came in, looking for somebody, and this one police tells me to empty my pockets. I say, 'What for, man?' He say, 'Oh, you wanna be a smart ass? I'll arrest your ass.' I say, 'Arrest me? For what?' He takes me to the station and what's the charge they put on me? Trespassing! Long as you on someone else's property, they can call it trespassing. They fuck with you just to fuck with you."

Nevertheless, Joe Maize had zero tolerance for the idea that the Mother's Day shooters deserved sympathy because they were poor and Black in a society that prized White and rich. "That dude is not the only person who came up through rough situations," he said hotly. "Deb is my dear friend, but I was a little mad with her when she said that stuff about forgiving them. Man, they shot you! She lucky she not dead. The way I look at it, an eye for an eye. I don't want those guys to do thirty years in prison. I want them under the prison."

"What do you mean, under the prison?" I asked.

"Dead and buried, that's what I mean," Joe replied.

Another African American musician, Tambourine Green, sympathized with some of Deb's message even as she also blamed Black people themselves. I met her during another second line parade (yes, I continued to attend second lines—I figured lightning wouldn't strike twice in the same spot) where she was performing with the venerable Treme Brass Band. With dark honey skin and a sparkling smile, she would have stood out in any crowd, but she was all the more noticeable for being the only female in the band. I introduced myself during a break in the music, saying that

I was trying to find out more about the Mother's Day shooting and had been one of the people shot that day.

"I'm very sorry that happened to you," she said. "There's way too much of that in New Orleans." The young men accused of shooting us obviously were wrong to have done that, she added, but their actions came as no surprise—they were responding to a message they had been hearing all their lives. Citing the lack of good schools and jobs for young Black men, as well as the poor or absent parenting she said was rife among Black families in New Orleans, she said that young Black men lashed out in rage at how they were cast aside and looked down upon by society at large. Choosing the same words Deb had used, Green said that the shooters' message was simple: "You don't respect me, why should I respect you?"

Ed Buckner also distanced himself from Deb's views. The first time I met him, we sat on his front porch, and he told me how sorry he was that I had been shot at his club's parade. When I said I was fine and the person I worried about was Deborah Cotton, Ed shook his head side to side as if in pain.

"Oh, I feel so bad for Miss Cotton," he said. "So bad. She really got tore up. I've never met her, but I wish there was something we could do for her. She has suffered so much."

I asked Ed what he thought about Deb's City Council statement pleading for mercy and understanding toward the accused gunmen.

"I was surprised she said that, to be honest," he replied. "I was interviewed on the news right after the shooting, and I called it what it was—a terrorist act. You don't have to have a turban on your head to be a terrorist. Those guys wanted to shoot somebody, and they didn't give a fuck about all the other people around. Right after the shooting, I wanted those guys dead. I mean gone. Just kill 'em."

Ed said he had mellowed a bit since then: "I know what it's like out there on the street, so I've found a way in my heart to have some forgiveness for these guys. They're going to spend the next forty years in prison."

"Is that the right outcome?"

"Definitely," Ed replied. "I want them to do serious time. I hope they use that time to learn that what they did was wrong. They made people afraid to go to second lines."

Even some of Deb's closest friends and family were bewildered by her call for forgiveness and understanding.

"I was in the hospital with Deb when she was preparing to make that statement," her mother, Carolee Reed, said. "I told her that she was free to do what she liked, but it wouldn't change my feelings. Life is about choices. There are millions of people who grew up in difficult circumstances like those young men did but did not make the choice to shoot people."

"I know what she means about how racism gives Black men a hard road in life," said Karen Gadbois, a journalist for *The Lens*, a local New Orleans news site, "and she's right about that. But is that really the most important lesson to draw from this? Deb came very close to losing her life. There's no excuse for that."

Deb's sister-cousin Le'Trese also was baffled by Deb's insistence on forgiving the two suspects, though Le'Trese wrapped her disagreement in a frame of admiration. She and Deb didn't talk about these issues during Le'Trese's first visit after the shooting, when Deb was still in the hospital, hooked up to tubes, and sometimes so exhausted that she fell asleep in mid-sentence. But later, after Le'Trese had read some of the comments Deb made about forgiving the shooters, she told her sister-cousin, "You're a better person than I am. Maybe someday I'll be that forgiving and wise."

"What did Deb say to that?" I asked.

"She just laughed," Le'Trese recalled. "We were both laughing. But personally, I couldn't fathom it. Me, I was angry. You're after some dude? Go find him in an alley, don't hurt all these innocent people!"

Detective Chris Hart likewise expressed great sympathy for Deb but also confessed that he and his fellow police officers "were kind of irritated with her after she came out on television and said, 'I forgive those boys, I can't testify against them.'" Having double-checked Deb's City Council statement, I pointed out that Deb had not said a word pro or con about testifying, only that she didn't want the suspects thrown to the wolves. Hart accepted the correction graciously, but he argued that the tone of Deb's message nevertheless left an impression harmful to the very people she cared about—disadvantaged African Americans. "It's not the forgiveness that bothered us," he said about himself and his fellow officers. "It was the implication that she wouldn't testify. Because [that shooting] was not just about what those guys did that day. Someone who could walk up to a crowd and shoot everyone around them, that's not somebody who should be out on the streets, because they'll do more of it. Eyewitnesses need to testify and bring those kinds of people to justice. Often, they don't, and the perps end up walking."

A hospital emergency room worker who saw the bloody carnage of gun violence in New Orleans on a daily basis also took issue with Deb's point of view. (Because this person might end up treating individuals involved in future shootings, I am withholding their name and other identifying details. To be clear, this person is not the doctor who treated my gunshot wound.) More than once, this emergency room staffer worked to save the life of a gunshot victim who, the staffer had reason to believe, was a shooter himself. More common, though, were patients like the sixteen-year-old boy whose brain was spilling down what was left of his face after a bullet blasted his eye socket to bits. "Mama, I don't wanna die," the kid wailed. "Jesus, please don't let me die."

"If people saw that kind of thing themselves, it would change their perspective on violence in this city," the ER worker said.

The shooters as well as their victims were almost always Black, this person added, and stopping the violence required not making excuses for it. "This is hard for some progressive White people to hear, but Black people suffer by far the most from this violence, and it's a form of racism to rationalize that violence on account of the systemic oppression Black people face," they said. "To me, that attitude can be summed up as, Black lives matter . . . sometimes. No. I say, Black lives matter *all the time*, whether they die in the custody of a White police officer or at the hands of other Black people."

This person recognized that social factors helped drive violent crime, it wasn't just bad individuals making bad choices. "We will not end the epidemic of violence in this city, or in any other major American city, until we have full inclusion of everyone in a fair economic system and a fair criminal justice system," this individual said. "At the moment, we have two parallel, unequal systems. In fact, the economic system is designed to be not for everyone—it's made for a few people to have a lot and most people to have next to nothing. But while we work on full inclusion, we've got to stop the people who are shooting other people. And that means putting them in jail."

Glen David Andrews hailed from one of the most renowned musical families in New Orleans. An older half brother, Derrick, played in the Rebirth Brass Band; a younger cousin, Troy "Trombone Shorty" Andrews, was the most famous New Orleans musician of the moment, selling out stadiums the world over. Growing up in Treme in the 1980s, Glen David loved playing and parading at second lines. "In the era I came up, second lines were the most fun thing in the world," he told me. He pointed to a photo on the wall of his Garden District apartment that showed Trombone Shorty's mother dancing in the street next to Uncle Lionel, a dapper-dressing drummer with the Treme Brass Band who personified second line culture in New Orleans. "Everyone was dancing at those second lines, everyone!" he said.

Andrews was a big guy who played stomping, upbeat music that left performers and audiences alike slick with sweat and excitement. The day before Mother's Day, I attended an outdoor show he and his band did on the campus of the University of New Orleans. One of the songs they performed, "Bury the Hatchet," was composed by the iconic Mardi Gras Indians band the Wild Magnolias. It featured a galloping beat and chanting vocals, and Andrews inserted additional lyrics of his own that denounced the gun violence that had afflicted his community for so long:

> *It's black people killing black people*
> *And that ain't cool*
> *Now it don't matter if you don't have a father . . .*
> *It don't matter if you have a cracked-out mother . . .*
> *It's not okay to go shoot up a second line*

Only after I had dived much deeper into the story of the Mother's Day shooting would the terrible irony of those final two lines become clear. Even now, it strikes me as spooky that I heard a good friend of Deb Cotton's sing, "It's not okay to go shoot up a second line," and then, less than twenty-four hours later, that is exactly what happened to her, me, and everyone else at that Mother's Day parade.

Like Ed Buckner, Andrews was particularly incensed that the Mother's Day shooters had chosen a second line parade as the place to settle a score. "Those guys couldn't have shot him some other place?" he said. "You only shot him there because you're trying to make a statement. Anyone coming to shoot someone is not part of second line culture. That culture is a celebration of life, not death. You don't belong there, and I have no sympathy for you."

Fingering his trumpet and blowing a quick flurry of notes, Andrews paused and said, more quietly, "Some Black people want to blame everything on the White man. But no White man is stopping you from going to a free public school. No White man is stopping you from studying, staying out of trouble, and deciding to better yourself. There's not many mothers and fathers still together in African American neighborhoods; fathers are either in the graveyard or in prison. And it's not okay for mothers to have five kids from five different fathers; it happens because none of those mothers had a father, either."

Andrews asked to see where I'd been shot, and I rolled up my pants leg to show him the bullet still embedded under my skin. Nodding his head, he said, "How can I hate a White man who came to my neighborhood to enjoy my culture and listen to my music and even got shot?"

Andrews said he knew Deb Cotton "very well" and regarded her as "a really good person who taught me a lot about forgiveness." Still, there was no mistaking how differently he viewed not only the Mother's Day shooting but also the larger problem of racism in the United States. Andrews refused to rationalize bad behavior on the part of young Black men just because they faced the poverty, poor schools, dead-end jobs, and other obstacles racism perpetuated. Deb, by contrast, insisted that those social factors had to be taken into account—indeed, they outweighed what any individual could be expected to muster against them.

The difference of outlook between Deborah Cotton and Glen David Andrews paralleled a divergence that had existed among African American leaders since the days of Booker T. Washington and W.E.B. Du Bois in the late 1800s. Both of those giants of Black liberation recognized and opposed racism, and both spent years working to make Black people's lives better. Their analyses of the underlying problem, however, and the tactics and strategies to overcome it, were quite different. Washington emphasized individual improvement by Black people: if they educated themselves, worked hard, and lived upstanding lives, they would better their own circumstances and over time Whites would grant them respect and social inclusion. Du Bois, on the other hand, believed that individual self-improvement was fine as far as it went, but it couldn't go very far in the face of structural impediments. Du Bois favored collective action to challenge and dismantle laws, customs, and institutions that discriminated against Black people.

Like Washington, Glen David Andrews put more emphasis on individual responsibility, even as he assailed the racism that he saw all around him. Like Du Bois, Deborah Cotton identified the overarching system of racism as the enemy and argued that only by targeting that enemy could Black people attain the freedom and prosperity they deserved.

Others I interviewed questioned whether the debate between individual versus social responsibility had to be either-or. Deb's friend Keith Twitchell suggested that synthesizing those two points of view was the better way. Twitchell worked with Deb at the nonprofit New Orleans Coalition on Good Governance—he was the group's executive director—and she later became his tenant and downstairs neighbor. Twitchell recalled being "horrified" when he heard that Deb had been shot. Four weeks later, visiting her in the hospital, "I saw her in her bed, surrounded by all kinds of medical apparatus," he recalled. "She was obviously in a deeply unwell physical state, and there was going to be a long road ahead. She was so weak."

Like many in New Orleans, Twitchell paid close attention to what Deb said after the Mother's Day shooting, but he had a relevant personal experience that most people did not share. "I had a friend who was murdered a few years earlier by four African American teenagers," he told me. "My reaction was similar to Deb's. On the one hand, I could not possibly condone this; I do think there has to be accountability. On the other hand, when you are a fourteen-year-old boy in New Orleans and you've got nothing—when you're basically living on the street because your home situation is a catastrophe and your only possession is your sense of respect on the street—any threat to that respect is a severe threat to you. And you will counter that threat.

"Some people want to make Deb out as a saint," Twitchell added. "Others think she was giving some sort of politically correct response. I think it's more complicated. For her to say, 'It's important to look at how these young men got to where they committed such a terrible act,' showed incredible spirit. I think that as someone who saw the bigger picture, Deb recognized that she had a platform to point out, 'I'm a person of color, and here's another way I've become a victim of institutional racism—by getting shot by people who had the cards stacked against them from the beginning.'"

Twitchell firmly rejected the suggestion that Deb was giving the accused gunmen a free pass. "We have to hold individuals accountable, but we also have to hold our social system, our educational system, and our political and economic system accountable," he said. "It's not either-or. It's both-and."

The next time I was in town Deb had recovered her health sufficiently for me to invite her to dinner at a nice restaurant in the French Quarter. I arrived first and ordered my usual New Orleans drink: rum with pineapple juice. I was halfway through it when I spied Deb at the entrance, a vision in red. A floppy burgundy hat swooped around her head, framing her face and giving her smile an extra dose of mischievousness. I stood to greet her as the hostess led her to the table.

"Well, don't you look dressed to kill," I said.

"Why, thank you," she said, her smile widening. "What's that you're drinking?"

"Rum and pineapple juice," I replied.

"Hey, that's my drink!" she said.

"Really? Shall I order you one?"

"Thank you, don't mind if I do."

It was good to see Deb looking healthier, and it turned out that she was as curious as I was about the Mother's Day shooting. "I'd really like to know what was behind all that," she told me. I shared some of what my reporting suggested so far. Ed Buckner, for example, had told me what he was hearing, the word on the street.

"You a White guy, so the streets won't talk to you the way they talk to me," Ed had said. "But the streets come up on my porch and tell me everything. Streets talk, streets kill, streets do all kinds of shit." And the streets, according to Ed, were saying that there had been two shooters that day, two targets, and that the shooting had resulted from a dispute—a beef, in New Orleans parlance—over drugs and territory.

"So this was all a battle for turf?" I asked Ed.

"Who knows," Ed replied in an exasperated tone. "Most of the time in New Orleans these are old beefs being refought years later. Somebody had a beef with somebody way back when, he shot that guy, then that guy's people take revenge on the first guy's people. Stupid shit! Those guys from the original beef are probably dead and gone, and these young men are refighting the same battle years later. It's like the Hatfields and the McCoys."

"That sounds pretty accurate," Deb told me. "Sad but accurate."

I told Deb that I had also spoken with Glen David Andrews. "Do you know him, the musician?"

"Sure," Deb said, grinning. "I used to date his cousin, Terrence. I hung out with all those Andrews guys a lot."

"Well, here's something amazing," I said. "The day before we got shot, I heard Glen David do a show, and during this one song, he started almost preaching in the middle of it, something like, '*I don't care if your daddy's in prison, I don't care if your momma's on crack, it's not okay to go shoot up a second line.*'"

"You are kidding," Deb said, slowly and deliberately.

"Nope. He and I talked about it during the interview."

"New Orleans is like that," Deb said. "There's coincidences stacked on coincidences and all these connections between people that are hidden . . . until suddenly they're not."

"I think there's something cosmic about this shooting," she added. "You have that story about Glen. I have my story about the shooter's face turning into my nephew's face. It probably sounds strange, but I've felt a spiritual connection with that young man, Akein. And I've always thought the reason that none of us died on that Mother's Day was that the spirit of the Mother Goddess protected us."

"The spirit of the Mother Goddess?" I asked, not sure she was being serious.

"Think about it, Mark. It's a miracle that I'm alive today. It's a miracle that no one else was killed. Those guys were shooting right at us, from really close. And no one died?"

"So, what should happen to them?" I asked. "Let's assume for the moment that the cops arrested the right guys. What should happen to them? A lot of people I talked to think you don't want them to go to jail. Is that true?"

"I think I've always felt the same way," Deb said, choosing her words carefully. "What gets emphasized at different times is maybe what makes the message sound different. Those young men are clearly dangerous. They have demonstrated they don't have the compassion and mental stability to live among us and not prey upon us. That, I've always been clear about. But the devastation is larger than them. They're an instrument of that devastation, but they aren't the cause of it."

Deb started weeping quietly. I offered my handkerchief.

"No one is born a predator," she said. "You're made into one—by your circumstances, where you live, who's raising you, what opportunities you have. If every day you wake up and you're struggling to make a bread and sugar sandwich because that's the best you can afford, even when you're working two jobs, that's the real source of violence and criminality."

"I hear you," I said gently. "What do you say, though, to what I heard from Glen and Joe Maize, and not only them—that racism is no excuse for violence? Glen said that there's a lot of us Black men who grew up in the ghetto who don't shoot people. He said that shooting up a second line isn't about Black and White, it's about right and wrong."

Deb's eyes suddenly flashed, and her words burst forth in a torrent.

"I get it that they have to be punished," she said, referring to the alleged gunmen. "I get it that they will probably spend most of the rest of their lives in prison. What I'm trying to emphasize is that they're not monsters. They're not animals."

"What do you mean, not animals?" I asked quietly.

"Black people have been thought of like animals since slavery," Deb said, speaking slowly and precisely, as if instructing a dim pupil. "During slavery, you had a system in which White people were able to get free labor from Black people and live in great luxury. To do that and still consider themselves moral, God-fearing Christians, White people had to tell themselves that Black people weren't really people—they were animals who didn't have the same mental capacities and emotional qualities White people did. When slavery ended and the Black people they had thought of like animals were legally their equals, many White people found that very hard to accept—financially and legally, but also emotionally. So, they *didn't* accept it. They held onto their old attitudes, passed them down to their children, and kept Black people down. That's what I mean when I say those young men are not animals. They are human beings, and they should be treated like human beings, even though they did something terrible."

Later, as I walked back to my room at the B&B, I thought back to that last exchange. It had clearly touched a nerve. Deb's critics were wrong that she didn't believe in punishment for the Black men accused of shooting us: that was a misinterpretation based on the two sound bites from her City Council statement. In truth, Deb was no simpleminded apologist for bad behavior as long as it was Black. What she was was an intellectually informed Black woman who saw the Mother's Day shooting in its historical context—as an outgrowth of the slavery her people had endured for centuries and whose aftereffects still lingered, polluting attitudes, stunting lives, and shedding blood all these years later.

8

"This Country Is Still Really Broken"

Seen the arrow on the door post
Saying this land is condemned
All the way from New Orleans
To Jerusalem . . .

See them big plantations burning
Hear the cracking of the whips
Smell that sweet magnolia blooming
See the ghosts of slavery ships

—"Blind Willie McTell"
by Bob Dylan

A forty-five-minute drive up the Mississippi River from New Orleans sits a stately mansion with a white-columned portico, white shuttered doors, and white stairs climbing to the second floor. From a distance, the Whitney Plantation looks like any of the other nearby plantations where, as tourist pamphlets back in New Orleans soothingly promise, visitors can "See the Old South." Behind its elegant front, though, the

Whitney is pursuing a radical agenda: telling the truth, the unsweetened truth, about slavery.

Exasperated that not a single plantation in Louisiana told what he considered "the honest-to-God-truth about slavery," John Cummings III decided to turn the Whitney property into a museum for that purpose. A retired White lawyer who made a fortune in real estate, Cummings was a civil rights activist in his youth, working with local African Americans to integrate the swimming pool in New Orleans's Audubon Park. Now, anticipating suspicions about why "a rich White boy," as he put it, had established a museum about slavery, he would tell reporters, "It was a lot of rich White boys who caused this problem, so it shouldn't be surprising if one of them is trying to do something about it now."

Doing something about slavery meant, to Cummings, educating people about what slavery actually was and how it continued to shape American life a hundred and fifty years later—a subject on which, he admitted, he himself had been woefully ignorant. Cummings had bought the Whitney property in 1999 purely as an investment. But with the purchase came the plantation's historical records, which documented that at least 354 slaves had worked this sugar plantation and been bought and sold like commodities—treated like horses or cattle rather than human beings. "Why didn't I learn this as a young man?" Cummings asked himself. Obsessed, he began devouring book after book about slavery. The more he read, the more appalled he became, not only by the horrors of slavery—the rape, murder, and mutilation, the endless dawn-to-dusk toil, the separation of children from mothers and fathers—but also by how little of this story Americans knew, especially White Americans.

Cummings believed that the racial divide in America was rooted in White and Black Americans' incomprehension of each other's perspectives on slavery. "Blacks," he said, "are screaming prejudice to the White side, and the White side is saying, 'Why don't they get over it? Why can't they get over it?'" He added, "The Blacks don't understand that the Whites don't know what the 'it' is. Unless you know what the 'it' is, don't ask the question, 'Why can't they get over it?'"

Cummings had stocked the grounds of the Whitney with artifacts from other plantations: seven slave cabins, a jail for punishing enslaved people who displeased their owners, and dozens of the metal kettles used to boil and refine sugarcane, a fantastically dangerous process that often resulted in workers getting burned or losing fingers or limbs. ("Brutality in cotton, death in cane," was the saying back then: sugarcane workers would last only seven to ten years on the job.) The Whitney also featured quotations from the slave narratives that the federal Works Progress Administration gathered by interviewing former slaves in the 1930s. "Who, us read! If you would have picked up a piece of paper, they would have slapped your damn head off," exclaimed one former slave.

Exhibits in the Whitney's visitor center put slavery in Louisiana in historical and international context, reminding me just how much I didn't know about this institution that has so profoundly shaped American history. A quote from Voltaire—"Slavery is as old as war and war is as old as human nature"—seemed to imply that slavery was an eternal feature of human society. I asked Ashley Rogers, the Whitney's director of museum operations, if the slavery practiced in the South was, then, simply an unavoidable example of man's inhumanity to man.

"I wouldn't look at it that way," replied Rogers, a young woman with light brown hair and a friendly, earnest manner. "You have to understand that the slavery that emerged in the United States was very different from the slavery that existed at other times and places in human history. Only here was slavery based solely on race, and only here did it become an inherited status. In the ancient world, you might be a slave, but that didn't necessarily mean that you were a slave for the rest of your life, or that your children were going to be slaves for their entire lives. That changed in the American South, especially in the 1800s with the Cotton Boom. As demand for cotton skyrocketed, there was increased demand for labor to produce that cotton. Making slavery an inherited status ensured an increasing labor supply, because enslaved women's children automatically became the slave owners' property."

Rogers elaborated on how the inherited status of slavery brought unfathomable suffering to enslaved women. "Julia Woodrich, an enslaved woman in Jefferson Parish [which bordered New Orleans], had a mother named Lucinda Logan. Julia said, 'My ma, you see, every time she was sold she had to take another man. Her had fifteen children after she was sold the last time. She was a good breeder.'"

Nauseating as it was, this anecdote did not surprise me, for I had recently read Harriet Jacobs's book, *Incidents in the Life of a Slave Girl*. If I could give a person only one book about slavery, it would be this masterpiece. As powerful and instructive a narrative as exists in the literature of American slavery, *Incidents in the Life of a Slave Girl* deserves a place on the same shelf as the writings of Frederick Douglass and W.E.B. Du Bois. (Indeed, scholar Henry Louis Gates Jr. included Jacobs's book alongside Douglass's memoirs in the 1987 collection *The Classic Slave Narratives*.)

Born in 1811, Harriet Jacobs was a slave in North Carolina who after twenty-one years in bondage escaped to freedom in the North, where she wrote her life story in hopes of advancing the abolitionist cause. Her book stands out because it describes slavery from inside the female experience of it, a relative rarity in the literature. Written as a memoir, her book delivers an indispensable insight: slavery in the American South was not only a system of economic exploitation, it was also a system of sexual exploitation, and the two were inextricably linked.

Incidents in the Life of a Slave Girl is a first-person narrative in which Linda Brent—Jacobs wrote under a pseudonym for fear of being captured and sold back into slavery—described how from the time of puberty she endured constant sexual threats and harassment from her White owner. Her prose is vivid but never explicit, in keeping with her devout Christianity and the cultural conventions of her time. "I now entered on my fifteenth year—a sad epoch in the life of a slave girl," she wrote. "My master [a married physician who was prominent in the local community] began to whisper foul words in my ear. Young as I was, I could not remain ignorant of their import."

To avoid his lecherous advances, Jacobs accepts the attentions of a young White man who expresses a desire to buy her freedom. The physician refused to sell her, even as she bore two children by the young gentleman, enraging the physician. The two children, however, were the physician's legal property, and he relished the price the "brats" would fetch when old enough to be sold. Jacobs resolved to prevent this fate for her children, even contemplating the most extreme of measures: "It seemed to me I would rather see them killed," she wrote, even by her own hand, than condemned to a lifetime of slavery.

A keen observer, Jacobs illuminated unexpected aspects of slave society, including how power relations could sometimes be less absolute than a simple master-slave relationship implies. Jacobs had the advantage of living in a small town rather than an isolated plantation, which gave her some leeway in dealing with her owner: "The doctor, as a professional man, deemed it prudent to keep up some outward show of decency." That did not deter him, however, from pressing his demands—sometimes with a razor against Jacobs's throat—when he could get her alone. Likewise, the physician was foiled when he resolved to sell at auction Jacobs's beloved grandmother, a woman who had worked most of her life for the doctor's mother-in-law. The mother-in-law had promised that, upon her death, Jacobs's grandmother would be freed. When the physician broke this promise, he was rebuffed by the town's other Whites: they refused to bid, allowing the mother-in-law's sister to buy the grandmother for a nominal sum and then free her.

The book's most heartbreaking passages describe how enslaved women were routinely separated from their children. Foreshadowing Deb Cotton's revulsion at modern African Americans being thought of as animals, Jacobs wrote that, "[Slave] women are considered of no value, unless they

continually increase their owners' stock. They are put on a par with animals." Slave mothers lived in particular dread of New Year's Day, for that
was the most common time for enslavers to buy and sell slaves. Once, she
wrote, "I saw a mother lead seven children to the auction-block. She knew
that *some* of them would be taken from her; but they took *all*. . . . She begged
the trader to tell her where he intended to take them; this he refused to do.
How *could* he, when he knew he would sell them, one by one, wherever
he could command the highest price? I met that mother in the street, and
her wild, haggard face lives to-day in my mind. She wrung her hands in
anguish, and exclaimed, 'Gone! All gone! Why *don't* God kill me?'"

What Harriet Jacobs did not describe—for how could she know?—were the
larger economic forces that encouraged this treatment of enslaved women.
Sexual exploitation of enslaved women was driven by two main impulses,
one physical, the other economic. The physical impulse was the lustful
desire of White men to rape enslaved women. The economic impulse was
to have those women produce offspring that could be sold or otherwise
commercially exploited. Toward that end, enslaved women were forced
to have sex with men not of their choosing—with their White enslavers
or with enslaved Black men selected by the enslavers—and surrender any
resulting children to the enslavers.

The Cotton Boom that transformed the South and the US economy in
the first half of the 1800s was the main driver of this second form of sexual
exploitation, and among its foremost profiteers was none other than Thomas
Jefferson, whose lofty assertions that "all men are created equal" and entitled
to "life, liberty and the pursuit of happiness" graced the opening lines of the
Declaration of Independence. Like other slaveholders in the Upper South
in the early 1800s, Jefferson was plagued by declining land productivity:
decades of intensive tobacco farming had depleted the soil at his Monticello

estate in Virginia, rendering agriculture less profitable. But a solution arose: an epochal technological innovation, the cotton gin.

Patented by Eli Whitney in 1793, the cotton gin boosted the productivity of cotton farming by a staggering factor of fifty, just as textile manufacturers in New England and Great Britain were demanding more cotton to service expanding markets. Suddenly land across the Deep South, which boasted the hot, dry climate where cotton thrived, became immensely more valuable, as did the labor used to grow cotton. As the US Army expelled Native Americans from their ancestral lands, White settlers pushed west from Georgia into Alabama, northern Louisiana, Mississippi, Arkansas, and Texas. "All the way to the Civil War, cotton and slavery would expand in lockstep, as Great Britain and the United States had become the twin hubs of the emerging empire of cotton," wrote Sven Beckert in his masterful history, *Empire of Cotton*.

Soon, however, the slaves who planted and picked all this cotton could no longer be legally obtained from Africa. A compromise provision in the US Constitution had mandated that the African slave trade would end in 1808, twenty years after the Constitution was ratified. Northern politicians intended the compromise to cause slavery's demise, anticipating that slaveholders would gradually run out of labor once imports from Africa halted. Instead, the fabulous profits made possible by the cotton gin reinvigorated slavery. The transatlantic slave trade wound down, but it was replaced by a domestic slave trade as the Cotton Boom's demand for ever more labor was met by breeding ever more slaves.

Enslaved females were commonly required to start having children in their early teens. Slave owners generally selected the biggest, strongest male slaves to sire offspring, and they did not shrink from employing castration to curb undesirable progeny. "Yo' knows dey ain't let no little runty nigger have no chilluns," Cornelia Andrews, an ex-slave interviewed in the 1930s, said in the dialect attributed to her. "Naw sir, dey ain't. Dey operate on dem lak dey does de male hog, so's dat dey can't have no little runty chilluns."

The cotton boom enabled Upper South slaveholders such as Jefferson to retain their luxurious lifestyles by shifting from raising tobacco to raising slaves. In a letter to the manager of his Monticello estate on January 17, 1819, Jefferson expressed dismay that five "little ones" had recently died. Apparently, what troubled the former president were not the moral but rather the economic implications of the children's deaths, for he ordered that henceforth childbearing females be excused from field labor to devote more attention to rearing offspring, the plantation's most valuable commodity. "A child raised every 2 years is of more profit than the crop of the best laboring man," Jefferson explained. "I must pray you to inculcate upon the overseers that it is not their labor, but their increase, which is the first consideration with us."

An estimated one million African Americans were displaced by the domestic slave trade, with many permanently separated from their spouses, parents, and siblings. Half of the sales of enslaved people across state lines "destroyed a nuclear family—many of these separating children under the age of 13 from their parents," historian Walter Johnson wrote in *Soul by Soul*, adding, "Slaveholders always had some reason for selling a slave—an estate to divide, a debt to pay, a transgression to punish. . . . What they rarely had when they sold a slave, it seems from the accounts they gave of themselves, was any direct responsibility for their own actions." In other words, slaveholders were at some level aware that what they were doing was morally wrong, but that awareness did not deter them.

Expanding in tandem, cotton and slavery were what first made the United States a global economic superpower. By 1820, wrote Beckert, "Cotton constituted 32 percent of all United States exports, compared to a miniscule 2.2 percent in 1796. Indeed, more than half of all American exports between 1815 and 1860 consisted of cotton. . . . It was on the back of cotton, and thus on the backs of slaves, that the US economy ascended in the world."

Nor was it only the South that profited from slavery. Since slaves were property, a legal and financial system took shape around the slave trade.

Just as today a homebuyer borrows money from a bank to purchase a given property, transacts with an insurance company to safeguard the property's value against fire or other disasters, and relies on lawyers throughout the process, so in those days slaveholders and traders relied on bankers, insurance agents, and law firms. Much of this legal and financial backing came from the North, notably New York City. So profitable and far-reaching were these financial dealings that, "On the eve of the Civil War, the mayor of New York proposed that the city secede from the Union to protect its economic relationship with the South," journalist Kathryn Schulz has written.

Nowhere profited more stupendously from the Cotton Boom than New Orleans, which more than any other city became the place where people went to buy and sell slaves. Other cities also had large slave markets—Charleston, South Carolina, in particular—but they lacked the geographical advantages of New Orleans. The city's location at the mouth of the Mississippi made it the gateway to the Deep South, the easiest destination to reach from the Upper South before railways and high-speed roads overtook sea travel. Traders redistributed slaves from New Orleans throughout the Deep South, shipping them up the Mississippi to northern Louisiana, Arkansas, and Missouri, or marching them by land to Texas, Mississippi, and Alabama. The cotton those slaves produced was then sent downriver to New Orleans for shipment to distant buyers, enabling New Orleans to profit on both the front and the back ends of the Cotton Boom.

The slave trade in New Orleans took place in two main locations: on Gravier Street, in what is today the Central Business District, and on Chartres Street at Esplanade Avenue, on the edge of the French Quarter. At both locations, slaves were confined in large pens that fronted the sidewalk. Traders were invited to inspect slaves in intimate detail, feeling their muscles and reaching inside their mouths to check their teeth, much as horse buyers would scrutinize beasts. Male, female, and child slaves were on offer. To make them as appealing as possible, sellers would dress them in decent clothes and apply oil to their skin. Once negotiations were completed and bills of sale signed, the purchased slaves were sent to new places of bondage and a fresh batch refilled the pens.

The cotton and slavery booms made New Orleans a bona fide world capital, renowned for its strategic importance, economic wealth, and cultural sophistication. Mad for music since its founding, the city amassed enough wealth by 1837 to sustain three opera houses. By the time the Civil War began in 1861, New Orleans was the second richest city in the United States, trailing only New York.

White elites throughout the South also profited spectacularly from slavery, and their wealth brought political power. By the eve of the Civil War, "most of the country's richest men lived in the slave states and . . . the nation's dozen wealthiest counties, per capita, were all located in the South," Bruce Levine wrote in *The Fall of the House of Dixie*. Thanks to the Electoral College, which Southern politicians demanded in 1783 as their price to remain in the Union, Levine noted, "nearly all the occupants of the White House [prior to the Civil War] were either slave masters (Washington, Jefferson, Madison, Monroe, Jackson, Tyler, Polk, and Taylor) or the allies and advocates of slave masters (van Buren, Fillmore, Pierce, Buchanan)."

"The past is never dead—it's not even past."

William Faulkner's imperishable line encapsulates how the long arm of slavery continues to reach out from America's past to stain its present and pervert its future. Perhaps for that reason, many Americans, especially White Americans, prefer to avoid the subject, taking refuge in the seductive lie White America has long told itself: slavery was wrong, but it happened a long time ago, ended with the Civil War, and has nothing to do with today. "Slavery remains the subject of a conversation that only one side wants to have and the other side continues to put off, decade after decade after decade," wrote Rochelle Riley in *The Burden: African Americans and the Enduring Impact of Slavery*. But slavery is where the story of race in the United States begins; omit the start of any story, and it's hard to understand the middle and the end.

"I don't think reparations for something that happened 150 years ago, for whom none of us currently living is responsible, are a good idea," Mitch McConnell, Kentucky Republican and the senate majority leader during much of the Obama-Trump era, said in 2019. This had long been the view of Republican leaders. Robert Dole, the GOP presidential candidate in 1996, had argued that the country's racial history should not be an excuse to implement programs such as affirmative action that, he claimed, discriminated against White people. "The people in America now are paying a price for things that were done before they were born," said Dole. "We did discriminate. We did suppress people. It was wrong. Slavery was wrong. But should future generations have to pay for that?"

At the Whitney, I asked Ashley Rogers what she thought of this line of argument: Was it fair to blame White people today for what White people did during slavery? She responded with a wan smile. Apparently, this was a question she'd heard more than once before.

"Nobody's blaming anyone," she said. "It sounds to me like the person asking that question just doesn't want to hear about the past, because it makes him uncomfortable. But we need to face and try to understand our past in order to make sense of the present."

I was interviewing Rogers not long after police in the St. Louis suburb of Ferguson, Missouri, shot eighteen-year-old Michael Brown to death and then left his body in the street for hours amid searing hot weather. The shooting triggered massive street protests and a violent police response that made headlines for days across the United States and around the world. The Ferguson uprising was a reminder, Rogers said, that when it comes to race, "this country is still really broken." She added, "Many White people don't understand that the reason Ferguson is so upsetting to Black people is the long history of Black bodies in this country. For decades after the Civil War, thousands of Black people were lynched across the South. Often, the local sheriff led these lynchings. Crowds of White people would bring picnics, take pictures, and send postcards afterward. That is the history we need to know and remember in order to understand today."

Bryan Stevenson, a civil rights attorney who established a museum in Montgomery, Alabama, to commemorate the victims of lynchings, cited historical records indicating that what he called "America's history of racial injustice" included roughly four thousand lynchings between Reconstruction's end in 1877 and 1950. Describing capital punishment as "a direct descendant of lynching," Stephenson wrote that, "African Americans make up less than 13 percent of the national population, but nearly 42 percent of those currently on death row."

In *The New Jim Crow*, attorney Michelle Alexander reported that similarly lopsided ratios characterized the rates of imprisonment in the United States, creating a "mass incarceration" system. Although "people of all colors use and sell illegal drugs at remarkably similar rates," she wrote, "Black men have been admitted to prison on drug charges at rates twenty to fifty times greater than those of White men." Fueled by a so-called War on Drugs that began during Richard Nixon's presidency in the 1970s and intensified under Bill Clinton in the 1990s, Alexander wrote, "In less than thirty years, the US penal population exploded from around 300,000 to more than 2 million, with drug convictions accounting for the majority of the increase." Clinton enthusiastically joined a Republican-led Congress to pass the Violent Crime Control and Law Enforcement Act of 1994. The measure contained a "three strikes" provision mandating life imprisonment for anyone convicted of a violent felony who had two prior convictions, even if those prior convictions were for lesser crimes. African Americans in particular ended up being incarcerated, accelerating a trend that would make the United States the world's incarceration capital. By the time Obama became president, New Orleans and Louisiana ranked as the most incarcerated city and state on earth: with 4 percent of the world's population, the United States held 22 percent of its prisoners.

History's grip on the present also manifested in the realm of economics, as Ta-Nehisi Coates demonstrated in 2014 in a landmark essay in *The Atlantic*, "The Case for Reparations." Owning a home had long been the most reliable way for an American family to accumulate and pass wealth to the next generation, and the US government encouraged home ownership through policies such as tax deductions and reduced-rate mortgages. Coates showed how federal practices were modified to make it all but impossible for African Americans to take advantage of such opportunities and advance their economic standing.

In response to the Great Depression of the 1930s, Coates explained, President Franklin Roosevelt launched New Deal programs to stimulate the economy and ease human suffering by putting more money in the pockets of average people. The Federal Housing Administration was established to make it easier for Americans to buy homes. The FHA insured mortgages against default, enabling lenders to accept smaller down payments and lower interest rates. But not all home purchasers were treated equally. "Neighborhoods where Black people lived were . . . usually considered ineligible for FHA backing," Coates wrote, and such "redlining" soon "spread to the entire mortgage industry, which was already rife with racism, excluding Black people from most legitimate means of obtaining a mortgage."

Blacks were likewise largely excluded from the Social Security and unemployment programs that Roosevelt championed. Each of these programs "excluded farmworkers and domestics—jobs heavily occupied by Blacks," Coates wrote. "When President Roosevelt signed Social Security into law in 1935, 65 percent of African Americans nationally and between 70 and 80 percent in the South were ineligible." Coates did not mention it, but the exclusion of farmworkers and domestics apparently was not Roosevelt's preference: a bloc of Southern lawmakers refused to vote for the bill without those changes. In any case, African Americans were deliberately prevented from getting ahead.

Coates's reporting was a powerful illustration of how the racial past of the United States continues to shape its present. In one of the finest closing lines in recent American journalism, Clyde Ross, an interviewee in Coates's article, declared, "The reason Black people are so far behind now is not because of now . . . It's because of then."

Before I visited the Whitney Plantation, I asked Deb if she wanted to come with me. I thought she might be interested, given all that she'd told me about how the legacies of slavery continued to resonate in American life.

"Naw, I'm not too interested in seeing that place," she told me.

"You're not?"

"If I went there with anyone, it'd be you, Mark," she said. "And you should go. But I'm gonna pass. I try not to dwell on that stuff."

Embarrassed, I suddenly realized that inviting Deb to tour a slavery museum was not so different from inviting a Jew to visit Auschwitz. All Jews know that the Nazi death camps existed, know the horrors inflicted there, know the awful numbers—six million dead—and the lasting suffering of the survivors. But they don't necessarily want to be reminded of all that by touring such a death camp and immersing themselves in the whole evil enterprise.

Deb went on to tell me about the time she had gone with a few friends to experience "Rodeo Day" at the infamous Angola prison in central Louisiana. One could hardly find a more overt link between the slavery of America's past and the mass incarceration of its present. Angola's inmates, nearly all of them Black, still grow and pick cotton beneath the watchful eyes of armed guards on horseback. What's more, the 18,000 acres of land where the prison was located had originally been owned by perhaps the greatest slave profiteer in US history, a man named Isaac Franklin.

Franklin amassed his fortune—six plantations in Louisiana, vast land holdings in Texas, and seven hundred slaves—by revolutionizing the slave trade, systematizing it into a commercially efficient operation. Combining financial backing and logistical organization, Franklin's company arranged recurring shipments of slaves from the Upper South to the Deep South, with New Orleans usually the destination point. The company's ships made money on both ends of the route, carrying slaves south and sugar, cotton, and molasses back north. After Franklin died in 1846, his widow leased out the four plantations that later became Angola prison—so named because many of Franklin's slaves hailed from that African region—to Franklin's nephew. The nephew and a subsequent owner used the kind of Black convict labor later described in Blackmon's *Slavery by Another Name* to grow cotton and other crops, often working the convicts literally to death. In 1901, the State of Louisiana bought the property and turned it into a prison. Over the course of the 20th century it became known as the most brutal and dangerous prison in the United States; in 1971, the American Bar Association called conditions there "medieval, squalid and horrifying."

"Rodeo Day" was an annual event at Angola, an opportunity for inmates to display their skills and compete against each other in front of visiting loved ones and the general public. Deb had gone partly out of curiosity and partly to show solidarity with the men who were incarcerated. But even someone as conscious as Deb about the demographics of mass incarceration in the United States was shocked by what she encountered.

"You could have been at Morehouse for spring break weekend!" she exclaimed, referring to the noted Black college. "You're sitting there in the grandstand, and everywhere you looked was all Black men. I mean, there was a sprinkling of Latinos and a few freckles of White guys, but it was like 99 percent Black. You'd see these faces and think that if things had gone differently in their lives, that man over there could have been your father, the man next to him could have been your uncle, those guys a row behind them could have been your husband and your brother. You saw how life was stacked against these guys because of their race, our race."

Deb never went back to Angola. Once, she said, was enough.

9

Crabs in a Barrel

Southern trees bear a strange fruit
Blood on the leaves and blood at the root
Black bodies swingin' in the Southern breeze
Strange fruit hangin' from the poplar trees
  —"Strange Fruit," written by Abel Meeropol,
  sung by Billie Holiday

Glenn Palmer was home for Mother's Day weekend when he saw the news. Slender, easygoing, with dark skin and short hair, Glenn was finishing his freshman year at Talladega, a historically Black college in Alabama that had been founded by emancipated slaves two years after the Civil War. "We regard the education of our children and youths as vital to the preservation of our liberties," the founders' mission statement declared. Many of Talladega's students hailed from New Orleans, six hours' drive away.

"My mother would freak if I wasn't there on Mother's Day," Glenn said later. "She was calling me for weeks—'I don't see you all year, and you can't come back for one day to see your mother?'"

Glenn's roommate at Talladega had gone back to New Orleans a few weeks earlier, only to call and ask if Glenn could bring back some clothes he'd left behind. Glenn said he'd be glad to do it.

Like Ed Buckner and so many other young Black men in New Orleans, Glenn grew up in second line parade culture. His father was a member of the Sidewalk Steppers Social Aid and Pleasure Club and often took his son to second lines when Glenn was a boy. "He had a truck, and he'd put my bicycle in the back so I could ride it during second lines," Glenn recalled. "I went every Sunday. Sometimes I'd go with my dad, or I'd go by myself. It's a magical thing, second lining. The atmosphere is even more overwhelming when you're with your family, because you feel right at home."

So the news that someone had shot up the Mother's Day second line was especially jarring in the Palmer household. Glenn was staying at his father's house that night (his parents had separated years ago), and like the rest of the city, he and his dad learned about the shooting on the TV news. When the Unblinking Eye video surfaced the day after the shooting, Glenn saw that, too. But nothing prepared him for what he saw on TV later that evening.

"I was eating a bowl of grits and the news was on," Glenn recalled. "I had just put the cheese on my grits when I heard them say the suspect's name was Akein Scott. I looked up, and there was his face on the screen."

Glenn was so shocked that he forgot he was holding the grits. The bowl fell from his suddenly lifeless hands and crashed on the floor.

Akein Scott was Glenn's college roommate. Glenn usually called Akein by his nickname, Keemie. But the Keemie whom Glenn knew at Talladega was as different as night and day from the wanton gunslinger Akein Scott was now accused of being.

"Brothers couldn't be closer," Glenn said of the two young men's relationship. They had not known each other back home—Glenn was from the Ninth Ward, Akein from the Seventh, a world of difference in New Orleans—but on campus they hit it off immediately. Glenn's assigned roommate was from the town of Talladega, so that roommate often stayed at his parent's house, and Akein's first roommate got expelled, so he and Glenn ended up de facto roommates. "We spent hours and hours talking about life and things we'd been through, all kinds of stuff," Glenn said.

In my interviews with Glenn, he struggled to reconcile the Keemie he knew on campus with the second line gunman that Akein Scott now appeared to be. At Talladega, Keemie was a homebody who skipped parties to stay in his room writing poetry. He was a clothes horse who wore bow ties to class and often cooked dinner for the rest of the dorm. Around older people, he was "always so polite, so respectful," Glenn said.

Keemie had been apologetic when he asked if Glenn could bring his clothes to New Orleans. "He called and said, 'Man, I know I got a lot of stuff, but can you bring it? I went and opened the door to his closet, and this *avalanche* of shirts pours out, nearly drowns me. He had lots of button-downs; he was always bringing them back from New Orleans."

"He dressed differently than everybody else at college, that's for sure," Glenn added. "Freshman year, you're away from home for the first time, everyone wants to look cool, so we're all wearing baggy jeans, torn T-shirts, that kind of thing. Not Keemie. He'd come out wearing a button-down shirt tucked into his pants, topped off with a bow tie. Just to go to class!"

At night, "the rest of us would be going to a party and we'd try to get him to come," Glenn recalled. "He did sometimes, but usually he stayed in his room. We'd get back like two in the morning and he'd say, 'Hey, y'all, listen to this poem I wrote. What you think?' He wrote raps mainly, about how we're all brothers and sisters, we shouldn't fight each other, we should live in peace, stuff like that."

When Keemie did go to parties, he was so picky about his clothes that it drove his dorm mates crazy. "He'd put on some outfit and ask us, 'How this look?'" Glenn said. "We'd say, 'Good, man, looking good.' He'd say, 'No, y'all don't know nothing,' and go put on something else. He'd change his clothes three, four times before we'd go out. We'd say, 'C'mon man, we gonna miss the party!'"

Keemie was just as fastidious about his cooking. "The food at Talladega was so bad, a bunch of us would pool our money, go to Walmart, buy food and cook it ourselves—jambalaya, red beans and rice, all kinds of stuff,"

Glenn said. "Keemie had like four hot plates. He was a good cook, but he wanted everything to be perfect, so it'd take him like six hours to make things. We'd fall asleep and he'd still be cooking." Glenn had an allergy to seafood that Keemie would tease him about. "I'd come into the room, the food smelled so good, and he'd say, 'Too bad, man! You can't have none a this here, it's got seafood.'"

On Mother's Day morning, Akein came to collect his clothes. He arrived at Glenn's father's place in New Orleans East "around ten or eleven o'clock," Glenn said. "We hung out and talked for a while, you know, 'How things going, man?' Keemie had family who were having a barbecue later, so he said, 'C'mon over. Don't worry, we'll have pork, but we'll have chicken, too.' He was teasing me. I'm Muslim; we don't eat pork. I gave him his clothes, we said goodbye, and that was it."

"I did try to see him later that day," Glenn added. "I had to go to my mother's first, but around four o'clock, I started calling him about the barbecue. He never picked up, never called back. It wasn't like Keemie not to answer, but I figured he might be with his girlfriend, and he'd call when he could."

The next night, after seeing Akein's face on TV, Glenn took a closer look at the Unblinking Eye video, which remained in heavy rotation on local TV. He paid especially close attention to the video's closing seconds, when the gunman had fired his last shots and ran away. The downward camera angle made it impossible for police to make a positive identification, but to a close friend the image was unmistakable.

"If you know Keemie, you know he's got a funny shaped head," Glenn told me. "He just does. You look at that video, the guy with the gun has that same head. You know that's Keemie."

By another one of the coincidences that pervade life in New Orleans, Glenn Palmer's high school history teacher was Leo Gorman—Flash Dance from the Mother's Day shooting. "Aw, man, he was my favorite teacher," Glenn said. "Any problem you had, you could take it to Mr. Gorman and he'd help you out. He taught me in tenth grade, and then he came back to see my graduation. Most teachers, when they gone, they gone, but he came back."

Stunned as he had been to see his bow tie–wearing roommate implicated in the Mother's Day shooting, Glenn was not entirely surprised. By the time Leo Gorman was teaching him high school history, Glenn knew full well how easy it was for a young Black man in New Orleans to get caught up in the wrong kind of life, fairly or not.

Police were a continual source of threat. "Tuesdays and Thursdays are the days they pull you over," said Glenn. "Especially if they see more than two people in a car, they pulling that car over. They ride behind you until they see you do something, you could swerve around a pothole, and they pull you over. They ask, 'You intoxicated? You got marijuana in the car?' If they don't like your answers, they find a pretext to haul you in and charge you with whatever. We got a saying down here: You may beat the charge, but you gonna take the ride."

Fellow Black people could be just as dangerous, Glenn said: "My youngest brother, he had a murder on him before he had his high school diploma. It's a long story, but it was basically self-defense. Some guy tried to do my brother something. But the guy had the wrong person, it wasn't my brother who did him wrong. The guy didn't believe it, he was on the edge of killing my brother, so my brother had to shoot first. He got charged with murder, and we had to go to court to prove self-defense. We had a good lawyer, an Arabic guy, did a good job. It cost us $15,000."

Nothing irritated Glenn more about Black people in New Orleans than how some of them tried to keep other Black people down, a pattern so widely recognized among locals that it had its own nickname: crabs in a barrel. "Nobody wanna see you make progress," Glenn fumed. "If you at the bottom of the barrel and you make it to the top, you have somebody in the middle trying to drag you back down. Some people, they don't want to strive and work for it. If I strive and work, I can help you, but I ain't giving you everything I made, it don't work like that. They wanna pull you down so they can see you right back with them: you don't make it and they don't make it. That's why people here don't get nowhere."

Akein was the antithesis of the crabs in a barrel mentality, Glenn said. "Keemie was what you call a 'hood star.' That's somebody who, if he just come up with $50,000, he's gonna give that to everybody in the 'hood. 'You got to pay your light bill? Here, take this.' If he didn't know you from a can of paint and he had two beers, he'd say, 'Here, take 'em.' See, Keemie was confident that he was gonna get out, whereas that other person might never get out."

The crabs in the barrel syndrome could sometimes turn deadly, with residents smiling at new neighbors even as they plotted to rob them. "They watch you move in and see, 'Hmm, they got a couple nice TVs, some nice furniture," Glenn said. "So they watch and plot 'til they see your routine: he leaves the house at 3:00 every day, so we gonna go in there 3:30. But maybe they watching *you* watch them, so maybe they be there waiting for you, and then people get shot. Or maybe they not waiting, but they know who robbed 'em. And they don't go to the police; they take care of it themselves. Before you know it, somebody's dead."

Although Glenn had zero doubt that the gunman in the Unblinking Eye video was his college roommate, he was careful to withhold judgment until he knew the whole story. "Not everybody look for the trouble that comes to them," Glenn said. "I don't know what put Keemie in that situation. He might have been making power moves other people didn't like, so they tried to hard him. There might have been a previous situation where he encountered these people, and now he had to do something first, like my brother did. Round here we say, 'I'd rather be judged by twelve than carried by six.'"

It was madness like this that convinced Glenn and his younger brother that they needed to leave New Orleans and not look back. Like Akein,

Glenn majored in business at Talladega. But after his first year, he decided
he wasn't learning enough to justify the $30,000-a-year tuition. He
transferred to a community college near New Orleans, planning to obtain
an associate degree. Then he and his brother would move to Houston to
work in the oil business. "You got twelve-year-olds walking around here,
carrying guns," Glenn said about New Orleans. "It's crazy. I'm done with
this place. I've done twenty-two years here, and when I leave, I won't miss
nothing. Not a thing."

From the time Akein Scott's face appeared on TV screens, barely twenty-
four hours after the Mother's Day shooting, it was only a matter of
time before he got caught. There was simply too much publicity to outrun.
The emergence of the Unblinking Eye video was the first nail in the coffin.
Once that video aired and Dashiki Guy's mother hustled him to the police
station, law enforcement knew that the shooter's name was Akein Scott. A
search of police records revealed that Akein Scott had been arrested weeks
earlier for illegal possession of a firearm, giving police his mug shot. Broadcast on TV the night after the Mother's Day shooting, the mug shot showed
a young Black man with short hair, wide cheekbones, deep-set eyes, and a
patch of peach fuzz at the center of his chin. Head tilted slightly to the side,
he seemed on the verge of smiling, as if he was amused to be photographed.

Blasting bullets into a second line parade and wounding twenty people
was bound to attract intense police attention, and the authorities struck
back fast and furious. Joining New Orleans Police Department officers
were federal agents with the Bureau of Alcohol, Tobacco, Firearms and
Explosives of the US Department of Justice and US Marshals Service. ATF
agent Joseph Frank heard about the shooting minutes after it happened and
sped to the scene. After taking his parents to church that morning, he got
an email from the NOPD command center: a dozen people had been shot

at the corner of Frenchmen and North Villere streets. By happenstance, Frank and his ATF partner, agent Josh Sherman, had started investigating suspicious firearms sales in that area a month ago. "For the next ninety hours, Josh and I basically didn't sleep," Frank later said. "It was all-hands-on-deck. With that number of victims and all the media attention, we had to get out there and show that we were out there."

"We went out and started rattling bushes," Sherman said. "We had contacts from our ongoing investigation, and we asked them what the streets were saying. The streets talk. When you go from house to house and hear, 'This group is beefing with that group,' you put that together with ballistics and other evidence and start to get a picture."

One source that provided no help, police complained, were two of the alleged targets of the shooting. Detective Rob Hurst interviewed Lennard Epps, a thirty-five-year-old father and dedicated second liner who was among the most seriously wounded. The fact that Epps was hit by five bullets led police to suspect that he was an intended target. Epps was in critical condition, breathing through a tube in his trachea, when Hurst arrived in his hospital room. As soon as doctors gave permission to remove the tube, Hurst identified himself as a police officer and asked Epps what he'd seen during the shooting.

"He immediately fell to the party line: 'I didn't see anything, I don't know what happened,'" Hurst said.

"It sounds like you didn't believe him," I said to the detective.

"Not much," Hurst replied. "I've had numerous people tell me over the years, including people who've been shot in the chest, 'I didn't see who shot me.' I'd say, 'Wait, you got shot from the front, so you had to have seen the guy!' Epps was hit five times, and he wants to claim he didn't see or know anything? I have a very hard time believing that. But you can't revictimize a victim by pressuring him to talk."

Meanwhile, Akein Scott had shown up at his Mother's Day family barbecue as planned. At that point, no one knew about the Unblinking

Eye video, so the young gunman may well have thought he was in the clear. Talking on his cell phone, in a conversation later reviewed by law enforcement officials, Akein sounded almost boastful about the shooting. Disparaging his older brother's skills as a hit man, Akein said, "Shawn's stupid ass keep falling down when he shoot."

But Akein and Shawn Scott soon realized they were in deep trouble. Mayor Landrieu held a press conference outside University Hospital, where Deborah Cotton and other victims were being treated. Landrieu made a point of absolving second line parades of responsibility for the violence, calling them "an important part of our culture." Instead, he urged people to come forward with information they might have about "who did this." He promised to be "very aggressive" in pursuing the culprits, pledging, "We will find them."

Akein and Shawn Scott fled to Texas, hoping to lie low. They had connections there, but they were turned away. Taking them in would have exposed the Texas contacts to charges of obstruction of justice and accessory after the fact; they wanted no part of that.

The brothers headed back to New Orleans. It wasn't the safest place for the city's two most wanted criminals to be, but they didn't have many options. They went to a house in New Orleans East, where a twenty-two-year-old woman, Bionca Hickerson, sheltered them. Hickerson was related to one of Akein and Shawn's older brothers, and she was not given a choice in the matter. "It was a case of, 'You *will* do this,'" detective Hart later explained.

But the authorities were close behind, as demonstrated when a SWAT team raided the Scotts' mother's house the next day. Gladys Scott lived in Uptown, about a twenty-minute drive across town from where her sons were hiding in New Orleans East. Her house was small, a single-story on a corner. Thinking that Akein and Shawn Scott might be inside, district attorney Joseph Cannizzaro ordered that a SWAT team hit the house.

It was a very tense moment, Hart recalled: the police feared that the Scott brothers might prefer to die in a blaze of gunfire rather than go to prison. Wearing dark battle dress uniforms for maximum self-protection, the SWAT team struck aggressively. "They had no-knock warrants," Hart recalled. "They knocked down a gate to get to the backyard and pulled the bars off a back door to make entry. I remember thinking, 'Jesus, I hope these guys are in there.'"

But the only person inside was Gladys Scott, and she proved of little help. For a woman whose property had just been demolished by a SWAT team, she was astonishingly calm. "She was very cordial," Hart recalled. "She accepted why we were there and was forthcoming with information, but nothing led us to believe she knew where her sons were. She said they didn't live with her anymore."

With the walls clearly closing in, Akein Scott prepared to turn himself in, but US Marshals got there first. By now, the Scotts had consulted a lawyer, who allegedly advised them to accept arrest in the short term and then fight the charges in court. But the marshals had already tracked Akein to the house in New Orleans East, and they hit the house Wednesday night around suppertime. Hurst remembered the timing well, because he had just pulled into a Popeyes across town when Hart called him: "We got him! Get over here!" Hurst gunned his BMW into traffic and raced to New Orleans East, breaking speed limits the whole way. "Man, I was *going*," he said.

US Marshals had secured the house by the time Hurst arrived. "There were four or five marshals standing out front, lots of police cars, but no media yet," Hurst said. "Chris stepped out of the house and asked if I had my recorder, so our case could be as airtight as possible. We went in, and there were five people inside, all of them African American: an older gentleman, two young females, and two young men."

In contrast to the knife-edge tension of the SWAT raid, the scene here was eerily calm, and no one was calmer than Akein Scott, according to Hart and Hurst. "He was sitting on a sofa immediately to the left when you walked in, just sitting there, his hands cuffed behind his back, but very, very calm," recalled Hurst. "I looked at him; he looked at me. He looked very confident. It was almost frightening how cocky he appeared."

"He was ready to go to jail when we got there," Hart said. "He had pretty clearly just had a conjugal visit with one of the young women. He was wearing three pairs of white wifebeaters, three pairs of shorts, and three pairs of socks." (Inmates in New Orleans jails were allowed no fresh clothes from outside, so locals facing arrest who knew the routine would bring as much clothing with them as possible.)

After transporting Akein Scott to the Fifth District police station, Hurst and Hart took turns interrogating him. The two detectives had conducted countless interrogations in their careers but had rarely, if ever, encountered a suspect like Akein Scott.

"We were asking, 'Why did you do this?'" Hart said. "We told him, 'Everybody in the world saw this. You didn't just shoot somebody who hurt you, you shot into a whole crowd of people. Other people won't understand that. This is your chance to explain yourself. Maybe you felt you had to shoot this person because he was threatening your family?'"

"But I saw no remorse," Hart continued, "which was very odd. Nine times out of ten, if you've got someone who did something terrible, you'll see it in their face. They may not tell you anything, but they will try to justify themselves. Or maybe they'll cry, or something. With him, it was like, how dare I question him."

Hurst was convinced that, deep down, Akein Scott wanted to talk. "I've been in a lot of interrogations and there are certain signs that a guy is getting ready to go," the detective said. "It's human nature; you want to tell your side of things. One thing they teach you in interrogation school is, 'Let them talk.' Well, Akein Scott wanted to talk. He was rocking back and forth, with his hands clasped in front of him and his elbows on his knees, and he was clenching his teeth, licking his lips, like he was about to talk. Then he'd bite down on his lip and stay silent."

"He stopped talking to Rob, so I went back in," Hart recalled. "You could see he was thinking about something that bothered him. But it wasn't that he'd shot all those people, or that he'd gotten caught. It was that he was being asked questions about it. Rob and I were saying, 'You've got to justify what you did.' And his attitude was like, 'I *don't* have to justify what I did.'"

Finally, Akein Scott looked up from the floor and said his first words since being taken into custody: "You know I got a lawyer?"

"Yeah," Hart replied, "I figured you had a lawyer."

"Well, I think I should talk to my lawyer."

While Akein was preparing to turn himself in, Shawn remained in hiding. After all, only Akein had been seen on the Unblinking Eye video. If Akein took the fall, maybe Shawn could stay out of prison.

If that was the strategy, it didn't work: Shawn Scott was arrested the following morning. A tip from a confidential source led NOPD officers to an apartment complex a few blocks from where Akein had been taken into custody. Officers saw Shawn Scott leaving the complex, alone. After they arrested him, the cops found a baggie of heroin in his pocket; apparently, he was hoping to make some quick cash.

Hart was astonished. "What was he doing out in public at all?" the detective wondered. "We couldn't believe it. And with a bag of heroin in his hands!"

Shawn Scott was a completely different character in the interrogation room than Akein had been. "We read him his rights, and I guess he just felt like talking," said Hart. "Rob said to him, 'Your brother was over here, on this side of Frenchmen, right? You see him on the video. And you were over there, shooting from the opposite side of the street, right?' And Shawn said, 'Yeah, I was over there.'"

Unlike Akein's arrest, which took place at night and without advance notification to the news media, television cameras were waiting when Hart escorted Shawn Scott out of the Fifth District police station for the drive to jail. Wearing a black baseball cap, a black patterned T-shirt, and a doleful expression, Shawn shuffled toward a police cruiser. Now there were pictures to go with last night's arrest of Akein. Soon, the story of the two brothers' capture was making fresh headlines, along with the fact that each of them had been charged with twenty counts of attempted murder.

Shawn Scott's arrest was the last time the Mother's Day shooting received national news coverage. A week later, Linda Usdin would read Deborah Cotton's statement at the City Council hearing. Deb's message of empathy and mercy was reported prominently by local media, but it got no coverage outside of New Orleans. The outside world, satisfied that the Mother's Day shooting was not an act of terrorism as conventionally defined, found no further significance in the story and moved on.

Tyrone "Tuffy" Nelson was a close friend of Deborah Cotton's and a fellow second line devotee who paraded almost every Sunday. And he had known Ed Buckner since they were youngsters; Ed was a few years older and would occasionally slide Tuffy one of his homemade pies for free. But what most distinguished Tuffy Nelson among the cast of characters connected to the Mother's Day shooting is that he seems to be the only person who was acquainted with both the hunters and the hunted: he was friendly not only with the Scott brothers but also with the guys they were targeting.

Tuffy had not attended the Mother's Day second line because "I heard an inner voice tell me I shouldn't go that Sunday," he later told me. But unlike his friend Deborah Cotton, Tuffy listened to that inner voice. So, when news of the Mother's Day shooting began spreading across New Orleans, he was still asleep after washing dishes on the midnight shift at the International House of Pancakes near his house in New Orleans East. His wife, Nettie, called him around 2:00 P.M. Still groggy, he snapped to attention when she said, "Somebody shot up the second line, and Lenny and them got shot."

"Where was it?" Tuffy asked.

"Frenchmen and North Villere," his wife replied.

"Okay, I know who did it," Tuffy said.

The reason he knew so quickly, Tuffy later explained, was that "I know who the killers are in that area and who would pull off something of that magnitude. There are a lot of killers in that area, but not all of them would do that."

After hanging up with his wife, Tuffy called Brian "Dubba" Benson, a cousin of the Scott brothers who was "like a son" to Tuffy. Dubba told Tuffy he didn't know anything but would ask around. Within minutes, Dubba called back and confirmed that two of the Scott brothers had been the shooters. Tuffy was also friends with Lennard Epps, the "Lenny" his wife had named as one of the victims, and Tuffy reminded Dubba of this fact. Tuffy said he was going to the hospital to watch over Lenny and that Dubba should tell his cousins: no more shooting. Tuffy was afraid someone in the FnD gang would go to the hospital to finish Lenny off. "Ain't none of them scared to shoot," Tuffy said of the FnD gang. "They'd want to get them dead, so there'd be no witnesses. But this shit got to stop!"

Tuffy knew such murderous violence all too well. In earlier days, he had sold and used voluminous amounts of drugs, particularly crack. He had shot people plenty of times and been shot himself more than once. He'd been in more fights than he could remember, just as he had lost track of how many times he had been arrested. He had served two five-year terms in federal penitentiaries.

Recently, however, after a brush with death, he had kicked his drug addiction with "the help of God," he said.

"Me and another guy were selling rocks and we decided to jack this one dude," he recalled. "The dude was getting married and wanted to buy a couple rocks to celebrate. He came over and gave us his money, but we decided to keep the money and not give him no drugs. We even took his wedding ring. He left but came back later and said we could keep his money, but he wanted his ring back. We told him to fuck off. He pulled a gun and shot at us, like a dozen times, from real close. I don't know how he missed. It had to be God who saved my life. That's when I decided, I got to give it all up to God." Tuffy became a Good Samaritan who served food to the homeless under the I-10 highway overpass.

Tuffy got his nickname as a kid from his willingness to fight. Barely five feet six inches tall, he was often underestimated, but he whipped larger foes time and time again. Part of his secret was that he had trained as a boxer, but more important was his ruthless attitude. "Most guys want to argue," Tuffy explained. "Not me. While they arguing, I'm fighting. I start getting it on, and I don't stop until they ain't movin' no more."

Tuffy sympathized with the Scott brothers; he understood how getting hurt early in life could make one want to hurt others, and oneself. "When you come from a home where you don't have love, you don't recognize love when it come to you," Tuffy told me. "'How you gonna love me, man? My own mama don't love me.'"

His mother was a heroin addict, his father a pimp. Tuffy saw the father only three times, terrified each time by this stranger with fancy shoes and bell bottoms who showed up without warning. When his mother's sister Lilly told him, "That's your daddy," Tuffy didn't know what the word "daddy" meant "because I didn't have a daddy," he told me. After his father was shot to death at age thirty-three, people told little Tuffy, "Your father died like a gangster," because it took six bullets to kill him. The adult Tuffy scorned that view. "My father didn't die like a gangster, he died like a ho," he told me. "He had a wife and children he should have been taking care of."

"I didn't know it at the time, but I was so angry as a kid," Tuffy continued. The truth about his mother's heroin addiction was kept from him when he was little; he was told she was diabetic and had to take insulin shots. Only when he was thirteen did his mother sit him down and say, "Look, this is why I couldn't raise you—because I was on heroin." He told his mom it was okay, "but that's not what I was feeling inside," he recalled. "I went out to the street and acted out what I was feeling because I couldn't tell her myself. I would fight the biggest guys I could find. I learned how to fight by being angry."

"Angry about what?" I asked.

"About what I didn't have. I wanted to know how it feel to be raised by a mom and a dad, because I had friends who *were* raised by a mom and dad. They wore the best clothes, their dads would take them places, watch their sports events, teach them how to drive. I wanted those things. My Aunt Lilly raised me, and she did her best, but she couldn't make much money. She only had a sixth-grade education."

When Tuffy took his anger out on the world, the world sometimes lashed back. One day, walking past a stranger's house, he slapped the mailbox to see how loud a noise he could make. A man sitting on the house's porch told him to knock it off.

"Fuck you," Tuffy yelled. "You not my father." To emphasize the point, Tuffy picked up a rock and broke all the windows of the man's car.

Enraged, the man on the porch yelled, "You little motherfucker! I'm a kill you."

The man disappeared into his house. Tuffy took off running. He looked back after a block. The man was chasing him, waving a gun in the air and shouting, "I'm a kill you, you little motherfucker!" Tuffy started running again, figuring his youth would save him, for surely the old man (who was probably all of forty-five, Tuffy said when recalling the story years later) would quickly tire. After two blocks, Tuffy looked back again. The man was still coming, still shouting, "I'm a kill you." Amped by adrenaline, Tuffy started running again. When he finally reached home, his grandfather was sitting on the front porch. Tuffy leaped up the stairs in two bounds and disappeared inside. The man with the gun arrived seconds later and, miracle of miracles, it turned out that Tuffy's grandfather knew him.

"You know that little motherfucker?" the man asked.

"Yeah, he's my grandson. What's the matter?"

"I wanna shoot that little fucker. He broke all the windows in my new car."

Tuffy's grandfather calmed the man down by promising to replace the windows. "But if my grandfather hadn't known him, that man would have come up in the house and shot me down," Tuffy said. "I'd a been dead, and he'd a ended up in the penitentiary. I was a bad kid, man. Bad."

The saving grace in young Tuffy's life was second line parades. The first band that captivated him was the Rebirth Brass Band. "When Rebirth first hit the streets, they were going to Clark High School on Esplanade," Tuffy recalled. "They'd come out of school in the afternoons and just start playing. The first song of theirs I remember was, 'Hey, Don't Go Nowhere, Rebirth's on Its Way.' I loved it, just loved it. Every day after school, we'd second line all through the Seventh Ward and Sixth Ward. We would just go!"

Because Tuffy was friendly with both sides in the Mother's Day shooting, he was able to supply one additional piece of information that, if true, propelled the tragedy to a still deeper level of perversity. The Mother's Day shooting, he said, was a case of mistaken identity.

According to Tuffy—and later corroborated by the law enforcement agents on the case—the target Akein and Shawn Scott were after was John "Little Manny" Taylor, and they did put three bullets into him. The reason Lennard Epps was hit with five bullets was that he and Little Manny were close friends who paraded together, and Epps was marching right next to Taylor when the shooting started. But according to Tuffy, and Tuffy alone, Little Manny was not the guy who'd been selling drugs in the Scott brothers' territory, the guy the Scotts actually had a beef with. "That was a different guy," Tuffy told me. "That guy wasn't at that second line because he was already incarcerated. Manny hung out with that guy, but he wasn't that guy."

"Are you kidding me?" I asked. "All this suffering and waste, and it turns out they were shooting the wrong guy?"

"Hell, man, you see that in a lot in New Orleans," Tuffy replied. "Beefs where one person say bullshit about somebody else, the story go round and round, and before you know it, people getting shot."

Glenn Palmer used almost the exact same words when I later shared Tuffy's claims that Akein Scott had gotten a life sentence due to a possible case of mistaken identity. "That happens a lot here," Glenn said. "Remember I told you, that's what got my brother his murder charge. People think they know who did them something, but lotta times they don't know. And they start shooting anyway."

Why was retaliation such a pervasive habit in New Orleans? The question gnawed at me. Deb once told me that Black people in New Orleans often took matters into their own hands after a loved one was shot because they didn't trust the police or the courts to deliver justice. That was especially so if the victim was, in the system's eyes, just one more drug dealer that the city was better off without. Instead, folks would decide, as a different source of mine put it, "we gonna take care of this ourselves."

But there was more to the retaliation impulse than that, Glenn said. I was telling him what a waste it seemed that so many Black people in New Orleans seemed determined to hurt one another over perceived wrongs. I quoted the song I'd heard Glen David Andrews sing the day before we got shot: *It's Black people killing Black people, and that ain't cool.* Why, I asked, was retaliation so deeply ingrained among African Americans in New Orleans?

"That's how we brought up," Glenn replied. "Retaliation is a must. Coming up, we taught by our mothers, 'If someone do you something, you do them back.' And if your mama find out you didn't fight back, she gonna say, 'Where they live at?' She gonna take you over there, and you better fight, or you gonna get an ass whipping from her."

"But why?" I persisted. "Why do that to one another when it only perpetuates the violence? Do White people in New Orleans do that too?"

"That I don't know," Glenn said.

I told Glenn a theory I'd heard from the hospital emergency room worker quoted earlier in this book. That person sometimes found themself trying to save the life of a young Black man who plainly had been shot in an act of retaliation. When the ER worker or their colleagues came to the waiting room to deliver updates on their efforts, one or more of the victim's loved ones would be on their cell phones, naming who the suspected perpetrator was and promising "he gonna get his."

The ER worker told me, "It seems it's often ego and pride driving these retaliations. A person's reputation is so important in these neighborhoods. Sometimes I've wondered whether that's a carry-over from slavery. A slave had virtually no power or individual agency. Even your own body didn't belong to you. So, any wealth that a Black person possessed had to come from somewhere else, including their status in other people's eyes. A slave couldn't get respect from White people, and the people a slave was around the most were other Black people. So that's who you demanded respect from, even if you had to beat them to get it."

This theory struck me as a variation on the crabs in a barrel syndrome commonly referenced in New Orleans: I can't get ahead in a White-dominated world, so you won't get ahead, either. I floated this idea with Glenn—that the modern-day craving for retaliation was rooted in the material injustices and psychological damages slavery had inflicted centuries ago. "That's the theory, anyway," I said. "What do you think?"

Glenn paused and thought for a few seconds. "I've never heard that before," he said quietly. "I think that makes a lot of sense."

10

The Obama Backlash

We have come over a way that with tears has been watered
We have come, treading our path through the blood of the
slaughtered
Out from the gloomy past
Till now we stand at last
Where the white gleam of our bright star is cast
　　　　　　　　　　　—"Lift Every Voice and Sing,"
　　　　　　　　　　　by John Johnson and James Johnson

Deborah Cotton was one of the fifteen million African Americans who voted to make Barack Obama the nation's first Black president in 2008, and she remained a fervent supporter of his throughout Obama's years in the White House. "I love, love, love Obama," she told me in one of our first conversations. "I love seeing a proud, brilliant Black man in the White House, and I love seeing Michelle and their daughters there with him. He's obviously a family man, he cares about ordinary people, he's even hip," she said, before adding with a devilish wink, "It doesn't hurt that he's also extremely good looking."

Recognizing the racial realities Obama had to navigate, many Black people muted their criticisms of America's first Black president when he said or did things that disappointed them. Deb, for example, never said a critical word about Obama, at least in my presence. Yes, she wished he did more to reform the criminal justice system that she and other activists were trying to overhaul. But Deb viewed racism as deeply embedded in American society, constraining even a well-intentioned Black president in ways both visible and not. She did not expect Obama to change the world overnight. "He's not a miracle worker," she would say.

Some 43 million White people also voted for Obama in the 2008 general election, many of whom seemed to view Obama's victory as proof that the nation had at last left its racist past behind. Certainly that's how plenty of White media pundits across the ideological spectrum interpreted the 2008 election. The conservative *Wall Street Journal* said it was time "to put to rest the myth of racism as a barrier to achievement in this splendid country." Liberal *New York Times* columnist Frank Rich accused journalistic colleagues who had warned that racism might obstruct Obama's rise of "antiwhite bias."

The fact remained, however, that a significantly larger number of White people voted against Obama than for him: fifty-five million White people preferred his Republican opponent, John McCain. Of course, choosing a White candidate over a Black candidate did not in itself make McCain's White voters racist. Many doubtless admired McCain's status as a Vietnam War hero; others may have favored McCain's Republican principles and policies. But a substantial portion of White America soon revealed itself to be driven by less lofty motivations.

"I want my country back" became the slogan of the Tea Party movement, which arose during Obama's first months as president. Beginning on April 15—federal income tax day in the United States—crowds composed overwhelmingly of White people denounced the new president at rallies in hundreds of cities and towns across the country. Some of the protesters carried signs depicting Obama as an African witch doctor, complete with a bone through his nose; other signs called him a Muslim or urged him to "Go Back to Kenya." The same racist insults were on display in a second round of Tea Party rallies on July 4, Independence Day, and yet again at hundreds more rallies in September.

Obama's ascent to the highest office in the land triggered a fresh episode of one of the enduring patterns in US history. Whenever Black people made real or even perceived gains toward freedom and equality—after the Civil War ended formal slavery, after Black people fleeing Southern terror moved to Northern cities during World War I, after the Supreme Court outlawed segregated public schools in 1954—an angry, often violent, backlash erupted among a large number of White people, White people who liked things the way they had always been, who thought Black people getting ahead meant White people were falling behind, who feared that the country they knew was vanishing in favor of a new order.

The starkest example in Obama's case was a dramatic increase in threatened and actual violence directed at the new president and his family. The threats began during the 2008 campaign, when Obama received Secret Service protection earlier than any candidate in history after the FBI registered a record number of death threats against him. As president, Obama received three times as many death threats as any of his predecessors, the *Washington Post* reported, with many carrying racial overtones. In one case, an assailant managed to fire seven rounds from a long-range rifle into the living quarters of the White House. Obama was not home at the time, but one of his daughters and her grandmother were, and his wife and other daughter returned minutes later.

In an illustration of Deb's point about the importance of White people talking with other Whites about race, the backlash triggered by Obama's election gained momentum in part because it was not condemned by enough *other* White people. The news media, an overwhelmingly White institution, was a prime example. The Tea Party rallies, although relatively small gatherings of hundreds rather than thousands of people, received extensive news coverage, with network television giving them much more airtime than much larger protests against the US war on Iraq had gotten. And despite abundant indications that Tea Party protestors' antipathy to Obama was driven at least in part by the color of his skin, prominent news outlets actively denied that race had anything to do with this outburst of animosity against the first Black president.

THE TEA PARTY ISN'T ABOUT RACISM, proclaimed the headline of a CNN article; Tea Partiers, the author explained, simply didn't like unrestrained government spending. At the *New York Times*, another powerful news outlet perceived as liberal, columnist David Brooks told readers that he recently wandered through a Tea Party rally on the National Mall in Washington, DC, and watched the almost entirely White crowd peacefully buying lunch from food stands manned by people of color. For Brooks, seeing these White people calmly accept Black people serving them food was sufficient evidence that "race is largely beside the point" for the Tea Partiers.

The actual truth was not difficult to discern. In June 2009, right-wing radio personality Rush Limbaugh began telling his millions of listeners that Obama had one thing in common with God: "God does not have a birth certificate." On July 15, 2009, Lou Dobbs of CNN ventilated the birtherism conspiracy theory at length on his national radio show. Five days later, Limbaugh returned to the theme, saying Obama "has yet to prove" that he was a natural-born citizen—as if the burden of proof for such a far-fetched accusation did not properly lie with the accuser. The next day, the controversy jumped from the right-wing fringe to the mainstream media when CNN aired a segment where a liberal and a conservative guest debated the accusation, which still had not been supported by any evidence. Days later, a woman holding her birth certificate and shouting, "I want my country back!" berated Republican congressman Mike Castle of Delaware at a town hall after Castle stated that Obama was indeed a US citizen. In the traditionally slow news month of August, the birther slander dominated cable news broadcasts at Fox, CNN, and MSNBC. By November of 2009, Representative Nathan Deal of Georgia and other Republicans in Congress were pressing Obama to release his birth certificate, a demand soon taken up by a thrice-bankrupted real estate mogul turned reality TV personality named Donald Trump.

Obama appeared to hope the birther issue would die out if he just ignored it. He was determined, he later wrote in his memoirs, not to soil the dignity of the presidency or give any oxygen to the controversy by talking about it. Besides, he added, "We had reams of data telling us that White voters, including many who supported me, reacted poorly to lectures about race. I knew I wasn't going to win over any voters by labeling my opponents racist."

Barack Obama and Deborah Cotton each had a Black father and a White mother, but in one fundamental respect their upbringings could hardly have been more different. Deb grew up culturally Black, raised by her Black father and his family in Texas and Oklahoma. Obama grew up culturally White. His Kenyan father and his White American mother separated shortly after he was born. Obama saw his father only once after that, spending a week with him when Obama was ten, and rarely heard from him. Young Obama was raised by his mother, with a great deal of help from her White mother and father. Barry, as he was called, lived full time with his grandparents from the time he was five until he was seven and then again for four years in high school. The fact that his biological father "looked nothing like the people around me—that he was black as pitch, my mother white as milk—barely registered in my mind," he later recalled.

This upbringing gave Obama a familiarity with White people that enabled him to make White voters feel comfortable with him in a way

that most Black politicians could not. In the process of ascending the electoral ladder, every politician enters countless rooms of people whose help the
politician wants, whether it be their votes, their endorsement, or their financial support. When those rooms are filled with White people, as is often the
case in the United States, a Black politician's first essential, if unstated, task
is to put those White people at ease. Conveying this subliminal message
came automatically to Obama, for he had been deeply loved by White family
members since his infancy, and he had loved them in return.

When Obama began visiting White districts in suburban and rural Illi-
nois in preparation for running for US Senate in 2005, his White assistant
"was a little nervous about how folks downstate might react to a Black
lawyer from Chicago with an Arab-sounding name," Obama later wrote.
But "what struck me most during our travels was how familiar everything
felt." He "heard echoes of my grandparents" in these White voters' "modesty
and their hospitality. In their enthusiasm for high school basketball. In the
food they served, the fried chicken and baked beans and Jell-O molds."

More than one Black observer speculated that only a Black man possessing Obama's affinity with White people could ever have a chance of
being elected president. "The thing is, a Black man can't be president
in America, given the racial aversion and history that's still out there,"
Cornell Belcher, one of Obama's pollsters, said in 2008. "However, an
extraordinary, gifted, and talented young man who happens to be Black
can be president."

But governing is very different from getting elected, as Obama soon
learned. As the opposition party, Republicans were expected to have differences with a president who was a Democrat. But congressional Republicans'
resistance to Obama went well beyond principled opposition, to hostility
and outright sabotage. The day after Obama was inaugurated, Senate
minority leader Mitch McConnell told his Republican caucus that their
number one goal would be to make sure Obama had "a failed presidency," an
ambition McConnell also announced in off-the-record editorial meetings

with major news organizations. Thus, at a time when the United States and world economies were in free fall due to the financial crisis Obama had inherited from his predecessor, George W. Bush, not a single Republican voted for the Obama administration's rescue plan. Similar lockstep opposition held true for the rest of Obama's presidency on health care, climate change, and nearly every other major issue.

Meanwhile, Republican leaders tacitly encouraged the birther accusation that Obama had no right to be president in the first place. When far-right Republicans in Congress demanded to see Obama's birth certificate, GOP leaders did not rebuke them for peddling unproven, racist conspiracy theories about the nation's president. Instead, they dodged reporters' questions or said they didn't know all the facts and looked forward to learning more, a not-so-subtle way to keep the controversy alive. Nor did GOP leaders repudiate Donald Trump when Trump revived the birther allegations in March of 2011. By the time Obama ran for reelection in 2012, the birther slander had so taken hold among the nation's Republicans that only 29 percent of them believed that Obama had been born in the United States and thus was legitimately president.

Republicans on Capitol Hill also obstructed the nation's first Black president through an unprecedented deployment of the filibuster, a feature of US governance rooted in the nation's racist past, as Sarah A. Binder and Steven S. Smith explain in their book, *Politics or Principle*. Never enshrined in the Constitution, the filibuster was simply a rule that proslavery senators such as John C. Calhoun of South Carolina started using in the 1830s to block passage of legislation that threatened what Calhoun termed "the positive good" that slavery did for slaves and enslavers alike. In pre-Obama times, senators of both parties had continued to use the filibuster to stall racial progress, but the tactic was deployed sparingly, not as a weapon whereby a minority could thwart the will of the majority on every issue facing the nation. Under Obama, Republicans invoked the filibuster a record fifty-five times and derailed numerous other bills simply by threatening to filibuster them. In their most brazen move, Republican leader McConnell refused to allow President Obama to fill a Supreme Court seat that became vacant in February of 2016, even though eleven and a half months remained in Obama's second term. "One of my proudest moments was when I looked Barack Obama in the eye and said, 'Mr. President, you will not fill the Supreme Court vacancy,'" McConnell later boasted.

Despite this unyielding opposition from Republicans at both the mass and elite levels, some Black activists and intellectuals were much less forgiving of Obama than Deb was. They complained that Obama did not even talk much about race, much less fight to reform the legal, economic, and social inequalities that afflicted Black people. Citing scholarly analysis of Obama's speeches, news conferences, and executive orders, Ta-Nehisi Coates observed that during Obama's first two years in the White House he "talked less about race than any other Democratic president since 1961."

And when Obama did address racial issues, this critique continued, he seemed to bend over backward not to threaten White sensibilities even as he scolded Black people for their supposedly lamentable behavior. "When he talks about race, Barack Obama blends the voices of Abraham Lincoln and Bill Cosby," commentator Eric Michael Dyson wrote. "He tackles the subject in largely moderate tones, and only when he must, a nod to the careful calculation of his bearded forerunner. And like the legendary comic—before his tragic fall from grace—both Blacks and Whites praise [Obama] for calling on Blacks to stop playing the victim."

Only after leaving the presidency did Obama tell his side of this story, revealing in his memoirs the political price he paid whenever he did speak more directly about racial issues. During his first summer in the White House, a White police officer in Massachusetts had arrested Harvard professor Henry Louis Gates Jr. for trying to enter his own locked house after Gates had misplaced his keys. When a reporter asked Obama about the incident, Obama replied that the officer may have "acted stupidly." White criticism was immediate, full-throated, and relentless. The TV networks made Obama's comments their lead story not just that night but for days on end. Police unions across the country demanded a presidential apology. Obama sought to quell the storm by inviting Gates and the officer to the White House to drink a beer together, but the damage was done. "The Gates affair caused a huge drop in my support among White voters, bigger than would come from any single event during the eight years of my presidency," Obama wrote in his memoirs, citing internal White House polling. "It was support that I'd never completely get back." The biggest drag on his poll numbers, Obama revealed in an interview with journalists, came from "White Southerners," especially those older than forty.

At the end of his presidency, Obama granted an extended interview to Coates, the leading African American writer of his generation. Coates had explained as well as anyone the double bind Obama faced as president. On one hand, Coates wrote, Obama was able to get elected and accomplish things in office only because he was a Black man who did not make too many White people uneasy. On the other hand, the need not to make White people nervous all but guaranteed that Obama would sometimes leave his Black supporters "quietly seething." Coates did not hesitate to criticize Obama's decisions when he disagreed with them, but he understood the forces that limited what a Black president could achieve. Perhaps for that reason, Coates gave his book on the Obama years, *We Were Eight Years in Power*, the subtitle *An American Tragedy*.

The key difference between Obama and himself, Coates wrote after the interview, was illustrated by their contrasting views about the man running to succeed Obama as president. With just a few months to go before the 2016 election, Coates thought that Donald Trump could win, despite his unconcealed racism. He did not think that Trump *would* win, but he thought it was possible, and not simply because Trump was only three to five points behind Hillary Clinton in most polls. Coates thought Trump might win precisely because racism was deeply embedded in the institutions and daily life of the United States. "Trump did not spring out of nothingness," Coates wrote, adding, "I can't say I knew White people would elect Donald Trump—and that is who did it—but I did not put it past them."

Obama viewed the situation differently—as he almost had to, Coates conceded, or he would not have been elected president in the first place. Obama possessed an "innate optimism and unwavering faith in the ultimate wisdom of the American people," Coates wrote. Coates regarded Obama as "a deeply moral human being, and one of the greatest presidents in American history," a status Obama achieved in no small part because he "had an ability to emote a deep and sincere connection to the hearts of Black people, while never doubting the hearts of White people."

But it was Obama's very ability to connect with Black and White Americans alike that "blinded him to the appeal of Trump," Coates argued. When Coates suggested that Trump's candidacy was "an explicit reaction to the fact of a Black president," Obama acknowledged that possibility but offered other less racially charged explanations. As Obama and Coates talked further, it became clear that Obama did not merely think Trump *would* not win. No, he assured Coates: Trump *could* not win.

Dread is not too strong a word for how Deb felt about Trump. She abhorred him as a blatant racist and sexist, but she also feared him and dreaded what he might do if he gained the White House. And like Coates, Deb thought that Trump very well could win the 2016 election.

I happened to be in New Orleans the night of the second debate between Trump and Hillary Clinton in October of 2016, and I asked Deb if she wanted to watch it together. She liked the idea and, typically, decided to jazz it up.

"My friend Linda throws these great parties on election nights," she said. "Let me call and see if she's having a party tonight. I'm sure she'd be happy for us to come."

Linda Usdin turned out not to be hosting a party that night—she was waiting for Election Night itself, she told Deb—so Deb called their mutual friend Annie LaRock. Deb, Linda, and Annie had been spending Passover seders together for years. Annie, a fundraiser for a local nonprofit, lived just a couple blocks from Deb's new apartment in Bayou St. John, a quiet, leafy neighborhood near City Park, well removed from the tourist bustle of Treme.

I swung by to pick up Deb, and we drove to Annie's place, a pleasant, roomy house wreathed in flowering bushes and trees, where she lived with her husband and two children. There were still a few minutes before the debate began—just enough time to pour a round of drinks and exchange quick nice-to-meet-you's. Annie had a sunny demeanor and a kind face that smiled often. I thanked her for letting Deb and me barge in like this.

"No, I'm glad you did," she replied. "I wasn't sure I wanted to watch this, especially by myself. Just the thought of Hillary having to go up against this creep makes me sick."

"I know!" Deb exclaimed. "He is *so* horrible. I turn off the TV when he comes on."

Then Deb flashed a mischievous smile and, glancing at me, said to Annie, "But Mark convinced me it was a good idea to watch tonight."

"I most certainly did not!" I said, laughing at Deb's shameless rewriting of our earlier conversation. "I said that as a reporter I had to watch the debate, and did you want to watch with me." Deb and Annie were both grinning as I continued, "In fact, Deb, if I recall correctly, it was *you* who suggested that we find a party where we could watch the debate."

"And I did find a party, didn't I?" Deb answered triumphantly, eyes dancing, pleased to have clinched the point.

The debate itself was as dispiriting as Deb and Annie had feared. Trump played the role of blustering bully, creeping up from behind to loom over Clinton as she gave her policy-heavy answers. The journalists moderating the debate were almost as infuriating. Like their colleagues throughout the media had done since Trump announced his candidacy fifteen months ago, they treated him like a normal candidate, not as someone who, without evidence, had repeatedly suggested that the current president of the United States was in office illegally.

Afterward, I apologized to Deb and Annie for inflicting such an unpleasant experience on them. Annie smiled and said, "Well, maybe some good will come of it. Now people can see what an awful person he is and they'll vote against him."

"Maybe," I said. "But that depends partly on how the media frames the story. And the media has given this guy a free ride on his racism from the get-go. I mean, the moderators tonight never mentioned that Trump has spent years alleging that Obama wasn't born in the United States, which would disqualify him from being president. Think about that: Trump stood on that stage, hoping to succeed a president who he implies is in office illegally. And the moderators never say a word about it, much less press Trump to explain himself. It's pathetic."

"Thanks a lot, Mark, you just made me more worried that Trump will win," Deb said. The three of us sat quietly for a moment until Deb broke the silence. "You know, lots of White people didn't like seeing a Black man elected president four years ago. And lots of those same people don't want to have a woman president now. There are plenty of men out there who just don't like strong women, especially a strong woman who'd be running the country."

Annie and I nodded our heads. Deb paused a beat, cracked her mischievous grin, and added, "And I'm not just talking about White men, either."

So, you couldn't say that Deb was surprised when Trump did in fact win. Horrified? Yes. Frightened? That, too. Deb had a pretty good idea of what four years of Trump would mean for racial justice in America, the focus of her moral concern and political activism. She sensed, as Coates would later write, that "In Trump, White supremacists see one of their own." At the 2016 Republican National Convention, journalist Joan Walsh had interviewed Richard Spencer, a founder of the alt-right movement, who a year later would be charged with organizing the "Jews will not replace us" march of neo-Nazis through the streets of Charlottesville, Virginia. "What's most important about Trump is the emotion," Spencer told Walsh. "He's awakened a sense of 'us,' a sense of nationalism among White people. He's done more to awaken that nationalism than anyone in my lifetime. I love the man."

America's failure to confront its racial past has had many consequences, but perhaps the most pernicious is how it has allowed the beliefs and policies that animated slavery to remain alive and socially acceptable throughout the century and a half since the Civil War. Trump's rise to power is the obvious contemporary example, but it has many antecedents. Like the Confederates whose states rebelled against the Union to preserve slavery, sparking the Civil War; like those Confederates' descendants who enforced racial segregation with beatings, lynchings, and other forms of terror for most of the 20th century; like their still later descendants who resisted civil rights advances in the 1960s, Trump and his followers represented a persistent strain in US history whose adherents have never fully accepted the outcome of the Civil War and the racial equality it mandated.

From the time he announced his presidential candidacy in 2015, Trump made little secret of his bigotry. In the announcement's opening minutes, he stereotyped all Mexicans as drug dealers and "rapists." The insult drew little attention at the time; most news reports emphasized the candidate's promise to build a wall along the Mexican border—a wall, Trump boasted, that Mexico would pay for. Soon Trump would vilify Muslims as an alien threat who should be barred from entering the United States. He would accuse a federal judge who was hearing a fraud case against Trump University of being unfair and "a hater" because the judge, who had lived his entire life in the United States, was of Mexican ancestry. When David Duke, the former Grand Wizard of the Ku Klux Klan, endorsed Trump's presidential bid, Trump would decline numerous invitations from reporters to disavow Duke's support.

Throughout the seventeen months remaining until Election Day 2016, Trump was never forcefully called out on his racism by the news media. Instead, all five major commercial TV networks—CBS, NBC, ABC, CNN, and Fox—broadcast hours and hours of Trump campaign rallies, live and without fact-checking, giving him millions of dollars' worth of free publicity. After all, the ratings were good and the profits big. "It may not be good for America, but it's damn good for CBS," Les Moonves, CBS's executive chairman and CEO, said in a comment he later claimed was a joke. Thus Trump got the benefits of mobilizing his right-wing base with racist rhetoric but didn't have to pay a political price with the larger electorate, many of whom would have recoiled from such prejudice.

Trump's 2016 candidacy was the logical extension of the modern Republican party's long history of kindling racist resentment among its White base. Fifty years ago, Republicans had chosen as their 1964 presidential nominee Barry Goldwater, an outspoken opponent of the Civil Rights Act that passed earlier that year, which outlawed segregation of public facilities such as restrooms and banned employment discrimination on the basis of race. (On the 1964 convention floor, GOP delegates beat and spit at baseball hero Jackie Robinson, the Black athlete who fifteen years earlier had broken the color barrier in the quintessential American sport.) President Lyndon Johnson privately mused after signing the Civil Rights Act that he had just lost the South for his fellow Democrats "for a generation," a prognostication that proved prescient. Although Johnson himself won reelection in 1964, in 1968 Richard Nixon won the White House with a "Southern Strategy" of appealing to White Southerners, including Democrats, who resisted the civil rights advancements of recent years. The Republican Party went on to dominate the South and, with it, presidential elections for most of the next forty years, propelling one "law and order" candidate after another into the White House: Ronald Reagan in 1980, George H. W. Bush in 1988, George W. Bush in 2000 and 2004, and Trump in 2016.

"Law and order" was code, what political operatives call a "dog whistle." Just as dogs can hear frequencies inaccessible to human ears, so White voters could hear in phrases such as "law and order" a politician's assurance that he would be tough on crime and, as the saying went, keep Blacks in their place. Reagan, for example, used a dog whistle when he launched his 1980 campaign in the same Mississippi county where three civil rights workers were murdered in the early 1960s by local Klansmen; Reagan even assured his audience that "The South will rise again."

Republican political operative Lee Atwater, one of the most skillful prac- titioners of dog whistling, later explained how the tactic evolved over time. "You start out in 1954 saying, 'nigger, nigger, nigger,'" Atwater said in 1981. "By 1968, you can't say 'nigger'—that hurts you, backfires [with non-racist Whites]. So you say stuff like, uh, forced busing, states' rights and . . . cutting taxes. . . . 'We want to cut this' is much more abstract than even the busing thing, uh, and a hell of a lot more abstract than 'Nigger, nigger.'"

The 2016 election results validated the fears that Deb, Coates, and other Black thinkers and leaders had about not only Trump but also many of the White people they shared the country with. Rather than penalize Trump for his racist outlook, a decisive majority of White voters in 2016 rewarded him. The final voting data leaves no ambiguity: the overwhelming support that Trump got from White voters was by far the biggest reason he was elected president. Whites chose Trump over Clinton by a lopsided 54 to 39 percent margin. Neither class, nor age, nor religion showed a stronger correlation than race to how Americans voted. If voting for Trump did not in and of itself make such voters racist, it certainly signaled that they were comfortable with electing a president who clearly was racist.

In a piercing illustration of Deb's belief that slavery continues to shape American life today, Trump won the presidency even though he lost the popular vote by a sizable amount. Hillary Clinton got 2.9 million more popular votes, but Trump won big in the Electoral College, where winner-take-all rules disadvantaged heavily populated states that leaned Democrat. Created in large part to protect slavery, the Electoral College was established because Southern politicians at the Constitutional Convention in 1787 refused to join the Union if the country's presidents were going to be elected by popular vote. The North's population at that time was significantly larger than the South's, and Southern politicians feared that if presidents *were* selected by popular vote, Northerners would someday vote to prohibit slavery.

With Trump's victory in 2016, the promise that Ronald Reagan made in Mississippi fifty-six years earlier was being kept: the South was rising again.

But so were its opponents. Even as the Obama years called forth a resurgence of White supremacy, they also gave rise to a powerful grassroots movement for justice that transformed the nation and inspired like-minded activists around the world. Two months and a day after the Mother's Day shooting in New Orleans, the Black Lives Matter movement sprang to life. It was a movement whose spirit Deb shared—indeed, a spirit she had anticipated in her activism and especially in her public response to that shooting.

On July 13, 2013, hours after a jury returned a not guilty verdict for George Zimmerman, a self-appointed neighborhood patrolman who had killed Trayvon Martin, a Black teenager in Florida, Alicia Garza went on Facebook and posted what she later called "a love letter to Black people." Anguished to see yet another African American die under suspicious circumstances and the killer not be held accountable, Garza, a twenty-nine-year-old racial justice organizer in Oakland, wrote that she was "sick to my stomach" that some White Americans were "cheering and celebrating" the not guilty verdict. Her post ended with the words, "Black people. I love you. I love us. Our lives matter." Garza's friend Patrisse Cullors read the

Facebook post and put a hashtag on it: #BlackLivesMatter. A third friend, Opal Tometi, built a social media platform where people who shared that sentiment could connect with one another.

Garza, Cullors, and Tometi—each of them a local racial justice organizer like Deb—hoped the Black Lives Matter rallying cry could "be a magnet for people who wanted to figure out how to fight back," Garza later said. They succeeded beyond their wildest dreams. Scores of Black Lives Matter chapters soon formed in communities across the United States (and later in Canada and the United Kingdom) as activists new and old got involved. The slogan Black Lives Matter not only captured the spirit of its historical moment, it also articulated "the animating principle at the core of Black social movements dating back more than a century," the journalist Jelani Cobb wrote. Rejecting the reformist stance and male-dominated hierarchies of previous Black organizations, Black Lives Matter grew into a mass cultural phenomenon and radical political counterweight—and sometimes critic—to the more accommodationist stance of President Obama. Trump, for his part, seized on Black Lives Matter to incite his right-wing base, attacking the movement as a violent bogeyman that epitomized everything wrong in an America governed by a Black president.

Deborah Cotton never met Garza, Cullors, or Tometi, but the four of them had strikingly similar analyses of how systemic racism worked and what to do about it. Just as Deb insisted that neither the Mother's Day shooting nor the related problems of crime and poverty could be corrected without combatting entrenched racism in the justice, economic, and education systems, so the Black Lives Matter cofounders rejected the idea that racism was mainly a problem of how White people treated people of color in each other's daily lives.

"The way that people understand racism in this country is about interpersonal dynamics, like racism is people being mean to each other," Garza said. Getting called the n-word or being unable to hail a taxi "sucks," she added, "but if that's all it was, let's just sing 'Kumbaya' together. But racism is a set of interlocking dynamics: One in three Black men can expect to spend some time incarcerated. . . . Black folks are on the low-earning end of the economy. Lots of people who are great people are implementing and protecting systems, practices, structures that fundamentally exclude, disenfranchise, marginalize Black people."

Black Lives Matter continued to grow during Obama's last three years in office, albeit for unwelcome reasons. Deadly shootings of Black people proliferated, and some were captured on video. There was the police killing of eighteen-year-old Michael Brown, which sparked days of riots in Ferguson, Missouri. New York police officers choked Eric Garner to death after they caught him allegedly selling illegal cigarettes. Cleveland police shot dead twelve-year-old Tamir Rice, whose toy gun they mistook for a deadly weapon. A South Carolina officer fatally shot Walter Scott while Scott was running away. A policeman in Minnesota killed Philando Castile when Castile tried to hand him his driver's license. Perhaps most appalling, the self-proclaimed White supremacist Dylann Roof murdered eight African Americans in the midst of their Bible study class at an iconic civil rights church in Charleston, South Carolina. These and numerous other examples of deadly violence against Black people simultaneously infuriated and validated the Black Lives Matter movement.

In January of 2017, Trump assumed the presidency and commenced governing like the White supremacist he had always been. When neo-Nazis marched in Charlottesville six months after Trump took office, carrying Confederate flags and chanting "Jews will not replace us," Trump defended them as "very fine people." In 2020, when the coronavirus began killing thousands of Americans while Trump prepared to run for reelection, he tried to escape blame by branding the disease "the Chinese virus" and then shrugged off subsequent hate crimes against Asian Americans. After Michigan's governor, Gretchen Whitmer, a Democrat, imposed public health restrictions to contain the virus, Trump urged supporters to "Liberate Michigan." When heavily armed White supremacists duly occupied Michigan's capitol and plotted to kidnap and execute the governor, Trump did not rebuke them. Spurred on by Trump's violent rhetoric, the frequency of targeted terror incidents doubled during his presidency.

In 2016, the Black writer Chauncey Devega had written a searing article in *Salon* titled, "What Kind of a White Person Do You Want to Be?" A forty-year-old Black man, Terrence Crutcher, had just been shot dead by police in Tulsa, Oklahoma. Crutcher was having car trouble at the time; his vehicle wouldn't move. He put his hands up after exiting the driver's side, witnesses said, but was gunned down on the spot. Devega had vowed to watch no more videos of police murders of Black people, he wrote, calling them "a type of pornographic violence, a digital-era version of lynching postcards." He was also tired of having to explain, yet again, how police violence was a legacy of slavery and the nation's failure to confront that legacy. The reason murderous violence against Black people continued, Devega argued, was that White America didn't care enough to stop it.

But White people could make a different choice, Devega added—in fact, some White people already had. In the 1960s, a young man named Paul Breines was one of numerous White people who joined the "Freedom Riders" movement of college students who traveled to the South to help Black people claim their right to vote. It was a perilous undertaking: racists were shooting Black people who dared register to vote, and their White allies, too. In a letter to his worried parents, Breines explained that he decided to go south after asking himself the question, "What kind of a White person do I want to be?" Devega implored today's White Americans to ask themselves the same question—and to remember that "silence and inaction in the face of such wrongdoing and bigotry are in fact complicity with them."

Four years later, large numbers of White people gave the answer Devega was hoping for. On May 25, 2020, a cell phone video of Derek Chauvin jamming his knee into George Floyd's neck for more than seven minutes left no doubt that a White police officer had just murdered a nonviolent Black man in broad daylight. George Floyd's murder gave rise to the biggest protest movement in US history: an estimated 14 to 26 million people took to the streets in all fifty states. A surprisingly sizable percentage of these protesters were White, an indication that Trump by no means spoke for all White Americans.

Black veterans of the 1960s civil rights movement welcomed the arrival of so many White allies. Echoing Deb's point about the importance of White people talking to one another about race, Nell Irvin Painter, an African American historian, told the *New York Times* that, "The great stall point after the civil rights movement was White people not being able to talk to other White people about Whiteness. That has to happen before anything can change. Now, many White people are stepping up and saying, 'Oh, we've got to talk about this.'"

The massive size of the George Floyd protests, and their unmistakable racial diversity, signaled that a new generation of Americans was putting into practice a fundamental principle that Martin Luther King Jr., Nelson Mandela, and other Black freedom fighters had emphasized: the struggle is not between people of different skin colors but rather between people of different moral perspectives.

"The struggle was never against White people; it was against the system of White domination," explained Kumi Naidoo, a former anti-apartheid activist in South Africa who went on to head the activist organizations Greenpeace International and Amnesty International. "Mandela kept making this point," Naidoo added, but Naidoo, then a teenager, didn't grasp it until, to his amazement, he watched TV coverage of White people in distant New Zealand disrupting a rugby match against the South African national team to protest apartheid. Martin Luther King Jr. made the same point years earlier to supporters in Birmingham, Alabama, where racial integration faced vicious opposition from local Whites. "I want you to understand me here," King declared. "We are *not* going to allow this conflict in Birmingham to deteriorate into a struggle between Black people and White people. The tension in Birmingham is between justice and injustice."

11

The Lost Boys of New Orleans

"As in everything in American culture, you have to face race. If you don't face race, you're not gonna fix the problems."

—Jon Batiste

Two weeks after Trump crushed the field in the New Hampshire primary to become the front-runner for the 2016 Republican presidential nomination, Deborah Cotton found herself facing Akein and Shawn Scott for the first time since the Mother's Day shooting. Just shy of three years had passed since the chaotic, bloody afternoon that changed each of their lives forever. Akein, nineteen years old at the time of the shooting, was now twenty-two. Shawn was twenty-six. Deb was fifty-one.

Miraculously, Deb had recovered sufficiently to resume a semblance of normal life, though she was still in the hospital a lot. She was on disability assistance but had regained the ability to eat, walk, talk, and basically function. She had even attended, briefly, a few second line parades. She wasn't worried about another shooting. "There's a lot of love for me on the streets," she explained.

Deb and the Scott brothers were sitting inside a federal courtroom in downtown New Orleans, but Deb was not there to testify against the young men. About that, she had always been adamant. She knew the two young men had to be punished, she told me more than once, but "I don't want to be part of the mass incarceration machine that sends so many Black men to prison." Months earlier, when I had gently passed along the news that the government, if it chose, could compel Deb to testify in the case, she had collapsed in sobs.

Now, instead of formal testimony, Deb was going to give a Witness Impact Statement, a voluntary description of how the crime in question had affected her. She was looking forward to it, she told me. "I won't be testifying against them," she explained, "I'll only be speaking my truth about the shooting and what we can learn from it. It will be my opportunity to speak to those boys face-to-face and connect with their humanity."

In fact, it was now officially impossible for Deb's words to help convict the Scott brothers: they had already pleaded guilty. After long negotiations, the brothers' court-appointed lawyers had reached a plea deal with the government. The Scott brothers would admit their guilt, sparing the government the time and expense of prosecuting them for crimes where the evidence of their wrongdoing was overwhelming. In return, the government would offer the Scott brothers the possibility of spending less than the entire rest of their lives in prison. The specific terms of the plea deal set the range of the brothers' imprisonment between a minimum of twenty years and a maximum of life. That day's proceeding would decide where within that range the sentences would actually fall.

The decision would be made by District Court judge Ivan L. R. Lemelle, and his decision would be final. As part of the plea deal, the Scott brothers agreed to waive all rights to appeal (except for the right, always protected in US law, to appeal on the grounds of inadequate counsel). So, there was no jury in the courtroom today. There was only Judge Lemelle, the defendants, their attorneys, the government's attorneys, and about two dozen members of the public.

The public gallery occupied the back third of the high-ceilinged, wood-paneled courtroom. A wooden railing separated the gallery from the front of the courtroom, where the jury box, tables and chairs for the attorneys, witness stand, and judge's podium were. The gallery's long wooden benches resembled church pews. Deb sat in the second row from the front, toward the right when facing the judge. Always fashion conscious, she was wearing a reddish orange jacket over a black skirt and red boots; her hair hung long and straight past her shoulders. With her were four members of her inner posse, all of them White: Stacy Head, Karen Gadbois, Meg Lousteau, and Ed McGinnis. A few seats away, sitting alone, was Ed Buckner, looking street elegant in a white sweater with orange rings around the biceps, his hair pulled back in a neat ponytail. On the left side of the gallery sat three African American women accompanied by young children who were all clearly part of the same family.

The jury box was mostly empty, but four seats in its front row were occupied by the Scott brothers. Four, because Akein and Shawn were joined by their brothers Stanley and Travis, ages twenty-two and thirty-one. Stanley and Travis had also signed plea deals, pleading guilty to related charges of drug dealing, weapons possession, and violence. The terms of their deals were virtually the same as those of Akein and Shawn: they would plead guilty and in return get a chance to spend only the next twenty years, rather than the entire rest of their lives, in prison.

All four Scott brothers were wearing neck-to-ankle prison jumpsuits; three of the jumpsuits were orange, one was scarlet. I recognized Akein and Shawn, both in orange, from their mug shots. Knowing that Travis was the eldest, I guessed correctly that he was the one in scarlet. By process of elimination, that meant the third brother was Stanley. Travis (not to be confused with the rap star Travis Scott) occupied the seat closest to the judge's podium. He was an imposing physical presence: tall, with muscular forearms and broad shoulders beneath short dreadlocks that hung around his ears. Shawn was slender, dark-skinned, with a quietly puzzled look on his face. Stanley was thicker, with almond-shaped eyes, medium height. Akein, also of medium height and build, stared into space as if living a dream he was struggling to understand.

I was seated in the front row of the public gallery. Deb sat a few feet away to my right. A few feet to my left was Akein Scott, the young man who had shot me and so many other people at the Mother's Day second line three years ago. I felt neither fear of nor anger toward Akein Scott, only a sad, nameless wonder that his life and mine had somehow intersected despite our vastly different backgrounds. Silently, I marveled at how young all four Scott brothers looked; Akein still had peach fuzz on his chin.

"All rise!" the court clerk intoned shortly after 9:30 A.M. A door swung open from the back wall. Judge Lemelle emerged in a black robe, mounted his podium, and sat down, a United States flag to his right and a Louisiana state flag to his left. Lemelle was sixty-five years old, a Louisiana native who had worked in New Orleans since attending Xavier University, the city's historically Black institution. Nominated as a federal judge in 1997 by President Clinton, he was heavyset, with prominent jowls and a red birthmark the size of a child's fist on his right cheek. He conveyed a stolid, no-nonsense sensibility. This was not the first time he was seeing the Scott brothers, nor they him; he had presided over earlier hearings in the case, so he was well acquainted with the evidence presented to date.

The government's evidence was summarized in so-called Factual Basis documents that were attached to the plea deal agreements they had made with the Scott brothers. Scrutinizing the documents before the hearing, I had to read them four or five times to penetrate their legalese and dense repetition of facts. The picture that emerged was devastating.

By accepting the plea deal, Akein, Shawn, Stanley, and Travis Scott were confessing that they and other members of a group calling itself the FnD gang had been selling heroin, crack cocaine, and other illegal drugs near the intersection of Frenchmen and Derbigny streets since at least 2006—seven years before the Mother's Day shooting. To assert control of that area against rival drug dealers, and to enforce cooperation from customers, victims, and witnesses, the FnD gang had routinely used "violence and threats of violence." This record of deliberate violence included at least three other shootings in addition to the Mother's Day second line assault.

The vocabulary of the FnD gang, as reported in the Factual Basis, was as colorful as it was foreboding. One favorite weapon, an AK-style rifle with a 100-round magazine drum, was named "monkey nuts." The generic term for any kind of gun was "rachet." If a gang member was armed, he was "toting rachets." A "birthday party" meant a murder. When Travis Scott sought to encourage customer loyalty by selling two bags of heroin for the price of one on certain Tuesdays, he named the discount days "Obama Tuesdays."

Travis was the undisputed leader of the FnD gang; his Factual Basis specified that he "would direct members of FnD to commit crimes of violence." Travis was also the man who once a month would buy FnD's supply of drugs from Merle Offray, "a high-level heroin supplier in the New Orleans area."

Akein Scott was portrayed as the gang's main enforcer. In each of the four shootings described in the Factual Basis, Akein was the triggerman, often joined by one or another Scott brother. According to an intercepted cell phone conversation, Akein had also urged the murder of two rival gang members.

The Factual Basis also provided previously undisclosed details about the Mother's Day shooting, including information about the intended target. When Akein and Shawn Scott fired handguns into a second line parade, they "intended to kill a rival gang member, J.T., with whom they had a 'beef,'" Count 19 of the document said. (The Factual Basis used initials to identify individuals; thus, Deborah Cotton was listed as D.C.) The rival gang member identified as J.T. was, I later learned, John Taylor, better known by his nickname, Little Manny, the young man who Tuffy Nelson told me had been targeted in a case of mistaken identity. The Factual Basis noted that, "at least four of the victims required multiple surgeries." That number squared with the estimate that EMTs at the crime scene had given detective Chris Hart when they projected three to four potential fatalities from the shooting. The motive for the shooting, the Factual Basis continued, was a dispute over territory: a rival gang had allegedly tried to sell drugs in the area the FnD considered theirs.

I don't know if Deb ever read the Factual Basis documents. I had summarized them for her weeks earlier, after they were publicly released when the plea deals were announced. At the time, she seemed to minimize their contents. It was a stretch, she told me, to characterize the Scott brothers as a gang. "I lived in South Central LA," she said. "The gangs there were the real deal. Even the cops were afraid of them." By comparison, the Scott brothers of New Orleans "were just members of the same family who sold drugs together." I pointed to the four shootings described in the Factual Basis and the atmosphere of violent intimidation the FnD members admitted to having enforced in their neighborhood. I reminded Deb that these were no longer mere allegations; these were crimes the Scott brothers were confessing that they had committed.

Of course, Deb and I both knew that many, many Black people over the years had accepted plea deals for crimes they had not actually committed. The reason often boiled down to the lesser of two evils. As Daniel Carty, a character in James Baldwin's novel *If Beale Street Could Talk*, explained, he had had marijuana in his pocket when police arrested him, and they gave him a choice: confess to having stolen a car that was missing and serve two years in jail, or face trial for possession of marijuana and risk spending twenty years in jail. "I didn't steal no car," Carty tells his friend. "Hell, I don't even know how to drive. But, you know, a marijuana charge could send me away for a long time." But not once in our many hours of conversation did Deb suggest that the Scotts' confessions and plea deals might be similarly tainted, and my interviews with their attorneys yielded no such indications, either.

"Be seated, please," Judge Lemelle said. Noting that the four defendants were seated in the jury box, six to ten feet away from their respective attorneys, Lemell asked the attorneys, "Is that going to be satisfactory for you in terms of communicating with them throughout this hearing?" At the time, I thought the judge was being remarkably gracious. Later I realized a more likely explanation: Lemelle wanted to foreclose the defendants appealing their sentences on the grounds of inadequate access to counsel.

The bailiff escorted the Scott brothers out of the jury box so they could walk the short distance to sit alongside their attorneys. As the four brothers stood, I saw silver metal chains encircling their wrists and looping around their waists. As they shuffled down the aisle toward the attorneys' table, I saw identical chains encircling their ankles. I couldn't help but think of the shackles their enslaved ancestors had worn.

No sooner had the Scotts taken seats beside their attorneys than Judge Lemelle threw a curveball: today's hearing, he announced, would not be a sentencing hearing after all. It would be an evidentiary hearing. Its purpose was to "determine whether or not the government can show some basis for any enhancements to possible sentences." I wasn't sure what that meant, but apparently it wasn't welcome news to the defense. Stanley Scott's attorney began voicing one concern after another, including whether he would have the right to offer objections during the proceedings.

At the time, neither Deb nor I comprehended the verbal legalese flying back and forth between the attorneys and the judge. It turned out that the government attorneys were hoping to convince the judge to give the defendants tougher sentences—to "enhance" their sentences toward the upper end of the twenty-years-to-life range stipulated in the plea deals. To support such enhanced sentences, the government wanted to present additional evidence. Which was why Stanley and Travis Scott's attorneys voiced one objection after another. But with only one exception, Lemelle was equally relentless, responding to each objection with a single word: "Overruled."

The first witness the government called was Ed Buckner. Like Deb, Buckner was, technically speaking, not testifying but providing a Witness Impact Statement. Asked what impact the shooting had on second line

culture, Ed said that after the shooting the heads of all thirty-nine Social
Aid and Pleasure Clubs in New Orleans had called an emergency meeting.
Their goal was "damage control," Ed said—figuring out how to keep this
high-profile attack from destroying public participation in a cultural ritual
Black people in New Orleans had inherited from their ancestors. "The
culture had been really damaged because of this shooting," Ed said. "You
had revelers and participants all afraid to participate, because they were
afraid that it could be another shooting." He added, "We had to do a lot of
convincing people that it would be safe, that it was not their fault, or my
fault, or none of the people that got hurt fault." Ed said that his club "did a
renew parade" three weeks after the shooting, "because we did not want to
be intimidated." The following year, the club resumed holding its parade on
Mother's Day for the same reason. Nevertheless, some of his club members
"had to have psychiatric help," and one family whose nine-year-old son
had been second lining for the first time decided to move away from New
Orleans. (This was a reference to Leo Gorman's nephew, Shiloh.) "They
just totally left town," he said. "I guess it was just too close for them."

I was shaken myself during Ed's testimony because the prosecution augmented it by showing the Unblinking Eye video. It was the first time that I
fully realized how lucky I was to have survived the shooting. Projected onto
a large screen at the front of the courtroom, this version of the Mother's Day
video was much better quality than what had run on television and social
media: this was the original video, not a copy, and government technicians
had cleaned it up to provide the clearest visuals possible.

I had watched the TV and online versions of the Unblinking Eye video
countless times by then, but only now was I able to pick myself out in
the crowd at the intersection of Frenchmen and North Villere streets. I
could see my yellow fedora and lime-green shirt near the right side of the
intersection while the gunman lay in wait on the left, his back against
the wall of the house on the corner. I saw myself drift a few feet to my left,
toward the shooter, as he strode forward, pulled a gun from his pocket,

and began to fire. As the crowd scattered, I was embarrassingly slow to react. The gunman was pointing his weapon directly at my fleeing back as he unleashed his final shots. No wonder I got hit.

But I was lucky. The video revealed that as Akein Scott advanced toward the crowd, he began firing his weapon while still on the sidewalk. Near the end of his barrage, however, he stepped off the sidewalk onto the street. The drop from the sidewalk to the street was no more than three inches, but those three inches were enough to change the destination of the bullet being fired in that split second. As Akein Scott's right foot stepped onto the street, the drop pulled the rest of his body down with it, causing his gunshots to angle down as well. Which explained why, once a doctor finally popped the slug out of my leg a year later, the bullet's nose was flattened: the bullet had ricocheted off the street before slanting upward into my leg. The impact with the pavement also meant that the bullet struck me with less force than it would have unimpeded. That simple twist of fate—Akein Scott stepping off the sidewalk in the moment he shot me—gave me a flesh wound in the calf, rather than a lethal bullet to the spine or the skull.

The atmosphere in the courtroom, already fraught, quivered with anticipation when the government called Deborah Cotton to the witness stand. Akein and Shawn Scott turned slightly in their seats to watch Deb stride up the gallery aisle to the front of the courtroom. Breathing hard, she looked a little nervous but ready.

In response to a prosecuting attorney's questions, Deb first offered her account of the Mother's Day shooting. She detailed the injuries she sustained, the fact that the doctors had not expected her to live, how she had undergone more than thirty surgeries and still had more ahead, and how she was now on disability because her injuries made it impossible to work full-time. She affirmed the importance of second line parade culture and said she had made a deliberate effort after Hurricane Katrina to help restore that culture by documenting and publicizing it.

"Second lines just would not be permitted anywhere else in the United States," she said. The fact that the shooting happened at a second line parade, she said, made it "more horrifying" than if it happened at some random place. Asked whether the city's second line parade culture had recovered from the shooting, Deb replied that, just like Hurricane Katrina hadn't managed to kill that culture, the Mother's Day "shooting didn't kill it. And we're going to just keep pushing. That's what we do as Black people. We just keep pushing."

Then came the moment Deb had been waiting for, when she was allowed to speak her truth to the young Black men who had changed her life forever that Mother's Day afternoon. Her statement, which she ad-libbed from handwritten notes, is quoted here at length:

"I have read some of the reports of the crimes that y'all have committed. I can never know the challenges you faced that caused the circumstances that you're facing now. It is possible by pleading guilty that you could get out one day, and you could possibly be getting out and being the age that I'm at. I'm fifty-one now. I'm old enough to be all of y'all's mother, and you're young enough to be my sons. I feel like, in a way, you are my sons."

Speaking slowly, with unmistakable emotion, she continued, "You are Black men that I have spent my entire life loving and working with and for. So I want you to hold on to what I'm saying to you today. I believe in you. I believe in your capacity, in your humanity. I believe in your ability to change. I believe that you have talents and value and worth. You have something positive to give. We haven't had the opportunity to see that yet. We haven't had an opportunity to benefit from it because you've been on the wrong path. This jail time that you'll be serving will be like a time out, for you to cool your heels, to think, to reconsider, to recalibrate, hopefully to recover your humanity, your dreams of what you want to do, to be."

Channeling the social engagement teachings of her Jewish background, Deb went on to say that "I want you to take this time to think about how you can improve the world, how you can repair the world. I'm pledging to you that I'm going to hold a vision of you on the right path until you can get out and bring that vision to fruition." Calling it "nothing short of miraculous" that all the people shot at that second line had survived, Deb said, "I'm here because God has more for me to do. Being here today to address you directly is just one of those things. I'm appearing before you to give you forgiveness, to give you support, to give you something to think about, to reflect on, to believe in, to hold on to, to depend on, to remember when you get down and you don't know how to get back up."

Then, in her closing words, Deb reiterated her spiritual beliefs while repudiating the conventional view of Black men who have committed crimes: "Because of God's grace, I survived; and he wanted me to come and tell you that there is more for you. There is more for you. There are people waiting out here to help you get more and be more. I ask that you don't give up. Some people would have you believe that you don't matter, that we just lock you up and throw away the key [and then] we have . . . four less criminals out on the street to deal with. But I believe in redemption."

As Deb finished speaking, a hush engulfed the courtroom. The Scott brothers' faces were impassive, but even courtroom veterans were visibly moved. Stanley Scott's attorney, the man who had been making so many objections an hour before, said he had no questions for Miss Cotton but did want to tell her, "You are one of the most gracious people I've ever been in the presence of." The judge said he wished he could be as "eloquent" as Deb was, calling her statement "a remarkable example, in your own words, of survival based upon your faith."

But, the judge added, "I do have to ask you a tough question." Did she have any opinion about the government's desire to enhance the penalties facing the defendants, "all the way up to life imprisonment?"

Deb was careful to acknowledge that "every person who was shot has their own truth and their own reality, and I respect that." Directing her gaze at the Scott brothers, she continued, "But for myself, I want to see you-all survive and come out and have a chance at life. I do. I really do." Turning to Judge Lemelle, she added, "I truly believe that given the opportunity and the time and the rehabilitation and the support, that they could be not only contributors and repay their debts to society, but that they could do great things. . . . So, I would like to see some options, some possibility for them to be free again."

After Deb returned to her seat in the gallery, the tone of the hearing grew considerably darker. The next witness was Shirley Johnson, who was questioned about an alleged crime not mentioned in the plea deals the Scott brothers signed. In other words, she was appearing only because the judge had granted the prosecution's request to present additional evidence to support possibly harsher sentences. Ms. Johnson was fifty-eight years old, Black, thin, and missing a number of teeth. She had never lived outside New Orleans. She had worked many years at the Avondale Shipyard on the Mississippi River, sandblasting the insides of US Navy vessels. Today, she would testify that Travis Scott had shot and killed her nineteen-year-old son Calvin.

Speaking in a spare but decisive voice, Ms. Johnson testified that the shooting had taken place in March of 2005, a year after she and her four children moved into a small house on Frenchmen Street near Derbigny. Asked what the neighborhood was like, she gave a one-word reply: "Hell." Pressed to elaborate, she said that on the first couple nights, there were gunshots, and "I told my children to hit the floor." Shown a photograph of a young Black man with long dreadlocks, she unhesitatingly identified him as "Travis." She didn't know his last name, but "he stayed on Frenchmen," a few doors down and across the street from her. Travis and her son were friends at first, she said, but their relationship turned hostile after T'Daryl, Travis's younger brother, shot her son in the arm in January of 2005. A few weeks later, her son shot T'Daryl, also in the arm, after which her son and his girlfriend moved "across the river" to the Algiers side of the Mississippi for fear of further retaliation.

Both Travis and Calvin sold drugs in the Frenchmen Street neighborhood, Ms. Johnson testified. She emphasized that she did not approve of Calvin selling drugs, "and he knew I didn't approve," but she couldn't stop him.

Seeking to head off this line of inquiry, Stanley Scott's attorney objected, telling the judge that the government was not "entitled to now just ask carte blanche anybody about anything they know that the Scott brothers might have done." Lemelle again overruled the objection.

Ms. Johnson said she saw Travis with a group of young people selling drugs every day at the corner of Frenchmen and Derbigny streets. Disgust dripping from her words, she said, "I was coming home from work, and they asked, 'Mom, you want to buy some?'" She told them, "I don't use drugs. And I'm not your mom."

On March 11 of 2005, Shirley Johnson had just gotten home from work and sat down in front of the TV set when she got a heart-stopping phone call: her son Calvin had been shot. In yet another ghastly New Orleans coincidence, her son was shot at an address that shared his surname: 1800 North Johnson Street. Frantic, Shirley Johnson hurried to the scene, ten blocks away. There, a neighbor lady told her that the wounded young man had already been taken to the hospital. At the hospital, her son's girlfriend told her what happened. She and Calvin were chatting in someone's yard when a car pulled up and Travis Scott jumped out with a rifle and started shooting. Calvin threw his body in front of his girlfriend, saving her life at the cost of his.

Shirley Johnson waited an hour at the hospital for the police to arrive; they didn't show. She returned home and called the station. Officers didn't come to her house to take statements for another week. By then, she testified, Calvin's girlfriend "was just too scared to talk."

Travis's attorney cross-examined Ms. Johnson, asking if she was aware that Travis had turned himself in after learning the police were looking for him, "and then they let him go." Yes, Ms. Johnson replied, but the reason Travis wasn't charged was that "we had an eyewitness that wouldn't testify [because she] was scared."

Throughout this back and forth, Travis Scott stared straight ahead, his face an expressionless mask. "In the courtroom, he didn't remember me until he heard my name," Shirley Johnson told me later. "I looked in his face when I got there. He had no idea who I was. He thought it was all over, he thought they'd got away with something. I looked at him [while testifying], because I wanted him to see me. And when he looked down, I said to myself, 'Got ya!'"

The next witness was James Lobrie. He too would testify about an alleged murder not included in the plea deals. Mr. Lobrie was a heavyset, middle-aged Black man, with sad, tired eyes. His son, James Gould, was killed in 2012. Mr. Lobrie admitted that his son had been a drug addict. After graduating from high school, his son had enlisted in the Navy, serving on the USS *Abraham Lincoln* in the first Gulf War. He "saw stuff that messed him up" during the war, his father testified, and got addicted to heroin. After a dishonorable discharge, his son returned to Louisiana, worked odd jobs, and tried to get treatment for his addiction, but with limited success.

James Lobrie worked as a school bus driver, and he happened to be driving a busload of kids through the Seventh Ward on February 3, 2012, when he saw blinking lights and yellow police tape cordoning off the intersection of Annette and North Villere streets. Behind the yellow tape, a white sheet was draped over what appeared to be a dead body. He told the kids, "This is why I try to get y'all off to school every morning, because now some parent is going to get a call saying their son or their daughter dead." Only later, when his daughter called, did James Lobrie learn that today he himself was that unlucky parent.

"My life ain't been the same since," Lobrie testified. "Your children supposed to be burying you, not you burying them." When he went to the morgue to identify his son's body, the wounds to the young man's face were so severe that burial was impossible. "They shot him up in the face so bad that they couldn't do plastic surgery or nothing to him," Lobrie said. "It was just, like, there was too many holes in his face. . . . I had to get him cremated."

Deb left the courtroom now; these last two witnesses must have been difficult for her to hear. From the beginning, she had given the Scott brothers the benefit of the doubt and urged others to do likewise. Today, she had declared that they did deserve punishment, but she had phrased that punishment in strikingly generous terms, referring to it as a "time out," like what a three-year-old might get after a tantrum. Now, a mother and a father of two young Black men had shared their bottomless grief at losing children to deadly gunshots, raising a fearsome possibility: perhaps the Scott brothers were not simply disadvantaged young Black men who made a single terrible decision one Mother's Day afternoon; perhaps they were stone cold killers who had murdered other young Black men, more than once.

Next to the witness stand came, one after another, three former members of the FnD gang, each wearing a prison jumpsuit. Wendell Jeremiah Jackson, Gralen Benson, and Richmond Smith had been "flipped" by the government—convinced to testify against their former compatriots in hopes of getting their own prison sentences reduced. It was a particularly dramatic turn of events in the case of Gralen Benson: he was the Scotts' cousin. The three men's testimonies were blunt, uncultured, devastating. They revealed some of the gang's innermost secrets: who the Scott brothers swapped guns with, how many murders they allegedly committed, why Akein and Shawn shot up the Mother's Day second line, and more of the code words the gang used among themselves.

"Sling iron" was the gang's slang for "to kill, like, shoot at people," Richmond Smith explained. Asked what Travis said about slinging iron, Smith replied, "If he got to, he going to sling it, no matter who get up in his way, you know. Yeah. He don't give a F. . . ." Travis often drove around the nearby streets, Smith added, accompanied by Akein and sometimes Smith himself, "trying to find they prey . . . trying to find somebody they beefing with." Asked what would happen if they found such prey, Smith replied, "shoot at them, try to kill them."

Although none of the three former FnD members witnessed the James Gould murder or knew the name of the victim, each of them said the Scotts had told them about a murder that sounded very similar. Wendell Jackson said Akein and Stanley had told him "in a boastful manner" about a shooting they had done on the other side of Claiborne Avenue, where they pulled up on the guy and Stanley jumped out of the car and started shooting, followed by Akein. The guy was hit, tried to run away, but eventually fell, at which point Akein allegedly stood over him and finished him off with a blizzard of bullets. Richmond Smith added further details, including the allegation that Travis gave the initial order to shoot, directing Stanley to "hit him."

Richmond Smith further testified that when he and Akein encountered each other in prison after the Mother's Day shooting, Akein bragged about how many murders he had committed. "You got two," Smith said. To which Akein allegedly replied, "No, I got four." The Mother's Day shooting, Smith added, was a revenge hit on Akein's part: "He said he did that because of his brother."

None of the Scott brothers showed any expression as they watched their fellow gang members betray them.

"What do you think of this bullshit?"

The judge had declared a bathroom break, and I had just finished washing my hands in the men's room when Travis Scott's attorney slung that question at me. Patrick McGinity had thinning snow-white hair combed back from a pink forehead and wore old fashioned two-tone shoes of white and brown. As he washed his hands, McGinity explained in a honeyed drawl that did not hide his disgust, "The government is in there asking for an upward departure, an enhancement, of the sentences. That's what all the stuff today is about. It's bullshit. They get you to plead to one set of facts, then they bring up all these other cases to paint our clients in the worst light possible."

We stepped back into the hallway, where McGinity explained "relevant conduct," a legal term that carried utmost significance for the government's case. "Relevant conduct" could be applied only during sentencing hearings that took place after a defendant made a plea deal but before the judge issued a sentence—in other words, hearings like today's. "Travis and his brothers signed plea deals that stipulated prison sentences of twenty years to life, but the government wants them to get life. That's what's going on in there," McGinity said, jerking his head toward the courtroom.

"That's how they do it," agreed his associate, a middle-aged White woman with alert eyes named Addie Fields. "And we can't challenge their case because we took the plea deal and didn't go to trial. But what the government is claiming about those murder cases, it's all hearsay. They don't have any eyewitnesses. It's what Calvin Johnson's mother heard on the street."

"Let me see if I'm understanding you," I said. "What you're describing sounds like a bait and switch. The government baits a defendant with one set of facts to get a plea deal. But after the defendant agrees to the deal, the government invokes relevant conduct and gives the judge additional information to support a harsher sentence. Is that it?"

"That's it," said McGinity.

"How can that be legal?" I asked.

"Well, a case challenging its legality is heading for the United States Supreme Court," McGinity replied. "But that doesn't help us today."

Irked as they were, McGinity and Fields were hardly surprised that the legal process was biased against their clients. McGinity had been a defense attorney for decades; Fields had specialized in such cases since 1995. Neither of them had illusions that the clients they defended were angels. But as certain patterns of behavior and outcome repeated themselves over the years, McGinity and Fields seemed to have concluded that the justice system was hopelessly stacked against young Black men from the ghetto.

"I've seen dozens of Travises during my years here, young Black men who grew up basically without parents," said Fields. "We're living today with the effects of the welfare law President Clinton signed in 1996. That law required welfare recipients to go to work or school to keep receiving federal benefits. Mothers who lived in public housing would lose that housing and their benefits if a felon was found on the premises. I suppose those reforms might have worked if the law provided some form of universal childcare, because if not, who's going to take care of the kids when the mother is at work or school? But that didn't happen, so kids ended up raising themselves. Families that were already fractured, Clinton's welfare law pushed them over the edge into total breakup. Kids would grow up without proper parenting and get into trouble with the law. That's when the two of us enter the picture, but by then it's too late. There are no good outcomes at that point, just degrees of bad."

"These are the lost boys of New Orleans," she added in a resigned tone. "I've seen it over and over. Travis and his brothers never had a chance, and there's a whole generation of kids facing the same plight. It's easy to blame the parents, but government policies shape the choices that parents make. Unless those policies change, we'll continue to have lost boys, and lost girls, all across this country."

Donald Harrison, one of the most eminent musicians of New Orleans, told me much the same thing in a separate interview. Harrison had grown up in the heart of second line culture in New Orleans as the son of the legendary Donald "Big Chief" Harrison. The younger Harrison studied under Ellis Marsalis Jr. and went on to play with some of the greatest jazz musicians in America, including Roy Haynes, Art Blakey's Jazz Messengers, and fellow New Orleans native Terence Blanchard. In 1999, following in his father's footsteps, he was named the big chief of the Congo Square Nation Afro–New Orleans Cultural Group. After Hurricane Katrina scattered many of his hometown's musicians and left behind few live performance opportunities, he had made a point of mentoring high school musicians, inviting them on stage to play with him to give them much-needed public exposure. He appeared in eleven episodes of the HBO series *Treme*, playing himself.

Despite his world-class accomplishments, Harrison told me, "You know, it's hard to love yourself as an African American. Because you don't really know who you are, you don't know the people you came from. Slavery separated African Americans from our families. We don't even know our real names." Harrison remembered the Mother's Day shooting, he said, and felt strongly that the young men accused of the crime had to be held accountable. He took explicit exception to Deb's opinion that those young men should be, if not forgiven, afforded mercy and understanding. Nevertheless, the idea that an African American of any age, sex, or background could lose faith in themselves within the ancient swirl of race in America was self-evident to Harrison. "It's not just that we don't know ourselves and our past," he told me. "It's also that society is saying we're not *worth* knowing, that 'you came from slavery, and you're no better than a slave.'"

On March 29, 2016, five weeks after the first hearing, many of the same faces were back in the same courtroom to witness the formal sentencing of the Scott brothers. In the public gallery, Deb was again accompanied by five close friends. Ed Buckner again sat alone. Shirley Johnson and James Lobrie, whose children the Scott brothers were accused of murdering, were there, seated separately. A contingent of the Scott brothers' loved ones again occupied the left side of the gallery. A middle-aged Black woman with tinted reddish hair turned out to be their mother, Gladys Scott. Joining her was a young woman in a formfitting blue sweater who was in charge of two little girls. Neatly dressed, the girls looked about four and six years old; the younger one had her hair pulled back in a bun, the older wore hers in impeccably braided cornrows. The older girl looked at me with doleful eyes that recalled the look on Shawn Scott's face after he was arrested.

The Scott brothers were again shackled and seated in the first row of the jury box. Travis was closest to the judge's podium, Shawn sat to Travis's right, then Akein, then Stanley. The brothers chatted quietly, their demeanors seemingly calm, even nonchalant. Travis stood and started making funny faces at the family members in the public gallery, silently mouthing, "You don't love me." One of the women may have mouthed loving words back, for Travis then pantomimed, with a playful smirk in his eyes, "You don't mean that."

At 9:54 A.M., Judge Lemelle called the hearing to order. Akein's attorney, Julie Tizzard, offered a final, spirited argument on her client's behalf, saying that the prosecution attorneys had previously told her that they would not include the murder of James Gould in their case. She added that she had informed them that if they did include the Gould murder, she would not advise Akein to accept the plea deal. Now, the prosecution had indeed included the Gould murder. Nor had the government proven its accusations, Tizzard maintained: for example, it had not interviewed even one eyewitness who said the shooter had run away in a completely different direction.

The judge looked down at his desk throughout Tizzard's discourse, but when she finished, he made it clear that the relevant conduct accusations would stand. "Relevant conduct is something the court can always use," he said. Lemelle reiterated that there was a looser standard of proof under relevant conduct: the prosecution did not have to prove its case "beyond a reasonable doubt," the usual benchmark; instead, a "preponderance of the evidence" was sufficient. In a crushing blow, Lemelle added, "The preponderance of the evidence indicates that Akein Scott was involved in that murder."

As the judge and Ms. Tizzard skirmished, I wondered how it felt for the two little girls across the aisle from me to hear the word "murder" repeatedly attached to Akein, who was likely their uncle or cousin. Their quiet, careful faces gave no hint.

After overruling a series of other objections from the Scotts' attorneys, the judge wiped his eyes and said, "I'm ready to proceed with the sentencing." First, he offered each defendant an opportunity to make a statement, beginning with Stanley Scott.

"First, I wanna say that I'm sorry to the victims of these crimes," Stanley began. "I pray every night to God to have a chance to raise my son." When Stanley said, "I want to apologize to my mama; I'm sorry for putting you through all this," his mother thrust her arms into the air and waved them back and forth, as if to absolve him. Stanley concluded with a poetic lament: "I was a child of the ghetto who grew up to be a man without a vision. The only love I knew was the love of the streets, until I was put in these chains."

Shawn Scott's attorney spoke on Shawn's behalf, arguing, "It's important to take into account some of the traumatic events in his youth. When he was five years old, a murder occurred in the household, which he witnessed. Not that this excuses what happened, but we hope you'll take that into account. We also ask the court to consider that his wife and two kids are here in court, and we'd like to have the possibility someday of his reunion with the family. Mr. Scott would like me to express his sincere remorse, especially for the Mother's Day shooting of 2013."

As Akein Scott stood up to make his statement, I watched Deb simultaneously stiffen and melt. "I would like to apologize to all the victims and everyone I put in harm's way," Akein began, reading from a piece of paper he held between his shackled hands. "I made mistakes in my life I'm not proud of. I've tried to improve my mind and become a more responsible person. I have asked God for forgiveness, and I understand that I have put my family and community through things. I wish I could take my decisions I made back."

Akein looked over at Deb and tried to speak her name, but all he could get out was "Miss . . . miss . . . miss." After three tries, he gave up and, almost in tears, said, "You asked about my dream. I had a dream to write poetry and become . . ." Again, he couldn't get the words out. Recovering slightly, he said, "I was in school for business management. I couldn't stay focused enough to pursue my dream." Again, his voice faltered as he stared down at his paper. This time, he gave up speaking altogether and silently sat down.

Finally came Travis's turn. In a strong but pained voice, he said, "I want to send my condolences to the victims' families. And I want to say I'm sorry to my mother, and to you, your honor. It's been a hard time, you know what I'm saying? . . . I tried to get away from this life and better myself and my family. But as you can see, the past catch up with you. I take full responsibility for my actions. I just want to say I apologize."

The judge then allowed the Scotts' mother, Gladys Scott, to speak. Standing in the public gallery, wearing a yellow and green striped top over black slacks, she said, "I raised nine boys and three girls by myself. It was kinda hard. I had three jobs. I'm apologizing to the people; whatever happened, I'm apologizing." Turning from the judge to her sons, she added, "I told y'all, you gotta be strong for your kids, you gotta trust in God. Y'all ain't no bad kids, you weren't then, you aren't now. . . . God made me strong and he can make you strong, too."

Then it was the prosecution's turn to speak, and Assistant US Attorney Matthew Payne responded, "The government has no doubt that these four young men had a difficult upbringing. . . . But this is not a case about one bad decision. This is about a long-term habit and plan of operating in a community in New Orleans and subjecting that community to fear and violence." He added, "The harm they caused was more profound than the twenty [*sic*] individuals who were struck by bullets [on Mother's Day] . . . The video shows numerous people running away in fear. The damage to the community was profound." Recalling how Deb portrayed second line parades as "a staple of the African American community in New Orleans," Payne added that, "This shooting endangered that culture."

Now it was Judge Lemelle's turn, and he began by invoking the greatest Black freedom fighter of the 20th century. "A wonderful human being once said, 'No one truly knows a nation until he has been inside its jails,'" Lemelle said. "'A nation should not be judged by how it treats its highest citizens but its lowest ones.' That quote comes from Nelson Mandela, who spent much of his life in prison because of the color of his skin and his belief in equality. He could easily have come out of jail with retaliation on his mind. What did he do? He came out with a message of love. Not a message of division, of hatred, of disrespect. He said what I guess the Good Book says, what every religion on earth says: 'You don't judge your own character by how you feel about yourself; you judge it by how you treat other people.'"

Listening to Lemelle begin with Mandela and the Golden Rule, Deb thought he was going to show mercy. He wasn't going to let the Scott brothers off entirely—he couldn't, under the terms of the plea deals—but it sounded like he wasn't going to give them full life sentences. I harbored the same hunch, and that hunch strengthened when the judge tilted his head to look the Scott brothers in the eye. "All of you in your statements today indicate a knowledge of that," Lemelle said. "You've got to put that into practice." Why would a judge urge the defendants to put the Golden Rule into practice if they weren't going to get out of prison someday?

But Lemelle then turned on a dime, telling the Scotts, "Your criminal history shows the opposite of that—an arrogance, a disrespect of others. The most heinous example was what I would consider a terrorist act, the attack on those people at the Mother's Day parade. You had to have known you were putting innocent lives at risk." The judge took a long pause, poured a glass of water from a metal pitcher on his desk, and took a sip. "Imagine one of your loved ones in that group of people," he continued. "Imagine the fear they would have had when shots rang out in a city that seems to be fraught with violence." A week before today's hearing, terrorist attacks in Brussels had killed thirty-two people and injured over three hundred. "Was your conduct any different than the terrorists who attack victims in Brussels and elsewhere?" Lemelle asked. "Are you terrorists? Your conduct that you admitted to seems to say that you are."

Then Lemelle's tone shifted again as he said that he forgave the defendants. Telling them that "even the worst human beings have goodness inside them," he urged the Scotts to "turn to that power within you when you feel disturbed or [feel] like retaliating against someone—turn like a flower turns to the light. Don't live in the darkness, kids. Don't live in the darkness."

Now that the moment of judgment had arrived, it felt impossible to guess how the judge would rule. He began with Travis Scott. Seated ten feet below and to Lemelle's right, Travis stared up at the judge, his eyes locked and intense. The judge looked down to read from a document on his desk.

"Travis Scott shall be imprisoned for life," he declared.

In the next instant many things happened at once.

In the jury box, Travis's eyebrows leaped as if someone had slapped him hard across the face. He looked across the room toward his lawyer, then to the security guard stationed between him and the judge, then back to his lawyer, and then silently mouthed, in obvious disbelief, "Life?"

In the gallery, his mother shouted, "No!"

Deb looked stunned, as if she couldn't comprehend what the judge just said.

Lemelle droned on about the specific terms of the sentence, assigning such and such many months in prison for count X in the plea deal, such and such many months for count Y, and so on. He said Travis Scott had the right to appeal this sentence, but only "to the extent it does not violate the agreement you made with the government." Which meant that the only basis for appeal would be a claim of inadequate representation by counsel.

"Do you understand your sentence?" Lemelle asked Travis. "Not do you agree with it, but do you understand it?"

In a weak, confused tone, Travis asked, "What is it?"

"I'll summarize it for you," the judge replied. "Life in prison."

Akein was next. There was not a sound in the room except the judge's penetrating voice. Again reading from a document in front of him, he declared, "Akein Scott shall be imprisoned for life." Akein began shaking his head slowly back and forth, leaned over, and whispered something to Stanley. As he had with Travis, Lemelle explained the specifics of the sentence, specifying how many months in prison each count carried.

Deb's face had the same stunned look as before, but now she was leaning forward and peering intently at the judge, as if trying to understand words spoken in a foreign language. But the judge's meaning was plenty clear. Travis and Akein Scott were each getting the maximum possible sentence: life.

Shawn and Stanley Scott, for their parts, were spared life in prison, but not by much. Shawn was sentenced to 439 months, which amounted to roughly 36 years. Taking into account time already served, Shawn would be in prison until he was fifty-nine years old. Stanley was given 480 months—40 years—meaning he could be released when he was sixty-four.

It was 12:50 P.M., two hours and fifty-six minutes since the hearing began. Akein was staring at the floor, his body rocking back and forth. Across the aisle from me, the Scott family's tiny baby started burbling. The judge looked at the defendants one last time; they did not look at him. "I pray for each of you, as I pray for all defendants, that you can find the light, the higher power and goodness within you," he said. Addressing the courtroom, he added, "I wish you peace. Court adjourned."

12

Hard Conversations

"You can't keep yourself tidy with racism around. It's everyone's misery."

—Deborah Cotton

That afternoon, Travis Scott was driven back to St. Bernard Parish Prison, where he had been incarcerated since his arrest a few months after the Mother's Day shooting. Now that he and his brothers had been formally sentenced, I was no longer prohibited from speaking with them. A twenty-minute drive downriver from New Orleans, the St. Bernard Parish Prison was a low concrete building with a parking lot out front that could accommodate a couple dozen vehicles. Looming across the sky behind it were exhaust pipes emanating from one of the scores of petrochemical plants whose toxic emissions gave the eighty-mile stretch of the Mississippi River between New Orleans and Baton Rouge the nickname "Cancer Alley." A few days earlier, I had written Travis a letter, which his attorneys passed along, explaining that I was a journalist who happened to be among the nineteen gunshot victims of the Mother's Day shooting. I said that I was writing a book about the shooting and his attorneys had given me permission to speak with him, if he agreed.

I sat in a small waiting room with painted concrete walls for half an hour before a guard opened a door in the far corner of the room. I followed the guard down a hallway a few steps before she ordered me to leave my cell phone with her while I spoke with "the prisoner." She opened a door on our left. The near side of the room was separated from the opposite side by a thick pane of glass. She pointed to a booth that contained an old-fashioned telephone receiver. I sat down, lifted the receiver to my ear, and waited.

Moments later, a different guard escorted Travis Scott to the seat on the other side of the glass. He was wearing the same scarlet jumpsuit he had worn in court. His short dreadlocks framed a broad, handsome face that was set in a neutral expression, neither friendly nor hostile. He looked me straight in the eye and picked up the phone.

"Hi, Travis. I'm Mark, the writer who sent you the letter about the Mother's Day shooting."

I formed my right hand into a loose fist and reached it toward him. Travis did the same, and we touched knuckles through the glass. I confessed to him that I was feeling nervous: I had never interviewed anyone through a wall of glass before. I didn't mention that I had also never interviewed anyone who had been credibly accused of murder.

"That's okay," Travis said. "It ain't hard."

I told Travis that both Deborah Cotton and I had been stunned by the prison sentences he and his brothers had received, and that we wanted to offer our forgiveness. I added that before I asked him my questions, he deserved to know a little about me. I told him that I had grown up on a farm in Maryland. I was raised in the church. I had virtually no face-to-face interactions with Black people until after college, when I moved to Washington, DC. My girlfriend and I rented a house where we were the only White residents for blocks around. I had written one of my first books on the second floor of that house; the neighbors used to call me the White guy in the window. Observing Black street life for hours on end from that window helped teach me the obvious lesson that people are people: our skin colors, histories, and cultures might be different, but Black and White and other people were the same inside, a truism that was reinforced years later when I spent many months working in various parts of Africa.

Travis took this in silently, his expression still neutral. I asked how he was getting along in prison.

"It's hard, but I'm a get through it," he replied.

"How do you manage?"

Looking skyward, he said, "I'm strengthened by my Lord and Savior."

Travis said he would answer my questions, "but I can only talk about what I know." Which did not include the Mother's Day shooting, he quickly added. On the day of the shooting, he said, he wasn't even in New Orleans. He was in Kansas City, having moved there with his wife and stepson five months before. On that Mother's Day afternoon, they were attending a baseball game at Kauffman Stadium; his stepson, he said, was "crazy about baseball."

I said I was pretty crazy about baseball myself, and Travis went on to explain that that particular game was not just any game: Travis had scored tickets to the last regular season appearance that legendary Yankee relief pitcher Mariano Rivera would make in Kansas City before Rivera retired at season's end to a guaranteed election to the Hall of Fame.

"The government know where I was that day," Travis said. "I got pictures of me and my son at the game. I showed 'em the [ticket] stubs. They kept asking me about that shooting, trying to make me say what they wanted me to say. I said, 'I can't tell you what I don't know.'"

Travis and I talked sports for a while, and I learned that he'd been a pretty good basketball player as a kid—good enough to be offered a scholarship to attend a private high school in Virginia. He attended that school for a year, he said, but it wasn't for him, and he returned to New Orleans.

Referencing the Mother's Day shooting, Travis told me that not only was he not involved with it but also that "I would never do something like that."

"Why not?"

"It's senseless," he said. "There's a million people out there."

"Why did you accept the government's plea deal then?"

"I got to protect my brothers," Travis replied. "I couldn't let them go through that by themselves. I'm like a father to them."

Travis explained that his brothers' biological fathers had been absent from the time they were born. As the eldest brother—Travis was five years older than Shawn, nine years older than Akein—Travis felt obligated to fill that parental role, even though he, too, was growing up without a father.

From about the time he was five, Travis had lived with his paternal grandmother in the 2000 block of Frenchmen Street. I asked if I could speak with her sometime, and he gave me her name and phone number. It turned out that his father lived just ten blocks away from Travis throughout Travis's youth. Nevertheless, the man rarely saw Travis, except on a birthday or other special occasion. (Later, when I interviewed Travis's father, Cleophus Benson, Mr. Benson told me he had not attended Travis's court hearing, nor was he aware of the exact crimes to which Travis confessed in his plea deal. Asked for his memories of Travis as a child, Benson said, "Travis was a good little dude. We didn't see each other much. He was doing his thing, I was doing mine.")

I expressed my sympathy that Travis's father had been absent when he was a kid. "Did that make you angry?" I asked him.

"No," he replied, without conviction. "Resentful, maybe."

Once he signed the plea deal, Travis knew he was going to spend at least twenty years in prison. But he was shocked and angry that the judge sentenced him to life.

"Yeah, I was watching your face when you mouthed 'Life?'," I said. "It was like you couldn't believe what you'd just heard."

The government "changed things around on me," Travis complained. During the plea deal negotiations, he said, the government indicated that if he took the deal, he would not receive a life sentence. "That's why I decided to plead out," he said. "Otherwise, I'd have taken my chances with a jury. It don't take an LSU grad to figure that out."

I chuckled at the LSU quip. Travis smiled back, a sparkle of gold gleaming from an inlay in his lower row of teeth.

The tone of our conversation shifted when I asked why Akein had found it impossible to say Deborah Cotton's name during his courtroom statement. Was it true, as one person close to the case (not Deb) speculated, that Akein had a speech impediment?

"No, he don't have a speech impediment," Travis replied, eyes flashing. "He just been through a lot."

"I can only imagine," I said, backpedaling. "You said he didn't have a father."

Travis sized me up for a moment, as if deciding whether to keep talking. His expression neutral again, he said, with force, "Worse than that. When Akein was a baby, one of our mama's boyfriends beat him so bad, he broke all his ribs and broke his arm. He was in a full body cast for months."

My mouth dropped open. I couldn't formulate words. My horror plain to see, I finally managed to say, "That's terrible."

"Yeah, that's terrible," Travis repeated in an almost mocking tone. Eyes blazing, he snapped, "You know, some people in the top classes think they there because they deserve it, because they work for it. And that people in the low classes are there because *they* deserve it, because they don't work for it."

Before I could say that I thought nothing of the kind, Travis demanded, with fury in his voice, "What if our situations was reversed? What if you was born into my life and had to hustle on the streets to raise your brothers, and I was the one who went to college and lived in Africa and wrote books? Who's to say you could have withstood all the pain and hardships I have? Maybe you'd have just killed yourself."

I had no answer.

⚜

I had given up counting the eerie coincidences woven through the Mother's Day shooting by the time I learned that the prison holding Akein Scott was located just a few miles down the road from the Whitney Plantation slavery museum. Akein's attorney also gave me permission to speak with him, and I wrote Akein a letter asking if I could come visit him and explaining why. When I told Deb that Akein had agreed to talk, she said she wanted to come with me.

I picked her up at her apartment in Bayou St. John around noon for the forty-five-minute drive. We took the northern route; a light drizzle spattered the windshield of my rental car as we passed Louis Armstrong New Orleans International Airport. Around the time that we climbed a high bridge to cross the Mississippi, the rain stopped, replaced by patches of gray clouds and a weak sun. Heading further upriver, we passed more Cancer Alley petrochemical plants. And then, on our left, an entrance sign announced the Nelson Coleman Correctional Center.

The prison was a single-story building about as wide as a football field is long. An American flag flapped out front; metal fencing topped with razor wire stretched around the building and out of sight. Deb and I had left the city early to make sure we wouldn't be late for our appointment with Akein, so now we had time to spare. We were sitting in my rental car, reviewing what we planned to talk about, when I spied another coincidence walking toward us.

"Oh, my God, Deb. Look behind you. See that woman with the two little kids? I think that's Akein's mother."

Deb looked out the passenger side window. "Are you sure?"

"Pretty sure. I saw her in court. Come on, we've got to say hello."

By the time Deb and I were out of the car, Gladys Scott was about twenty feet away, walking slowly across the parking lot. Besides the two little kids, a young man in his late teens accompanied her. When the distance between us closed, I looked the Scott brothers' mother in the eye and said, "Mrs. Scott?"

"Yes?" she said, glancing over.

"My name is Mark Hertsgaard. This is Deborah Cotton, and we're here to visit your son, Akein."

"Yes?" she repeated. She stopped walking, pulled a box of Skittles from her purse, and popped a couple in her mouth.

"He's expecting us," I said. "Deb and I were two of the people shot at that Mother's Day second line. We're here to give him our forgiveness."

Gladys Scott absorbed this news with no apparent impact. "I just been in there myself," she said.

I waited for her to say more. She didn't. Deb availed herself of the silence to ask, "How's he doing?"

"Oh, he straight, he straight," she answered. "The good Lord watching over him."

"I hear that," Deb said, nodding. "In times of trouble, put your faith in the Most High. He will not desert you."

"That's right," Gladys Scott said, nodding, "that's right." Without another word, she walked off, the teenager and two little ones trailing behind.

"Well, how about that," I said to Deb. "We tell her that her sons shot us and we're here to offer forgiveness, and she doesn't say, 'I'm sorry,' or 'How you making out?' Nothing."

Deb, true to her generous nature, only murmured, "It's got to be pretty hard to meet someone your kids have shot."

Inside the prison, a clerk escorted Deb and me to a low, square room filled with rows of booths, each containing a video screen the size of a laptop computer and, next to the screen, a telephone receiver. It turned out that Deb and I would not see Akein in the flesh; he was elsewhere in the complex, his face visible only on the video screen. Deb and I had agreed in advance to split the time allotted for our visit; we took turns handing the phone back and forth. Having written the introductory letter that his attorney had forwarded to Akein, I went first.

The screen suddenly filled with the face of a young Black man wearing a tight purple skullcap. Again, I silently marveled at how young Akein Scott looked.

"Hi, Akein? Can you hear me? This is Mark Hertsgaard, the writer who sent you the letter."

"Hi, Mr. Mark. Yeah, I hear you. How you doing today?"

"Fine, thanks. Like I said in my letter, I have Deborah Cotton with me. I'm going to pass her the phone in a second, but first I want to repeat what my letter said: neither of us bears you any ill will. We are here to offer our forgiveness. We also want to ask some questions. As I mentioned, I'm writing a book about the Mother's Day shooting. And Deb would like your advice for the work she's doing on racial justice."

I handed the phone to Deb, and she began with the lighthearted banter that New Orleans folk routinely use to lubricate conversations with strangers. I couldn't hear Akein's half of the conversation, but judging from the grins and chuckles I could see on the screen, he and Deb seemed to be getting off to a good start. I heard Deb remind Akein of what she'd said in court—that she believed in him and his brothers and wanted to support them while they were in prison. She asked about Akein's poetry and urged him to keep writing. She said she strongly disagreed with the judge's sentences and hoped that the sentences might be reduced on appeal. She added that she was working on keeping other young African American men from ending up in prison, and she thought Akein's ideas could be invaluable to her work.

"Looking back," Deb asked him, "what are one or two things that could have made a difference for you? Things that maybe you didn't have but could have really used."

I watched Akein answer instantly and at some length. Later, Deb told me that his immediate reply was, "family support." He added, "My mama tried, but there wasn't no man around, and a woman can't make that many boys do right. Boys do what they wanna do unless there's a man to teach 'em, guide 'em, and punish 'em when they wrong."

Deb handed me the phone, and I reminded Akein that I was writing a book, which meant I had to ask him some questions. I said I had already interviewed his lawyer and his brother Travis, and I hoped to interview his other brothers as well. Before I could continue, Akein spoke up to say that the police had the story of the Mother's Day shooting wrong: he alone was guilty of the shooting; his brother Shawn was innocent.

"My brother didn't do nothing," Akein said. "He wasn't at that second line. I was the one did the shooting."

Taken aback, I responded, "Are you saying that Shawn wasn't part of the Mother's Day shooting?"

"Yeah," Akein replied. "I did that shooting."

Having heard Deb tell me twice in no uncertain terms that she had seen Akein in profile as he shot into the crowd, I knew that Akein wasn't telling the truth. He was trying to cover for his brother, the same strategy he and Shawn seemed to have followed shortly after the shooting, when Akein surrendered but Shawn remained in hiding. But our time was short, so I pressed on.

"Why did you do that? Why would you shoot up a second line, when there were so many innocent people there?"

It was the most obvious question Akein could be asked, yet it seemed to catch him off guard. Just as he was unable to utter Deb's name during his courtroom statement, now he seemed incapable of speech. He looked down at the floor, bit his lip, shaking his head.

I tried again: "Do you remember what you were thinking?"

Finally, without looking up, he murmured, "I thought I was protecting my brother. It was like déjà vu. I thought someone was shooting at my brother, and I had to protect him."

I tried another tack: "Someone who knows you said that you and Shawn were on drugs that day. He said you took some of those one dollar pills that make a person do things they wouldn't do in their right mind. Is that true?"

This time Akein just stared at the screen, silent. After a few seconds, speaking in as gentle a tone as I could muster, I told him I was sorry, but I had to ask these questions: as a journalist, it was my duty to tell the story as accurately and fairly as I could. I added that I wanted readers to understand how he and his brothers had found themselves in that situation in the first place.

"I gather that you and your brothers faced tough times growing up," I ventured, trying to at least get him talking again.

"Yeah," Akein replied. I waited for him to say more; he didn't. I wanted to ask about Travis's claim that Akein had been beaten so badly when he was a baby that he ended up in a full body cast, but Akein clearly wasn't ready for that topic, and anyway, our appointment was almost over.

"I hope you and I can talk more sometime," I told Akein. "In the meantime, is there anyone in your family who might speak with me?"

Suddenly animated, Akein began giving me elaborate directions on how to send letters and make phone calls to him in prison. "And you should talk to my grandma," he said eagerly. "I grew up with her, she know all about me." He managed to give me her name and number just before the video screen went dark, terminating the visit.

Back at the reception desk, Deb transferred $20 into Akein's prison account so he could buy toiletries and make phone calls to the outside world. She was silent as we crossed the parking lot and got in my rental car. Knowing that she, as a Black woman, would have better luck asking Akein's grandma to speak with me, I asked if she'd make the call. She did, and within five minutes, I had an appointment to visit Miss Jean Snowden later that afternoon.

The sun was low in the sky as we pulled out of the parking lot for the drive back to New Orleans. I thought that Deb would come with me to talk with Akein's grandmother, but she suddenly nixed that idea. "This visit stirred up lots of emotions for me, Mark," she said. "I can't do another one today. Can you drop me at home first?"

"Sure, Deb. I'll fill you in later."

We drove in silence, again passing the petrochemical plants that, like the prison, occupied land that had once been filled with plantations

❧

Jean Snowden, Akein's grandmother, was working as a home nursing aide, taking care of an elderly White woman who had dementia. She invited me to the woman's home in the suburb of Metairie, and we sat at the dining room table while the woman watched the news in the living room. Miss Jean looked to be in her early sixties, with a round, pleasant face and the calloused hands of a lifelong member of the working class. Beside her on the table rested a clothbound Bible. "I carry my Bible everywhere," she said. "I always used to tell Akein, 'You got to stay prayed up in life.' You stay prayed up, the good Lord will take care of you."

Like Akein's college roommate Glenn Palmer, Miss Jean had spoken with Akein—whom she, too, called Keemie—on that fateful Mother's Day morning.

"He called me three times that morning to wish me happy Mother's Day," she recalled. "He said, 'I love you, grandma, I love you.' He said he had a card and a present for me, and he'd call me later to bring it over. But he never did."

Jean Snowden was not Akein Scott's biological grandmother. She met him when he was a toddler, after his Aunt Vanessa had moved in downstairs, renting a spare room from Miss Jean in Central City, a low-income neighborhood plagued then, and now, with high rates of crime. Miss Jean was raising a grandson who happened to be about the same age as Akein, and the two boys became fast friends, as did Miss Jean and Aunt Vanessa. For snacks, the two women would give each boy a piece of bread and a glass of sugar water. "I can still see them, sitting at the table with their bread and sugar water, Akein just as happy as he could be," Miss Jean said.

To hear her tell it, Akein was an eager, enthusiastic student. On days when Vanessa had to work early, Miss Jean made sure that Akein got out the door in time for school. If he missed the bus, "Well, then I'd drive him to school before I went to work," she said. Little Akein loved marching off to school, book bag in hand, she said, and when he got home, he couldn't wait to tell her what he had learned that day. In high school, Akein had a mentor, Willie Gray, who, along with Miss Jean and Aunt Vanessa, got him to take the idea of college seriously. Miss Jean and Vanessa were beyond proud the day Akein left for Talladega, the first in his family to attend college.

How such a seemingly angelic child had grown into a young man who confessed to the biggest mass shooting in modern New Orleans history was a genuine mystery to Miss Jean. The day after Akein's mug shot first appeared on television, she ran into the pastor of Edgewater Baptist Church, which she and Akein had long attended. "Was that Keemie on TV?" pastor Chad Gilbert asked. Miss Jean replied that, sadly, yes, it was. The pastor dropped to his knees and wailed, "Let's pray!"

"I wish I could talk to him about it," Miss Jean said about Akein and the Mother's Day shooting. "I would just ask, why did he do that? Did he need money or something?" She had not attended his sentencing hearing, she added, "because I knew I would break down, and he doesn't need to see me do that."

Miss Jean gave me contact information for Akein's Aunt Vanessa, and it was by speaking with her and two of her sisters—Gilda and Jacqueline—that I learned the details of what happened to Akein as a baby: how he was beaten mercilessly by his crack-addicted mother's crack-addicted boyfriend. I verified the sisters' story by interviewing other family members and cross-checking the accumulated information with court and police records.

Baby Akein was two months shy of his second birthday and just starting to talk on the day he was brutalized. At the time, his mother was living with a man named Kenneth Allen. This was in 1995, and New Orleans, like many American cities, had been in the grips of the crack epidemic for more than a decade. Gladys Scott and Kenneth Allen were among the countless victims. The two met after Gladys lost her previous residence and moved in with her cousin, Sam Smith, at 2627 Delachaise Street in Central City. Like Gladys Scott, Allen had been homeless before he moved into the house on Delachaise. It was a crowded abode, for Gladys brought five of her children with her. They ranged in age from son T'Daryl, who was nine, to Akein, who was not yet two.

On May 19, 1995, while Gladys Scott was out, Kenneth Allen apparently became furious that baby Akein would not stop crying. In response, he hit the baby, and hit him, and hit him. Akein's Aunt Jacqueline told me that Allen hung Akein on the back of a door "like you would hang up a dress, and he hit that baby with a stick so bad, he broke his ribs and arm."

When Gladys Scott got home, she found her baby shrieking for no apparent reason. She took him to Children's Hospital, where Akein was x-rayed, diagnosed, treated, and encased in a full body cast. As required by law when encountering such injuries, hospital staff notified Child Protective Services. Gladys Scott was arrested on the spot for child endangerment and taken directly to Orleans Parish Prison.

The beating of baby Akein helped explain a small but telling detail in the Unblinking Eye video. As the gunman was firing with his right hand, his left arm swung upward to balance his aim. As it swung, the left forearm appeared to twist outward at an unnatural angle. That twist was because baby Akein's broken left arm had never healed properly after he left the hospital, and the family lacked the money to get the problem corrected. "It didn't fall right," Miss Jean told me about Akein's left arm. "It kinda turned outward."

Horrific as it was, the beating of baby Akein turned out to be but an initial blast of violence that triggered an even bloodier explosion. Five of Gladys Scott's children were in the house when Kenneth Allen was beating baby Akein. The older two children—T'Daryl and a sister, Brittany—soon told their older siblings, who lived with relatives across town, what happened. The next day, two of those siblings—Craig Scott, eighteen, and Michael Scott, twenty—went to the house to confront Allen. The brothers exchanged angry words with Allen then shot him in the head. That act of vengeance earned Craig and Michael Scott life sentences at Angola, formally known as Louisiana State Penitentiary. (I tried to visit Craig and Michael Scott, but prison authorities denied my requests.)

With Gladys Scott now in jail for child endangerment, her remaining children were dispersed among various relatives. The five youngest were taken in by her sisters Vanessa and Jacqueline. It was a continuation of a longstanding pattern, the sisters told me. Gladys was the eldest sibling, and from the time she first gave birth, at age sixteen, she sooner or later handed each of her children over to their grandparents, who would house, clothe, and feed them. Gladys's mother and father raised her first three children (who came from two different fathers): Michael, Tywanna, and Craig. Her next three—Cleophus, Crystal, and Travis—were raised by their paternal grandmother, Mary Benson. Ultimately, Gladys Scott had fourteen children with five different fathers. (In court, she had said she had twelve children, but that did not include two who died—one during childbirth, another after two days of life.)

"My sister had a man problem—she had too many," Vanessa told me. "She'd go from one to the next." Jean Snowden, with her deep religiosity, put it more gently: "I guess she just had a bed for everyone."

According to her sisters, alcohol and drug addiction were frequent demons for Gladys Scott and influenced her choices in men. Kenneth Allen was not her first partner who abused drugs; so did Daryl Robertson, the father of the five children who were living with Gladys when Kenneth Allen beat baby Akein. "Daryl was involved with Akein when he could be, but he was on drugs a lot and in and out of jail," said Vanessa.

I made numerous attempts to speak with Gladys Scott to hear her side of the story. Some weeks after Deb and I encountered her in the penitentiary parking lot on our way to visit Akein, Gladys Scott called Deb to complain about "the White reporter" asking questions about the Mother's Day shooting. She didn't want that White Reporter to publish anything about her and her children, she told Deb. I got Ms. Scott's number from

Deb and called her. She picked up, and we had a fifteen-minute conversation that consisted largely of a monologue on her part.

Gladys Scott said that no one else raised her kids or knew anything about them, and that the allegations made in court about them were lies told by jailbirds. She made the intriguing statement that she had attended the Mother's Day second line parade where the shooting took place—"I was out there too," she said—but before I could ask further, she changed the subject. Despite the injustices done to her kids, she continued, she was not worried about them going to prison. She had given her life to God when she was sixteen, she explained, "and I believe He's going to let them walk out the doors someday." I asked if she and I could speak face-to-face. She agreed, and we made an appointment to meet at her house the next day. But she didn't show, nor did she respond to additional phone calls and letters from me.

One more tragic coincidence in the Mother's Day shooting now came to light.

Initial news reports had accurately stated that two of the nineteen people shot that day were ten-year-old children. One was Lennard Epps's daughter, who suffered a graze wound across her back. I spoke with her when I interviewed Epps; she told me that getting shot "hurt—I cried."

The other ten-year-old was Ka'Nard Allen. Two days after the Mother's Day shooting, Ka'Nard got written up in the *Times-Picayune* because this was the second time in less than a year that the young man had been shot. At his tenth birthday party, held the previous May in his grandmother's yard in Central City, three men suddenly opened fire with an AK-47 rifle and handguns. Ka'Nard suffered a flesh wound in the neck. His five-year-old cousin, Briana Allen, died at the scene from a bullet to the abdomen. Ka'Nard's mother, Tynia Allen, testified before Judge Lemelle about the Mother's Day shooting, recalling how, when she heard the *pop-pop* of bullets flying, she yelled, "Run, Ka'Nard, run!" This time, Ka'Nard had sustained a flesh wound in his right cheek.

What neither Ka'Nard nor his mother knew about the Mother's Day shooting was that he had been shot by a member of his own family. I learned this from Akein and Shawn's long-lost father, Daryl Robertson. I tracked Mr. Robertson down after the court hearing—he had moved to California many years ago—and we spoke briefly by phone. I said that I was one of the people who had been shot at the Mother's Day second line and that I was a journalist who was writing a book about the shooting.

"I'm sorry that happened to you," Mr. Robertson replied, adding, "I have a grandson who was involved in that shooting."

"Do you mean Akein?" I asked.

"No, not my son," he said. "My grandson."

"What's his name?"

"Ka'Nard Allen."

I was so taken aback I nearly dropped my phone. After a long pause, I said, "Do you mean that ten-year-old boy with the graze wound to his cheek?"

"Yeah, that's him," Mr. Robertson said. "That's my grandson." Mr. Robertson then said he had to leave for work. I subsequently called and left him numerous messages, but he never replied. (About a year later, Akein told me from prison that his father had died recently from cancer.)

I later spoke with Tynia Allen, Ka'Nard's mother. She confirmed that Darryl Robertson was her son's grandfather, via a different mother than Gladys Scott. "He raised me," Ms. Allen said about Darryl Robertson. "He's my stepdaddy, my brother's daddy."

I asked Ms. Allen if she knew that the two confessed gunmen, Akein and Shawn Scott, were Darryl Robertson's sons by blood. No, she did not know that, she said in a surprised tone. She rushed off our phone call and did not respond to further inquiries.

In short, without knowing it, Akein and Shawn Scott had almost killed their own nephew. If one or the other brother's trigger hand had shifted its aim by a millimeter or two, the bullet that grazed Ka'Nard Allen's cheek might instead have blasted fatally into the boy's eye or throat.

After Ka'Nard Allen's mother hung up on me, I sat at my desk for a long time, trying to come to grips with this news. I thought about calling Deb, as I sometimes did when I'd made a breakthrough in my investigations, but I decided against it. This news would only break her heart.

Another jolt came a few weeks later when I interviewed Shirley Johnson, the woman who testified that Travis had killed her son Calvin. The day we met, Miss Shirley was propped up in a hospital bed at University Medical Center, preparing to have surgery. Doctors, she said, had "found a mass in my arm." I'd gotten Miss Shirley's phone number from Josh Sherman, the second federal agent on the Mother's Day case. Miss Shirley was a prime example, Sherman told me, of why he and his partner, Joe Frank, worked so hard to bring lawbreakers to justice—because when criminals continued to roam the streets, decent people like Shirley Johnson paid the price, whether through the loss of a murdered child or simply through enduring the fear and danger of living near drug dealers who didn't hesitate to sling iron.

While getting to know Ms. Johnson, Sherman had made a special effort to connect with her remaining son, Eric, who hoped to become a lawyer someday. But shortly after the sentencing hearing for the Scott brothers, Eric, age twenty-one, was found shot to death. The news saddened but did not surprise Sherman. "The last time I visited, I was asking Eric about his grades," he recalled. "He and I had always had a good rapport, but that day he couldn't look me in the eye."

Eric's girlfriend had brought their infant daughter to the hospital to visit her grandma; Miss Shirley sat the baby on her lap, grasped her tiny wrists, and swayed her gently back and forth, smiling and cooing. Miss Shirley told me that her son Calvin, like the Scott brothers, had grown up without a father. Her husband had not been able to stay off drugs, she explained, and eventually she decided it would be easier to raise her children without him rather than "keep cleaning up his messes." However, Miss Shirley's own father was an active presence in Calvin's life, teaching Calvin that "a father take care of the house, a father pay the bills and make sure his kids have things," she told me. For example, when Miss Shirley awoke at 4:30 every morning to go to work in the shipyard, it was Calvin who got the younger children dressed, fed, and off to school before heading to school himself.

It took my breath away when Miss Shirley confided that she had lost three of her five children to gun violence. Besides Calvin and Eric, she said, "My baby girl was found in bed with a bullet in her head, age twenty-one. I always felt that her boyfriend did it, but they didn't have any proof." She recounted this with astonishing calm but added, "Nobody who don't walk in these shoes, they don't know. I'm only here through the grace of God. I didn't go cuckoo, I didn't do drugs. My daddy used to tell me, 'God gives you your children for a little while, then he take 'em back.' That's the only thing got me through it, that they wasn't really mine."

When I shared the story of Akein Scott's brutal beating as a baby and explained how the subsequent murder of his mother's boyfriend separated the Scott brothers from their incarcerated mother, Miss Shirley sympathized—but only to a point.

"I can understand what Akein went through, and his mother and his brothers and them," she said. "But they was out there taking life, and they need to see the ripple effects on other people. Like me: I don't trust people now. I don't do second lines; I don't do Mardi Gras. I got three children gone. That hurts more than I can say. I don't want no one to retaliate, I just want them to stop killing each other."

A nurse entered the room and announced that visiting hours were almost over. Before I left, Shirley Johnson provided me with one of the saddest of all the coincidences that pervaded the Mother's Day shooting.

"I'm very sorry to ask you this, Miss Shirley," I said, "but I have to check: when did your son Eric die?"

Without a moment's hesitation, she replied, "May 12, 2016."

I looked at her, stunned. Could it really be that her third child to die from gun violence had been shot three years to the day after the Mother's Day shooting—a shooting that itself took place three years to the day after the TBC band's Brandon Franklin was shot to death?

"Did you say May 12, Miss Shirley?" I asked.

Recognizing my amazement, she nodded. "May 12, 2016," she repeated in a firm voice. "Three years to the day."

Sharing all this news with Deb was not an easy conversation.

We were supposed to have dinner before I left town, but at the last minute she canceled, casually explaining that she had to check into the hospital. Her nonchalance reminded me of a flight attendant I knew who thought nothing of flying from London to Los Angeles for a long weekend. "It's like taking a bus for me," she'd say. Deb was like that about going to the hospital; since the shooting, it had become as routine as going to the grocery store was for other people. "I just have to have some tests," she said.

So, we talked by phone after I returned to San Francisco, one of those conversations where you talk for hours, backtrack, detour, and talk some more. There was a lot to tell, and a lot of it was delicate to relate.

Deb told me that the "spiritual connection" she had felt with Akein Scott from the instant she watched him firing into the second line—as his face morphed into the face of her nephew Austin—had deepened since she and I had visited Akein in prison. She had exchanged emails and letters with him, encouraging him to keep writing poetry, adding that maybe she could get it published. She had contacted the new court-appointed attorney who was handling the appeal of his life sentence and offered to testify on his behalf. She was praying for him.

So when I told Deb about the beating of baby Akein, and the revenge murder the next day that sent two of his older brothers to Angola prison for the rest of their lives, the news pained her like a physical blow. She was amazed by all the secrets my reporting had uncovered, and she lamented that this new information had not been mentioned in court. When I told her about my jailhouse interview with Travis and the fierceness of his question, "What if our situations was reversed?" she gasped, "There but for the grace of God go I."

But I also had to tell Deb what Shirley Johnson and Darryl Robertson told me.

In her hospital bed, Miss Shirley had spoken in much greater detail about the death of her son Calvin than she'd been able to do in court. "Everybody in the neighborhood knew it was Travis who did it," she told me, recalling those days of ten years ago like they were yesterday. A few days after her son's death, she said, "a young boy who hung around with Travis came to my door and said, 'Travis and them are sorry they shot Calvin.' All I could say to him was, 'Get off my porch.'"

I told Deb about Miss Shirley having lost three of her five children to gun violence and her calm dignity in the face of that unimaginable pain and desolation. I added that Miss Shirley nevertheless sympathized with the Scott brothers' difficult upbringing, even as she maintained that there was no excuse for them to be "out there taking life." I told Deb that I found it inconceivable that Miss Shirley was lying about Travis killing her son. Which, in turn, suggested that the prosecution's portrayal of Travis, and by extension Akein, as killers was probably accurate. What's more, thanks to my conversations with Darryl Robertson and Tynia Allen, it seemed clear that Akein and Shawn had shot their own father's grandson, ten-year-old Ka'Nard Allen—an eerie example of the "self-hate" among Black men that Deb had mentioned in our first phone conversation almost three years before.

When I finished, Deb was silent. Over the phone it was hard to tell how she was taking all this, but it couldn't have been easy for her. Ever since the Mother's Day shooting, Deb had insisted that the two young gunmen deserved mercy and understanding. She had said that the Scott brothers didn't even sound like a real gang, not compared to the murderous criminal enterprises she recalled from her years in South Central LA—the Scotts were just a family that sold drugs together. But this new evidence made it hard to deny that Akein and his brothers had very likely taken the lives of two other young Black men and had shot and almost killed their own nephew during the Mother's Day shooting. Surely those three young Black men were as deserving of mercy and understanding as the Scott brothers were.

"I'm sorry, Deb," I finally said. "I know this is hard. But I promised you when we started this that I'd do my best to find out what happened and tell the truth about it. And these seem to be the facts, as best I can determine."

"No, no, it's okay," Deb said, her voice quiet and sad. "I'm glad you told me. We need to know, we do. My heart still breaks for Akein and his brothers, but it also breaks for Miss Shirley and the father who lost a son—I can't imagine the pain they must feel. I don't blame you for telling the truth, Mark. This story is on chronic repeat in New Orleans, and we have to face the truth before we can break the cycle."

"What do you mean, break the cycle?"

"The cycle that's behind all this violence," Deb said, "where racism drives poverty because Black people don't have access to decent education and jobs, and poverty drives drug dealing as a way to make a living. And then drug dealing gets people addicted or shot, and the cycle starts over again. This is a systemic problem, and not just in New Orleans. What Akein and his brothers did was reprehensible, I know that. But racism shapes people's actions even if they don't realize it. Remember how I told you at the start of all this that racism can kill Black people even when a Black finger pulls the trigger?"

Not for the first time, I was humbled by Deb's generosity of spirit, her keenness of intellect, her open heart. From her City Council statement onward, Deb had expressed strong, if unpopular, opinions about the Mother's Day shooting. Now she was confronted with new facts that starkly challenged those opinions. But she did not tune out, deny those facts, or deflect the issue. No, she listened and took in the new information, including the uncomfortable parts. And then, on that basis, she sought a fresh way forward that was still aligned with her moral values—her desire, in the words of her Jewish faith, to help "heal the world."

"I think that's a righteous way of looking at it, Deb," I replied. "Thanks for talking so bravely about this."

"You've broken my heart many times in this conversation, Mark, I won't deny it," she said. "But I'm glad we talked about this. These are the conversations we all have to have if we're ever going to break the cycle."

How many of the rest of us are ready to have these hard conversations? How many of us will listen with the kind of open mind and heart Deb did, listen even when it's hard, even when it challenges our preconceived notions, and then incorporate what we've learned into our outlook, and seek a fresh way forward?

The beginnings of an answer emerged on my next trip to New Orleans. Now that the legal case was closed, I was also permitted to interview the prosecution side of the Mother's Day case: the NOPD officers who worked the crime scene, the federal agents who helped figure out who did the shooting and how to find them, the US attorney's office lawyers who argued the case during the plea deal negotiations and the hearings before Judge Lemelle. Having now uncovered some of the back stories of the Scott brothers, I wondered how these agents of the law and others close to the case would respond to this new information.

The first person I spoke with was Joe Maize. His musical career seemed to be going fantastically well. He and the rest of the TBC band were on the road a lot, playing gigs in Texas and beyond. They were under consideration for a Grammy nomination. In addition to his TBC work, Joe was also playing in a second band, where he was handling lead vocals, which "is kinda fun," he said. After congratulating him, I asked if I could share some information about the Mother's Day shooting that hadn't come out in court. I reminded him that he had told me, some months ago, that he thought the Scott brothers should be put not *in* prison but *under* it. He still felt that way, he assured me. I then told him about the horrors the Scott brothers had endured growing up, including the horrific beating of baby Akein by his crack-addicted mother's crack-addicted boyfriend. Did any of this affect Joe's opinion about Akein Scott and his brothers?

"No, it don't change my mind," Joe said heatedly. "Because at a certain point, you have to *want* to be like that. Those guys had other options. I know a guy, his mama smoked crack, he didn't have no father, but he never got into gangster life. He didn't have parents, but other people started helping him—teachers maybe, I'm not sure. That guy made it through school and ended up as a cop. You don't have to be a gangster."

I also spent more time with Ed Buckner. Sitting on his porch overlooking Elysian Fields Avenue, Ed was not surprised to hear about the deprived, violent childhood the Scott brothers had. Nevertheless, he thought Judge Lemelle had no choice but to issue harsh sentences. "That judge is a New Orleans boy, and he looked carefully at the videotape," Ed told me. "That was sure no attempt to shoot someone and get away. That was an attempt to show everyone out there, 'You fuck with me, I'm gonna kill *all* you sons a bitches.' The judge knew that these were very dangerous young men."

Reiterating his profound respect for Deb Cotton, Ed said, "One thing that always gets me is the large amount of suffering this lady went through, and she still has the humbleness and graciousness to want to save life. That takes something, to be that forgiving after that much suffering. Every time she went into another surgery, it was another opportunity to feel angry at those young men. Instead, she tells the judge, 'I don't want those young men to be put away for life.' That's a powerful woman."

Ed's main concern now was to keep something like the Mother's Day shooting from happening again. The Scott family, he said, "is still in trouble. Social workers need to get into that situation quick, or we're gonna see the same thing happen again. Because the ghetto don't change. The people in it change, they rotate it in and out, but the ghetto don't change. The hood is still there. The same corners where they sold dope forty years ago, they selling it today."

Preventing additional violence was also the priority for the police, federal agents, and prosecuting attorneys on the Mother's Day case. As US attorney for the Eastern District of Louisiana, Kenneth Polite was the senior federal official overseeing the prosecution of the Scott brothers. An African American in his late thirties, Polite (pronounced, Poe-LEET) had grown up poor in the Lower Ninth Ward, raised by a single mother. He nevertheless attended Harvard University and Georgetown Law School before making a rapid ascent up the Justice Department bureaucracy. His elite education had not blinded him to the realities of his hometown, however; indeed, Polite said he had firsthand knowledge of the world the Scott brothers inhabited.

"I lost a half brother to the streets of New Orleans in 2004, when he was twenty-four years old," Polite told me. "He and I grew up in very different circumstances. We shared a father, but I was fortunate to have a loving mother who made sacrifices. My half brother did not have the same level of parental support or the commitment to academics that I did. I suspect that his death was in retribution for something he'd done, and that the person responsible for his death was killed not long after. So, I've seen this within my own family."

After expressing my condolences, I told Polite what I had learned about the Scott brothers' upbringing—how baby Akein had been brutalized by his crack-addicted mother's crack-addicted boyfriend, grew up without the guidance or support of a mother or father, and at age nine got recruited into the drug business by his older brother, who sometimes had Akein hold the gang's guns because, as a juvenile, he wouldn't go to jail for possessing a firearm. I added that some people, such as Deborah Cotton, felt that the Scotts' disadvantaged childhoods should be taken into account when sentencing them. Others pointed out that many people who grow up in tough neighborhoods do not become drug-dealing gangsters. What did Polite think?

"There are no excuses for a crime like that," the US attorney replied. "Let me tell you about one of the more poignant cases this office has worked on, the prosecution of a street gang that had much the same demographics as the Mother's Day case. One member of the gang was responsible for babysitting a four-year-old boy on a daily basis. He would take that four-year-old with him when he was dealing drugs, when he was firing weapons. We had some truly heartbreaking footage of that four-year-old in a car with one defendant and a drug purchaser. You see the boy looking at their hands doing the deal, you hear the vulgar language. That's what that little four-year-old boy is surrounded by. It brings home the intergenerational perpetuation of violence that we deal with, and the helplessness of some of the young men in these situations. Where do we expect that four-year-old to be in twenty years if we don't hold accountable the people who put him in that position?"

The examples of Kenneth Polite and Joe Maize's friend, two young Black men who overcame terribly challenging childhoods, made it sound like making a successful life was a matter of individual effort. If those two young men could stay out of trouble and get out of the ghetto, why couldn't the Scott brothers?

Keith Twitchell, Deb's former colleague at the Committee for a Better New Orleans, answered that question by recalling his close friend who'd been shot dead by young Black teenagers. "I understand the argument that not all impoverished fourteen-year-olds end up shooting people," Twitchell said. "But the fact is that different people can respond differently to the same set of circumstances. Even people raised in the same family can respond differently. Remember that Sly and the Family Stone song, '*One grows up who loves to learn, one grows up who loves to burn*'? These things are a mixture of nature and nurture. We can't just say, 'Those poor kids grew up in a bad neighborhood, that's why they went wrong.' But neither can we say, 'Other kids grew up in that neighborhood and they turned out fine.'"

Joe Frank, the ATF agent who grew up on the grounds of Angola penitentiary, had seen the Scott brothers' same story play out time and time again during his career in law enforcement. "You can't arrest your way out of this problem," he said. "You can't build enough prisons. You've got to deal with this before it gets to the criminal justice system. Just look at the criminal history of the Scott brothers: Shawn Scott is a six-or-seven-times-convicted felon. Obviously, it's not working just to arrest them."

Joe Frank was no soft-on-crime liberal; it was his duty as a law enforcement officer, he said, "that when a Travis Scott comes across our path, we make sure they don't do it anymore [by putting them in prison]." At the same time, Frank believed that punishing individuals without addressing the circumstances that shaped those individuals was an endless, dubious approach. When I told him about the brutal beating of baby Akein, Akein's brothers' murder of the man who beat him, and the dysfunctional parenting that contributed to all that violence, Frank was not surprised. "When you dig deep into someone like Travis Scott or Akein Scott, and you see how they grew up, you kind of get it how they came out the way they did," Frank said. "If you grow up around violence from the time you first walk and talk, what are you going to do when you're grown up?"

Scholarly research supports Frank's point. Children who have been exposed to violence are thirty-one times more likely to behave violently themselves, according to a study in *Criminal Justice and Behavior* by Richard Spano, Craig Rivera, and John M. Bolland. Thirty-one times!

NOPD detective Rob Hurst, Chris Hart's deputy on the Mother's Day shooting, also viewed gun violence as more a social failure than an individual's failure. Hurst, who was White, grew up on a farm in Wyoming where he worked long hours, often in brutally inclement weather, from the time he was a little boy. But he had no doubt that his upbringing was immeasurably easier than that of many Black youths he came to know as a detective on the streets of New Orleans. "Growing up on a farm, you worked hard, but you knew you were loved—not only your own family but everybody in the community cared about you," Hurst told me. Referring to the Scott brothers, he added, "These poor children, they were handed a horrible lot in life. They had each other and no one else. I'm in no way surprised that they learned to handle any sort of situation with violence, because physical expression of emotion is the only thing they know. They have no conflict resolution skills. All conflicts get resolved by the gun."

"Having done this work for twelve years now," Hurst added, "there are kids who I first met when they were six or seven. Now they're nineteen or twenty, and you see them turning up dead. It's horrible."

"Don't they know that the drug business is going to get them killed?" I asked.

"Yeah, they know," Hurst replied. "I've interviewed so many of these guys. They know they're either going to end up in prison or dead by the time they're twenty-five. But they don't know that there are other options. They don't see any way out."

13

"The Truth Hurts, But Silence Kills"

We're gonna name Lee Circle
After Allen Toussaint
Tear those monuments down!
—"Wild Magnolia" by To Be Continued
and Glenn David Andrews

When Deb told me that "these are the conversations we have to have if we're going to break the cycle," she was thinking foremost of her beloved New Orleans. But she would be the first to concur that the same conversations are needed across the United States. Deb regarded poverty, drug dealing, and gun violence as systemic problems rooted in America's long history of slavery and racism and their perpetuating social structures, none of which were unique to New Orleans. One could find the same interlocking problems, ATF agent Frank told me, in Chicago, Detroit, Oakland, and other cities. The problems were perhaps easier to notice in New Orleans because they manifested in more extreme ways there, but then life in general was often more extreme in New Orleans.

Deb's belief that having the hard conversations was the only way to "break the cycle" brought to mind the truth and reconciliation process that Nelson Mandela and his compatriots launched in South Africa after the fall of apartheid. The anti-apartheid struggle had profoundly shaped both Deb's and my racial consciousness. Straight out of college, I'd been fortunate to work at the Institute for Policy Studies in Washington with scholars and activists who were key organizers of the anti-apartheid movement in the United States. In 1986, they organized a series of mass arrests at the South African embassy; day after day, hundreds of people would line up and attempt to enter the embassy, which would get them arrested by the local police, a sustained spectacle that generated global media coverage and pressure on the apartheid regime.

The embassy protests were organized by Roger Wilkins, a former US Justice Department official who was among my mentors at IPS, and Randall Robinson, a gifted activist who would soon publish *The Debt*. the first general audience book to argue that African Americans were owed reparations for slavery and subsequent forms of discrimination. The day I was arrested, our protest was led by Desmond Tutu, the archbishop of Cape Town, who had won the Nobel Peace Prize two years earlier in recognition of his decades of work against apartheid. Barely five feet tall, Tutu was a bundle of energy at the protest, his face beaming as he sang freedom songs and pumped his fist in the air as vigorously as protesters half his age.

In 1990, after public pressure at home and abroad forced South Africa's government to release Mandela after twenty-seven years in prison, Wilkins helped organize Mandela's triumphant tour of the United States. I joined a packed crowd in the Oakland Coliseum that erupted in jubilant applause the instant Mandela took the stage. Not long after, attending a conference of scholars and activists in Amsterdam, I spent hours walking the city's rain-slicked streets talking politics with Thabo Mbeki, who a decade later would succeed Mandela as South Africa's second democratically elected president. Later, I visited Robben Island, the desolate, wind-blown slab of rock off the western coast of South Africa where Mandela and other political prisoners had been imprisoned for so many years. My tour of the grounds was guided by a former inmate who described the conditions he and others endured in stoic terms that nevertheless left no doubt of the material and psychological horrors the regime imposed to try to break their spirits.

For her part, Deb got interested in the anti-apartheid struggle a few years later, after her racial and political awakening following the Rodney King riots. After a stint as an organizer with the Service Employees International Union, she moved to the Bay Area to pursue a degree in African American Studies at San Francisco State. SF State was the first university in the country to offer such a program, and the campus had been a politically active place since the student protests of the 1960s. One day, Deb attended a campus forum where a guest speaker named Azibuike Akaba talked about his work with Black-led labor unions in South Africa, a core element of the country's anti-apartheid movement. Deb was enthusiastic about what she heard and approached the speaker afterward to ask a few questions. A few questions led to a few more questions, which turned into grabbing a cup of coffee. Before long, Deb and Az, as he was called, were a couple, living together in a group house in Berkeley known as a local nerve center of political and cultural activism.

Deb was no dilletante about the South African liberation struggle, Az later told me. "Deb was a fun person, but she was serious about social change," he said. "She was interested in the anti-apartheid struggle for its own sake—it was Black people fighting for freedom and self-determination—but also for what it might teach about making change in the United States."

One of the most inspiring things Nelson Mandela did as president of South Africa was to help establish a truth and reconciliation process to heal the wounds inflicted under apartheid. At the time, South Africa had just fought a bloody civil war after nearly 100 years of repression of the Black and mixed-race majority by the White minority. Although actual combat between the South African military and the liberation forces had mostly ended, feelings remained raw and distrustful on both sides. It was far from clear that South Africa would not descend back into violence, much less that it could evolve into a unified country with freedom and equality for all.

South Africa's Truth and Reconciliation Commission was designed to enable South Africans, in the words of their new constitution, "to transcend the divisions and strife of the past, which generated gross violations of human rights, the transgression of humanitarian principles in violent conflicts and a legacy of hatred, fear, guilt and revenge. These can now be addressed on the basis that there is a need for understanding but not for vengeance, a need for reparation but not for retaliation, a need for *ubuntu* [an African word connoting communal and interpersonal solidarity] but not for victimization."

Many victims of apartheid wanted the perpetrators of that system to be punished and reparations paid to the survivors, much as former Nazi officials had been punished via the Nuremberg trials after World War II. But that approach was not available to South Africa, Tutu explained in his book *No Future Without Forgiveness*, because the war between the South African military and the liberation forces had ended in stalemate. With pressure for reform growing inside the country and internationally, the White government and the liberation movement had reached a negotiated settlement: apartheid would be replaced by a democratic system of governance where people of all races could vote for their elected representatives, but officials of the apartheid regime would not be prosecuted for their past actions. That settlement made possible the "miracle," as Tutu called it, of South Africa's "relatively peaceful transition from repression to democracy." The security forces of the apartheid government would never have supported this negotiated settlement, Tutu explained, if they thought it could result in them going to prison for their past actions. What's more, "While the Allies could pack up and go home after Nuremberg, we in South Africa had to live with one another."

To satisfy both sides of this conundrum, the Truth and Reconciliation Commission conducted a nationwide conversation about what had happened during apartheid. Victims were invited to testify about injustices they or their loved ones had experienced. Security officials were allowed to apply for amnesty from prosecution, provided they told the whole truth about their past wrongdoings. The proceedings were broadcast by South African public television and radio so the entire country could follow each and every development.

The slogan the Commission chose to build popular support for its mission was, "The Truth Hurts, But Silence Kills." The Commission aimed to establish a truthful record of the horrors that apartheid had inflicted upon South Africa, present this truth to the South African people, and thereby lay the groundwork for a reconciliation among contending segments of the population so the country could heal and move forward.

South Africans were riveted by the hearings, starting with one of the opening witnesses. A woman whose husband had been murdered by security forces when she was twenty years old sat in front of the microphones and unleashed what one commissioner later called "a primeval and spontaneous wail from the depths of her soul . . ." that "transformed the hearings from a litany of suffering and pain to an even deeper level. It caught up in a single howl all the darkness and horror of the apartheid years." Alistair Sparks, a leading South African journalist, wrote that the hearing shattered the complacency and blindness many White South Africans had long indulged. "White South Africa, which had voted for the policy [of apartheid] in ever-increasing numbers for half a century, was confronted with the appalling facts of the crimes committed in its name," Sparks wrote. "And there could be no escaping them, for these were . . . confessions, by the perpetrators themselves."

Toward the end of his book, Tutu ventured that the United States might also benefit from a truth and reconciliation process. In words that could apply to the Scott brothers in New Orleans, Tutu wrote that the victims of apartheid "often ended up internalizing the definition the top dogs had of them. . . . And then the awful demons of self-hate and self-contempt, a hugely negative self-image, took its place in the center of the victim's being. . . . That is the pernicious source of the destructive internecine strife to be found, for instance, in the African American community. Society has conspired to fill you with self-hate, which you then project outward."

"It may be," Tutu added, "that race relations in the United States will not improve significantly until Native Americans and African Americans get the opportunity to tell their stories and reveal the pain that sits in the pit of their stomachs as a baneful legacy of dispossession and slavery. We saw in the Truth and Reconciliation Commission how the act of telling one's story has a cathartic, healing effect."

Barack Obama, Bill and Hillary Clinton, and numerous other public figures in the United States have suggested convening a national conversation about race. There was little follow-through, however, and some observers have questioned whether merely talking was much of an answer to the underlying problems. Tutu heard similar complaints about South Africa's truth and reconciliation process. Rejecting the idea that it was merely a naïve, rhetorical exercise, he wrote that, "Forgiving and being reconciled are not about . . . patting one another on the back and turning a blind eye to the wrong. True reconciliation exposes the awfulness, the abuse, the pain, the degradation, the truth. It could even sometimes make things worse. It is a risky undertaking, but in the end, it is worthwhile, because in the end dealing with the real situation helps to bring real healing."

❧

South Africa is not the only country to use a truth and reconciliation strategy to address such dilemmas; Canada, Rwanda, certain South

American countries and, perhaps most notably, Germany have also employed variations on this approach. How the process was implemented varied from one country to the next due to differences in history, culture, legal systems, and more, but the animating vision and principles have been much the same. In the aftermath of systemic mistreatment of a people by a government or society—Nazi Germany's extermination of Jews and other persecuted groups, Hutus' genocidal slaughter of Tutsis in Rwanda, Canadian governments' land theft and cultural obliteration of indigenous peoples—a national conversation was convened. The conversation aimed to document, acknowledge, and publicize what had happened, understand why it happened, make amends, and prevent such atrocities from recurring in the future. The amends have ranged from providing victims with the emotional validation of having their truth heard, to providing legal and financial compensation for damages, to official apologies for past misdeeds and pledges that "never again" would they be tolerated.

Exactly how a racial truth and reconciliation process would operate in the United States is a complex question that deserves a book of its own, but it's important to note that reparations and reconciliation are two distinct things. A racial truth and reconciliation process might lead to reparations; it might not. In South Africa, it didn't; in Germany, it did. Germany not only paid reparations to descendants of Jews and other victims of Nazi terror as well as to the state of Israel, it also officially apologized for the horrors of the Nazi era. Perhaps most importantly, it injected into Germany's mass consciousness an understanding of the crimes of Nazism by erecting monuments, establishing museums, teaching the truth in schools, and so forth.

Personally, I favor reparations, even as I recognize, as Ta-Nehisi Coates has written, that the legal and political challenges of paying them are immense. But whatever one's opinion about them, to debate reparations before engaging in a truth and reconciliation process risks dooming both by putting the cart before the horse. Opinion polls have long shown that a substantial majority of White Americans oppose reparations. But that's hardly surprising, considering that most White Americans have never learned the truth about what slavery was and has long done to life in the United States. Without such knowledge, how could anyone understand why reparations might be warranted?

The very phrase "truth and reconciliation" makes the point: if reparations or any other form of reconciliation is the goal, the necessary first step is to tell the truth. In the wake of the neo-Nazi march in Charlottesville, in the opening months of the Trump presidency, the activist and scholar Bryan Stevenson said that only after Americans face and acknowledge the truth about their past can they hope to transcend it and consign such outbursts of racist hatred to history. "Our nation is a nation that needs truth and reconciliation, and incidents like Charleston and Charlottesville just reinforce that," Stevenson said. But, he added, "You have to tell the truth before you can get to reconciliation, and culturally we have done a terrible job of truth telling in this country about our history of racial inequality."

Stevenson sought to improve America's racial truth-telling by establishing the Legacy Museum and the National Memorial for Peace and Justice. Located in Montgomery, Alabama, on a site where enslaved people once were held captive, the museum not only documents the workings of slavery in the old South, it also explains how that system evolved after the Civil War into racial terrorism, followed by decades of legal segregation, and eventually the inequalities of present-day America, especially the presumption of guilt that leads to the wildly disproportionate incarceration of Black people. In 2019, Todd Strange, the White mayor of Montgomery, credited Stevenson with sparking a reckoning with the city's history, telling the *New York Times*, "We're confronting our past. We're owning the issues Bryan is talking about."

Stevenson's work was not unique; a host of kindred initiatives arose during the Obama-Trump era. The Whitney Plantation began educating visitors about slavery in 2014. The National Museum of African American

History and Culture opened in Washington, DC, in 2016; it too, documented how the cruelties and exploitations of slavery had shape-shifted into Jim Crow and subsequent manifestations of brutality and inequality. Also in 2016, volunteers founded an organization named Coming to the Table to connect White and Black Americans who shared slavery-era ancestors; the group's goal was to "transform the nation's legacy of slavery and racism" by acknowledging "the racial wounds of the past." Bill Sizemore, a White journalist at the *Virginian-Pilot* newspaper who discovered he had blood relatives who had been enslaved by his White ancestors, told those Black relatives at a family gathering (which Sizemore's White relations boycotted), "White Americans have a lot to atone for, and we need to say it plainly. My family stole your family's liberty, their labor, and their human dignity. And I'm sorry."

Facing unpleasant truths about America's past is not easy, but no one should blame themselves for being unaware of those unpleasant truths in the first place. America's schools, churches, legal and political systems, news media, and other cultural channels have obscured or denied the truth about race and slavery since before the birth of the United States. Teachers, parents, clergy, coaches, neighbors, and employers have passed down, often unthinkingly, habits of word and deed to younger generations, just as those habits were passed down to them. These sorts of inherited patterns are part of what makes racism a systemic condition rather than an individual shortcoming.

"We in America were not taught African American history," Joseph Riley Jr., the White mayor of Charleston, South Carolina, said after the Bible class massacre in 2015. "It was never in the history books, and we don't know the story." John Cummings, founder of the Whitney Plantation museum, said much the same after buying the plantation and seeing its records of enslaved people who had been bought and sold as if they were livestock: "Why was I never taught this in school?" As recently as 2017, a survey of US high school textbooks conducted by researchers with the

Southern Poverty Law Center found that only 8 percent of high school seniors could identify slavery as the central cause of the Civil War. "Slavery is hard history," the researchers wrote, adding, "We the people have a deep-seated aversion to hard history because we are uncomfortable with the implications it raises about the past as well as the present."

But being uncomfortable can be helpful, according to Emmanuel Acho, a TV sports commentator and former professional football player who launched a video series after the murder of George Floyd called "Uncomfortable Conversations with a Black Man." Born in Texas to Nigerian immigrants, Acho grew up as one of the few Black kids in his schools; like Deb, he was at ease with White people and familiar with White culture. Which made it easier for him to open the book version of his video series by addressing White people, convincingly, as "Dear White friends, countrypersons: welcome." Promising "a safe space" where White people could ask questions and "learn things you've always wondered about," Acho said that he was "not sure if we can cure racism completely, but . . . I believe an important part of the cure, maybe the most crucial part of it, is to talk to each other." At times, these conversations will be uncomfortable, he said; indeed, most chapters in Acho's book contain a passage headlined, LET'S GET UNCOMFORTABLE. In a chapter that summarizes the history of White privilege along with current examples of it, Acho writes, "This country won't change in a significant way until the majority of White Americans acknowledge and address their White privilege. Let's practice. You, dear reader, have White privilege. It's okay. Just sit with it for a minute: embrace it. Your discomfort means that the medicine is doing its job."

Late night TV host Jimmy Kimmel put the matter more squarely to fellow White people, some of whom resisted the notion of White privilege on the understandable grounds that their own lives weren't very privileged. After all, the income of White working-class Americans, adjusted for inflation, has not increased over the past forty years, while the richest 10 percent of the population, and especially the richest 1 percent, have accumulated ever larger shares of the country's income. None of that, though, invalidates the reality of White privilege. As Kimmel put it, "White privilege does not mean your life has been easy. It just means the color of your skin hasn't made it harder."

Truth and reconciliation does require willing partners, however—in particular, White people who are ready to ask themselves the question posed earlier in this book: What kind of a White person do I want to be? Shortly after the Charleston church massacre in 2015, a White man named Garry Civitello called in to a nationally televised talk show about the massacre and asked, "How can I be less racist?" Heather McGhee, a Black scholar and activist appearing on the show, praised Civitello for his openness and his desire to change, and suggested he start by getting to know some Black people and reading some Black history. Civitello and McGhee exchanged phone calls and emails and eventually became friends. Civitello, who resided in rural North Carolina, ended up not voting for Trump in 2016, even though nearly all the White people around him did. In a comment countless Americans might echo if they read the history books McGhee recommended to him, Civitello marveled that, "There are so many things I did not know that I thought I knew."

Not long after the Mother's Day shooting, New Orleans became a stirring example of what a racial truth and reconciliation process for the United States could look like in practice. And jazz musicians were at the heart of the action, both as artists who articulated the urgency of change and as activists who helped push political leaders, including the White mayor, out of their comfort zones and into truth-telling.

John Boutté, the singer who composed "Down in the Treme," had favored a truth and reconciliation process since first learning about South Africa's example. "When they did it in South Africa, I said, 'What are we waiting for?'," Boutté told me. "We as a country need to fess up to the wrongs we've done and try to right the ship. I don't think anybody has ever stepped up as a US president and said, 'We really screwed up with the whole slavery thing and the genocide of Native Americans. We're sorry, and we want to fix it.' Until you do that, you can't really move forward." A national truth and reconciliation project would be ideal, Boutté added, but the project could also "happen from the bottom up, from the grassroots. In some ways, that's better. Racial truth and reconciliation can be integrated into school curricula. It can take place in churches. We gotta sit down and talk about this stuff without hollering and wanting to kill one another."

In late 2014, mayor Mitch Landrieu had called Wynton Marsalis, the internationally renowned trumpet player, to ask a favor. The two men had known each other since high school days, when Landrieu's father, as mayor of New Orleans, had championed justice and equality for Black residents—and got shunned and attacked by White friends and voters for it. New Orleans was going to celebrate its 300th birthday in 2018, and Landrieu was assembling a committee of high-profile people to plan and publicize a program of events highlighting the city's recovery since Hurricane Katrina. Landrieu asked if Marsalis would serve on the committee. Marsalis told the mayor he would, but he wanted something in return.

"Take down the Robert E. Lee statue," the musician said.

Landrieu didn't see the connection. Marsalis responded by asking the mayor whether he had ever thought "about what Robert E. Lee means to someone Black," and whether a statue to the Confederacy's top general truly reflected how the city wanted to be seen on its tricentennial anniversary. Marsalis reminded Landrieu that Louis Armstrong was one of the many locals who left town because "they didn't feel welcome" in a city where racism remained so visible and entrenched. Marsalis conceded that getting rid of the monument would be a "big political fight" but maintained that "it's the right thing to do."

Grassroots racial justice activists in New Orleans had been making the same argument for years, but Landrieu credited this conversation with Marsalis as a turning point in his thinking. The mayor tried to imagine himself as a Black father explaining the Lee monument to his Black daughter: why did her city maintain a monument to a man who led the fight to keep people with her skin color in bondage? As a father himself, Landrieu said, he couldn't answer that question.

Landrieu began to educate himself on the history of Confederate monuments in his city and, more broadly, the history of slavery. Just as for John Cummings of the Whitney Plantation slavery museum, Gary Civitello, whose TV friendship with Heather McGhee propelled him to ask deeper questions about race, and the author of this book, Landrieu underwent an eye-opening journey. As a high school student in the 1970s, he later wrote, he was taught about the military battles of the Civil War—though the war was referred to by its Confederate-friendly term, the War Between the States—but he was not taught about the realities of slavery, which gave rise to that war. Landrieu had spent his entire life in New Orleans and had been mayor for five years by this time, but only now did he learn that New Orleans had been "the largest slave market in America." The more he read and pondered, the more he came to believe that "the history we learned was purposefully false history."

That was also the case, Landrieu discovered, about the history of the Lee statue and other Confederate monuments. Defenders of Confederate iconography insisted that there was nothing racist about a Confederate flag or monument; they were simply symbols of Southern heritage and memorials to the thousands of soldiers who lost their lives fighting for the Confederacy. The actual history taught a different lesson. Most of the monuments were not erected immediately after the Civil War to honor fallen Confederate soldiers; rather, they dated from the 1880s and later decades, when White supremacists were reasserting their dominance across the South during the Jim Crow era. The Lee statue in New Orleans, for example, was erected in 1884. "The

Confederate flag was only put on top of the South Carolina statehouse in 1962," Eric Foner, a renowned historian of Reconstruction, pointed out. "It was put there as a rebuke to the civil rights movement. It was not a long-standing commemoration of Southern heritage. It was a purely political act to show Black people in South Carolina who was in charge."

Black people in New Orleans had received similar messages in the 1960s from other parts of the White power structure, and with conse-quences that still lingered fifty years later. "You can't talk about New Orleans today, about the lack of jobs and other economic problems, without talking about the past," Asali DeVan Ecclesiastes, a community development aide to Landrieu, told me. Perhaps the most dramatic example occurred in 1966, when the federal government rammed Interstate 10 through the Claiborne Avenue corridor, a thirteen-acre rectangular park straddled by retail shops that had long been the commercial and cultural heart of Black New Orleans. "Highway 10 destroyed 326 Black-owned businesses that employed hundreds of Black residents of New Orleans," Ecclesiastes said. "None of those business owners got compensation. The ripple effects, in terms of lost jobs and Black buying power no longer building wealth in the Black community, are incalculable." In an even more overt example of racist policy, said Ecclesiastes, Mayor Victor H. Schiro in the 1960s diverted millions of dollars of federal money intended to install sewage lines in the city's overwhelmingly Black Seventh Ward, using it instead to develop the upscale Lakeview neighborhood. Citing city records, she said that the mayor justified diverting the money by declaring, "The niggers don't need that."

After the Charleston massacre, Landrieu later wrote, "I doubled down on my conviction" that the Confederate monuments had to go. A week later, he publicly apologized for slavery, the first major US politician to take that step. The necessary first move toward reconciliation, he said in his apology speech, was to acknowledge that "something bad happened." He added, "On this day, let me, as the chief executive officer of this government, in this city that at one time in history sold more people into slavery than anywhere else in America, apologize for this country's history and legacy of slavery." Landrieu added that African Americans in his city were still oppressed by slavery's legacy; every time they drove past the Lee statue or the monument to Confederate general P.G.T. Beauregard at the entrance to City Park, they were reminded that their city still celebrated men who had fought to keep their people in bondage.

Soon after, the To Be Continued band joined with Glen David Andrews to write "Wild Magnolias," a song illustrating that reparations for past wrongs could take various forms beyond the financial. Set to a squalling beat and propelled by explosive horns, the song's lyrics repeatedly declared, "Tear those monuments down!" The verse explained what should take their place: "We gonna name Lee Circle, after Allen Toussaint." It was Black defiance at its most uncompromising. The TBC and Andrews weren't asking for anyone's permission to take down those monuments. They weren't suggesting that it might be a good idea. They were announcing that those monuments were coming down, whether White supremacists liked it or not.

But removing the monuments proved to be a politically fraught and dangerous task that demonstrated that the road to truth and reconciliation is by no means smooth and easy. Landrieu learned that some White people still harbored considerable sympathy for Confederate symbols and ideas. After the City Council voted 6 to 1 in favor of the mayor's proposal to take down the offending monuments, opponents filed lawsuits that blocked implementation for the next eighteen months. Meanwhile, Landrieu and his family received face-to-face denunciations and even death threats from enraged White people, just as his father had in the 1970s when he dared to stand up for Black people's rights. After the courts upheld the city's right to remove the monuments, private companies that applied to do the removals were attacked on social media and harassed. Most companies withdrew their applications; one did not—until its chief executive's car was firebombed. "We knew [our plans] were being monitored by White nationalists," Landrieu recalled, calling their intimidation "terrorism by any other name, despite what President Trump is too cowardly to say about one part of his 'base.'" Mitch Landrieu had been handily reelected in 2014 with majority support from Black and White voters alike. Now, polls indicated that he had lost half of his White support—just as his father had before him.

Unable to hire a crane to remove the Lee statue, the mayor found himself facing what he later called "the very definition of institutionalized racism. You may have the law on your side, but if someone else controls the money, the machines, or the hardware you need to make your new law work, you are screwed." This was "exactly what has happened to African Americans over the last three centuries," he added.

The city finally prevailed after it hired a Texas company and "took extraordinary security measures to safeguard equipment and workers," increasing the project's cost by a factor of five. Landrieu got "a great deal of favorable attention in the national media" for taking the monuments down, he recalled, "but in my hometown, the tide has not so quickly turned." His son, who attended the same Jesuit high school his father had, later wrote that, "For the two days after the removal, I walked down the school hallway bracing myself as my classmates yelled out 'nigger lover' and 'your dad is ruining the city.'"

During these same years, Landrieu was also spending a good deal of time and political capital trying to halt the epidemic of gun violence that young Black men in New Orleans were inflicting on one another. An article in The Atlantic about Landrieu's NOLA For Life program described one of its core crime-fighting tactics, something Landrieu called the "call-in." The mayor regularly called in groups of inmates and parolees for private discussions with him, the chief of police, and other key officials. The inmates, wearing prison overalls and handcuffs, sat on one side of the room; the parolees, who as free men wore civilian clothes, sat on the other. Most of these young men were between sixteen and twenty-four years old, the demographic most likely to shoot and be shot. The mayor stood between the two groups and delivered a message that was part carrot, part stick. If the men committed crimes in the future, he warned, the city would make sure to imprison them. But if they left the criminal life behind, the city would help them make a fresh start—help them prepare for and find jobs, kick drug addiction, and learn parenting and other life skills. Landrieu stressed that he and his aides were talking with the men not only because they were determined to make New Orleans a safer city, but also because they cared about them and didn't want them to end up dead or in prison.

The story of Mitch Landrieu's evolution—from a White person who thought of himself as racially enlightened into a White person who got awakened by a challenging conversation with a Black acquaintance and then went on to educate himself about his country's real racial history and make amends through not just words but deeds—is the kind of transformation a racial truth and reconciliation process could foster among Americans nationwide. Hoping to encourage such transformations, Congresswoman Barbara Lee, Democrat of California, introduced legislation in the aftermath of George Floyd's murder in 2020 to establish a United States Commission on Truth, Racial Healing and Transformation. Its mission would be to "examine the effects of slavery, institutional racism, and discrimination against people of color, and how our history impacts laws and policies today." (Lee reintroduced her legislation in 2023, arguing that "Every challenge we face today—from health disparities laid bare by the COVID-19 pandemic, to economic inequality and poverty, to environmental racism—can be traced back to four hundred years of systemic, government sanctioned racism.")

Landrieu acknowledged that it had taken him too long to leave his blind spots behind, and he expected the same would be true for others, especially White Americans. "We are all capable of" what he called "transformative awareness," he wrote in his memoir, *In the Shadow of Statues: A White*

Southerner Confronts History, "but we come kicking and screaming to a sudden shift of thinking about the past. To get there, we have to acknowledge that we were inattentive, insensitive, myopic, or God forbid, hateful in our earlier view." The alternative, Landrieu argued, was that racist "hatred" and "violence" would persist and intensify, not only in New Orleans but throughout the United States. Describing what he had learned after going through the ultimately successful process of removing Confederate monuments from his city, the mayor of what was once North America's largest slave market wrote, "Here is what I know about race. You can't go over it. You can't go under it. You can't go around it. You have to go through it."

Even as the shadow of Donald Trump was looming over American politics and daily life, Deb scored a great success in her professional life: getting a new job she absolutely loved. The Alliance for Safety and Justice was a nonprofit organization that worked to reform the criminal justice system, including the mass incarceration of Black and other people of color. Having nearly been killed in the most notorious mass shooting in the modern history of New Orleans, Deb brought instant credibility to her new post. A few weeks after Trump's election, she was invited to address a conference in Baton Rouge, Louisiana's state capital, where government officials and legal experts were considering alternative policies to incarceration. The first speaker to address the gathering, Deb told me afterward, was an older White woman who had lost her son to gun violence. The woman urged the assembled experts to "think long and hard before" they implemented any such alternative policies; the woman felt strongly that her son's killers should never be allowed back on the streets.

"Then I got up and gave my story, about how I was a survivor of a violent crime," Deb told me. "I said that the young men who shot me and the other people on Mother's Day should be punished, but I didn't think they should spend the rest of their lives in prison. I said I thought those young men could redeem themselves and make a positive contribution to society if we would consider alternatives to life in prison. After the panel was over, a long line of people came up and wanted to talk with me, take my card, have me come speak to their organization, and whatnot. That felt so good. My statement and presence sent a very different message than people usually hear from victims of crime."

"As I was driving back from Baton Rouge," Deb added, "I was thinking, 'This is really kismet, me doing this kind of work right now. It's exactly what I'm passionate about doing and have the skills to do.' During the first year after the shooting, I often felt like I didn't want to live anymore. I wasn't going to take action myself, but many days I thought, 'Just let me go.' Now, I feel like if getting shot was what put me in the position to do this work, then I'm glad I was shot."

"Wait—are you serious?" I asked. "Glad you got shot? I'm glad you survived, but I'm sure as hell not glad you were shot."

"Yeah, I'm serious," Deb replied. "That's just how I feel."

In her new job, Deb was spreading the same truth and reconciliation message she had been preaching from the time we were shot at the Mother's Day second line parade. The White woman at that conference in Baton Rouge had her version of truth: the killers who took her son's life should never see freedom again. And Deb had her version of truth: even people guilty of terrible transgressions can be redeemed. Airing both points of view so people could hear and discuss ideas they hadn't previously encountered and perhaps change their minds—what was that but an attempt to use truth to forge reconciliation?

But Donald Trump's arrival in the White House forced to the surface a challenging question about a truth and reconciliation strategy: What do you do when one side of the conflict isn't interested in reconciliation—and doesn't have to accept reconciliation, because that side still wields enormous power? Most countries that have employed a truth and reconciliation strategy were able to sidestep this conundrum for a simple reason: the side that had mistreated people was militarily defeated before truth and reconciliation was attempted. In Germany, Allied armies had routed the Nazis. In Rwanda, international peacekeepers had forcibly halted the slaughter (albeit later than they should have). In South Africa, the regime was fought to a military stalemate that amounted to a de facto defeat, for the stalemate coincided with enormous pressure from the international community to end apartheid. (Canada is an exception to this trend; there, moral suasion and political pressure did get the federal government to acknowledge the mistreatment of indigenous people.)

None of those conditions applied in Trump's America—not when he was president, not later, when he was trying to overturn his 2020 election defeat, and not later still when he was campaigning to retake the White House in 2024. Trump's power was grounded in the cultlike support he enjoyed from the majority of Republican voters—enough support that Republican officials on Capitol Hill and across the country continued to defend him no matter what he did. The idea that Americans should learn the actual truth of the nation's racial history—and perhaps unlearn much of what they previously believed—as a step toward racial reconciliation was a complete nonstarter for Trump and his followers. Indeed, they gleefully weaponized the very idea of facing up to America's history, condemning it as "critical race theory."

Rather than accept the fact that Trump lost the 2020 election, he and his cult simply insisted, against all the evidence, that he had won, and his victory was being stolen. Some sixty-one court rulings, many of them by judges Trump himself had appointed, found no evidence of fraud. Determined to remain in power anyway, Trump incited a mob to storm the Capitol on January 6, 2021, to prevent Congress from certifying the election results. Shattering windows, attacking police with clubs, and spearing them with flag poles, Trump's mob—some of them wearing Nazi insignias and carrying Confederate flags—swarmed the halls of Congress, shouting death threats against Vice President Mike Pence and Speaker of the House Nancy Pelosi. The assault left seven people dead and injured more than 140 police officers, although shaken lawmakers did return that night to certify Biden's election.

The larger conflict remained far from resolved, however, for Trump continued to claim that he was the rightful president, and most Republican voters and politicians continued to support him, despite the overwhelming evidence. "Trump and his party have convinced a dauntingly large number of Americans that the essential workings of democracy are corrupt, that made-up claims of fraud are true, that only cheating can thwart their victory at the polls . . . and that violence is a legitimate response," journalist Barton Gellman wrote a year after January 6. Warning that Trump and his followers would not accept defeat in any future elections, Gellman was one of numerous observers to warn that a deeply divided United States was in danger of descending into a form of civil war. (Indeed, some members of the January 6 mob had worn sweatshirts on which were printed the words, MAGA CIVIL WAR, 1/6/21.)

The January 6 insurrection was grounded in the same White supremacist ideology that championed slavery before the Civil War, and that ideology's current manifestation threatened to spark a modern variation of that bloody conflict. Michael Luttig, a retired federal judge who was conservative enough that President George W. Bush had considered nominating him to the Supreme Court, spoke to this point when testifying to the special congressional committee that investigated the January 6 assault. As horrible as that assault had been, Luttig argued, an even greater danger loomed: Trump and his followers remained determined to subvert American democracy by rigging election procedures to ensure that their side won no matter what. The January 6 insurrection, Luttig continued, had brought the United States "face to face with the raging war that it had been waging against itself for years," propelling the nation to "a foreboding crossroads with disquieting parallels to the fateful crossroads we came to over a century and a half ago."

"We are in the midst [of] a cold civil war," Carl Bernstein, the Watergate journalist and author, likewise said. "It goes back twenty, thirty years, the origins of this cold civil war. Trump ignited it. It's no longer cold. It's reached the point of ignition."

But Trump, by himself, could not inflame a full-scale second Civil War; what gave his rhetoric political force was that a sizable portion of the population enthusiastically embraced his calls to do whatever it took, including spilling blood, to crush political opponents and reinstall Trump in the White House. Thus, when Trump wrote in September of 2023 that the nation's top military officer, the chairman of the Joint Chiefs of Staff, General Mark A. Milley, deserved "DEATH" for telling Chinese military officials that the United States did not plan to attack China in the final days of Trump's presidency, Trump's supporters, both among grassroots Republicans and on Capitol Hill, did not criticize or distance themselves from him. When Trump said at a November 2023 campaign rally that his political opponents were "vermin" that he would "root out" when he returned to power—wording, as President Biden noted, that "echoes language you heard in Nazi Germany in the 1930s"—rank-and-file Republicans and their party's representatives in Congress again did not rebuke him. When Fox News personality Sean Hannity, in a December 2023 interview, gave Trump the opportunity to disavow any intention of "abusing power as retribution" if he won the 2024 election, Trump corrected him, declaring that he would indeed be a dictator, but only "on day one. We're closing the border and we're drilling, drilling, drilling. After that, I'm not a dictator." This time, many Republicans outright applauded Trump or said that he was only joking in order to drive liberals crazy. Meanwhile, Trump remained by far the frontrunner for the party's 2024 presidential nomination.

What made these and many similar statements by Trump so menacing was not only their obviously authoritarian agenda—it was that tens of millions of Americans applauded him for saying them out loud and clearly hoped he would follow through on that agenda. More than a few of Trump's supporters also made it clear that, if the 2024 election went against him, they would gladly employ violence to overturn the results. As this book went to press in February of 2024, it was that combination—a brazenly racist, authoritarian leader and unswerving support for that leader from a sizable mass of violence-prone supporters—that made a second American civil war such a plausible possibility.

True, demographics and other social trends were running against Trump and his modern-day Confederates. Younger Americans of all backgrounds were notably more progressive on matters of race and equality than their elders were. But would opponents of Trump turn out in 2024 to vote in large enough numbers to block his return to the White House? Would they turn out even if Trump's supporters used intimidation, as Trump urged, to deter them from voting? And if the election results did go against Trump, what then? How would the rest of the country respond if he and his supporters made good on their fantasies of launching a second civil war to "make America great again?"

As the future awaited, the question of America's trajectory dangled. "The essential underlying conflict," wrote US Representative Jamie Raskin, Democrat of Maryland, who had led the second impeachment case against Trump after the January 6 insurgency, was whether the American people were "capable of putting the pathologies of political White supremacy behind us once and for all. More than 150 years after the end of the Civil War, will we finally reject and transcend racism in this century? Or has it become such a necessary tool for maintaining right-wing political power and social control that we are bound to see it wielded in perpetuity through dangerous new forms of propaganda and self-deception?"

In the face of the combative intransigence Raskin described, what chance does a truth and reconciliation strategy have of healing America's long festering racial wounds? I have no ready answer to that question, but many people and organizations of impressive skill and determination are working on the problem. I've written about some of them in this book: the Whitney Plantation slavery museum outside of New Orleans; Bryan Stevenson and his work at the National Memorial for Peace and Justice; Mitch Landrieu and the musicians—Wynton Marsalis, Glen David Andrews, and the To Be Continued Brass Band—who pushed him to "tear those monuments down"; the Coming to the Table organizers of family-to-family conversations; and the Smithsonian Institute's National Museum of African American History and Culture in Washington, DC.

Another example of de facto truth and reconciliation work was the 1619 Project, a long-form journalism initiative backed by the *New York Times* that aimed "to reframe the country's history by placing the consequences of slavery and the contributions of Black Americans at the very center of the United States' national narrative." Conceived and edited by Nikole Hannah-Jones, the project won the 2020 Pulitzer Prize for Commentary and was expanded into a book that was adopted in countless classrooms across the country. Nor was such work taking place only in the United States. "London, Sugar and Slavery," an exhibit at the Museum of London, powerfully illustrated "how the trade in enslaved Africans shaped London." The first sentence presented to visitors to the museum set the tone: "Behind the growth of London as a centre of finance and commerce from the 1700s onward lay one of the great crimes against humanity."

The assumption underlying such efforts was that one must change individual people's hearts and minds before the larger society's politics, economics, and other systems can change. Changing hearts and minds, in turn, requires that people face the truth of what happened and talk constructively about it. That kind of dialogue can lead people to act differently out in the world, influencing everything from how they treat others at work or on the street to what kind of leaders they elect to political office. As Stevenson said in response to the election of Trump in 2016, "If we had done the work that we should have done . . . to combat our history of racial inequality, no one could win national office after demonizing people who're Mexican or Muslim. We would be in a place where we would find that unacceptable."

But changing hearts and minds, much less the larger political and economic choices they shape, does not happen overnight, and in the meantime Trump and the forces he represents are loose on the national stage. So to repeat: What use is a strategy of truth and reconciliation in a country so deeply polarized that more than a few experts feared that it could lose its democracy and even descend into some form of civil war?

After Deb took her new job in criminal justice reform, I wondered if she would gain any insights to this puzzle. Maybe her truth and reconciliation work at the local level in Louisiana would carry lessons for how to deal with Trumpism at the national level. After all, outside the New Orleans city limits, political sentiment in Louisiana ran bright red. Trump beat Biden in the state by twenty points in 2020, so Deb would be interacting with people across the political spectrum as she pursued racial truth and reconciliation and its intellectual cousin, "restorative justice." As defined by the Centre for Justice and Reconciliation, a nonprofit that works on these issues throughout the world, restorative justice "repairs the harm caused by the crime. . . . It emphasizes accountability, making amends, and—if they are interested—facilitated meetings between victims, offenders, and other persons." The meeting Deb and I had with an imprisoned Akein Scott was a small example of restorative justice. Restorative justice can also be applied to heal conflicts between communities or countries. In her new job, Deb would be arranging activities to hold accountable victims and offenders alike, including the systemic racism that she blamed for much of the violence in New Orleans.

As Deb pursued this work, I was also curious to know how her new experiences might affect her feelings about the Mother's Day shooting. A few readers of an early draft of this book questioned the notion that

the Scott brothers' story carried the moral lessons Deb ascribed to it. The
Charleston massacre of Black people attending a Bible class—sure, they
said, that tragedy did carry such lessons, because those Black people were
shot by an avowed White supremacist who hoped to ignite a race war. But
the Scott brothers had shot other Black people for no reason other than a
feud between two drug gangs. How could such an attack be elevated into
an uplifting commentary about race in America?

Deb and I had talked about this more than once. She thought the Scott
brothers should be imprisoned—"They've shown they can't live among
us"—but she also thought they could be rehabilitated. And there had to be
a way to stop the cycle. This stance embraced a credo voiced by many public
defenders, including the lawyer inherited by Travis Scott when he sought to
appeal Judge Lemelle's life sentence. "Every human being is more than what
they did on the worst day of their life," Michael Admirand, a young White
man, told me. Joe Maize and Glen David Andrews were right that not
everyone born into desperate situations ends up a drug-dealing gunslinger,
but more than a few do—not necessarily because they are bad people but
because a certain percentage of people facing such challenges is bound to
fall short. As Coates argued in a public debate with Mitch Landrieu about
violent crime and the Black community, government policies "herd certain
people into certain neighborhoods. We deprive these neighborhoods of
resources, of jobs. . . . And then we're shocked that the murder rate is high
there. Why are you shocked?"

It's understandable that people want a consistent moral framework for
dealing with issues as charged as race in America. But race in America does
not afford such a framework, partly because the dilemma is rooted in profound
trauma. In her City Council statement after the Mother's Day shooting, Deb
lamented that the young Black men accused of the shooting had been "separated from us by so much trauma." But in a broader sense, perhaps all Americans have been separated from one another by the trauma of racism and slavery,
a trauma their nation has never fully faced, much less put right. To be sure,

Black people have suffered incomparably worse from this trauma than White people have; I'm not suggesting any kind of moral equivalence here. Rather, I am ventilating a perspective expressed by a number of African American activists and intellectuals I interviewed for this book, including Deb.

According to this perspective, it's precisely because White people are at some level aware of how vile and immoral slavery was that they—some of them, anyway—resist facing that fact and taking steps to address it. Landon Williams, a senior organizer for the Black Panther Party in the 1960s, said in a 2017 interview that all people of color experience racism in the United States, but Black people get the harshest treatment of all. That's because White people, if only subconsciously, feel guilty about slavery, Williams argued, and seeing Black people reminds them of that guilt. "So they may hate the Native Americans because . . . they were here first," Williams explained, "or they may hate the Latinos because they just crossed the border lately . . . [but] they hate us because they know what the crime of slavery was and they wish we would just go away. And we don't [go away]."

"Slavery is not something that started and stopped 150 years ago," said Andrea Queeley, the professor of African American history quoted earlier in this book, who also happened to be a close friend of Deb's. "But every time we try to face the problem, the reactions are so strong, because [White] people don't want to face their demons. Instead, they project their own sins onto the people they oppressed. It's like during the lynching era. Why do you think White men were lynching Black men and accusing them of raping White women? Because that's what White men had been doing since the dawn of slavery in this country—raping Black women."

Deb made a very similar point to me about how White Southerners psychologically came to terms with the end of slavery. She said, as quoted earlier in this book, "When slavery ended and the Black people they had thought of like animals were legally their equals, many White people found that very hard to accept—financially and legally, but also emotionally. So, they *didn't* accept it. They held onto their old attitudes, passed them down to their children, and kept Black people down."

Processing and overcoming trauma is a messy, difficult process for individuals and societies alike, and success is far from guaranteed. But the alternative is messy and difficult as well. Until a trauma is brought into the open and worked through and amends are made, the trauma will persist—or, as Deb put it after hearing the full story of the Scott brothers' criminal behavior, the cycle will stay stuck on repeat, and more lives will continue to be scarred, or worse.

I looked forward to Deb and me having another of our long, soul-searching conversations about all this. I imagined the two of us sitting on her front porch in the moist glow of early evening in New Orleans, perhaps a couple of rum and pineapple juice cocktails at hand. We would explore the pros and cons of the contending points of view, debate potential remedies, relish our mutual respect and affection, maybe even enjoy a few laughs. Alas, we never got the chance.

14

One Last Second Line

I went down to the St. James Infirmary
Saw my baby there
Stretched out on a long white table
So cold, so sweet, so fair
Let her go, let her go, God bless her
Wherever she may be . . .

—"St. James Infirmary Blues"—traditional

On June 29, 2016, three months to the day after the Scott brothers received their sentences from Judge Lemelle, Deb suddenly found herself involuntarily committed to an addiction treatment facility. I got the news while changing planes on my way to New Orleans. Deb and I were supposed to have dinner that night; I was calling to confirm the time and place. When she answered the phone, she was too embarrassed to tell me where she was, but she made it clear she would not be available for dinner.

"Is something wrong, Deb?"

"Yeah, my friends, that's what's wrong," she replied with a mirthless laugh. "They decided I needed a twelve-step program, so they put me in this rehab center."

"A rehab center?"

"Yeah," Deb said. "For opioid addiction."

"Opioids? I remember you talking about that the last time I was in town. You said you were a little concerned about your reliance on painkillers, and you were looking into some programs for dealing with it."

"Good memory, Mark! I *was* looking into programs, and I found one I liked. That's what really pisses me off. My friends put me in this place that *they* chose, without asking me. They staged an intervention on my ass, can you believe that?"

I didn't know what to say.

"This is so embarrassing to have to tell you," Deb continued. "But I'm not staying here. The law says they can't hold a non-consenting adult for more than seventy-two hours, and I am definitely not consenting to this bullshit."

Despite the circumstances, I had to chuckle at Deb's vehemence, which got her chuckling, too.

"How long are you in town?" she asked.

"I leave next Wednesday."

"Cool, we can see each other before you go," Deb said. "Can I ask you a favor?"

"Sure."

"If you're not busy Sunday, can you give me a ride home from this place?"

"Of course."

A few hours later, after checking into my usual B&B, I called Deb's friend Karen Gadbois, the reporter at *The Lens* who'd been one of the first friends at the hospital the afternoon Deb was shot. Karen sounded agitated. She confirmed that she and other members of Deb's inner circle had staged an intervention.

"We think Deb is in trouble," Karen said. "She isn't getting better. Instead of getting counseling to work through the emotional trauma of that shooting, she's focused on trying to save those boys who shot her. It's crazy. Meanwhile, she's spent through all the money we raised for her. I'm talking six figures. It's all gone. And she's way too dependent on pain pills. We talked to her therapist and decided we had to stage an intervention."

I knew that Karen and the rest of Deb's inner circle had kept vigil at her bedside from the night she was hospitalized and intensively cared for her for months afterward. Deb herself had told me that "they just wouldn't let me die," and that she loved them for it. If these folks who knew Deb so well had become concerned enough that they forced her into rehab, that was something to take seriously.

"You really think Deb's an addict?" I asked.

"No question," Karen said flatly. "She nods off, misses appointments, doesn't pay her bills. We've pointed this stuff out to her and said, 'Face it, you're an addict.' She wouldn't listen. So, we made the decision that we would no longer enable her behavior. We would no longer clean up her messes or do any of the stuff we'd routinely done these past couple years. That's an important part of this approach—no more enabling from friends and loved ones. So, if she calls you, don't enable her."

Now I felt caught in the middle. I did not tell Karen that I'd already promised Deb a ride home from the rehab facility.

When Deb called me on Sunday, I was on a bike ride, exploring parts of New Orleans I hadn't seen up close before. I was just following my nose, enjoying the tropical air after the permanent cool of San Francisco, when I found myself at Bunny Friend Park in the Upper Ninth Ward. Seven months earlier, a mass shooting eerily like the Mother's Day shooting had taken place in that park. At 6:15 P.M. on Sunday, November 22, 2015, as hundreds of people gathered for a live DJ performance, two rival gangs unleashed a hail of gunfire. Seventeen people were injured, including a ten-year-old, though none were killed.

I remembered Deb telling me that Juicy grew up across the street from this park. Bunny Friend had been his playground, the place where he'd gotten his nickname from always carrying around a juice box. Pulling my bike to a halt, I tried to picture the scene on the night when those seventeen people were shot, but it didn't come into focus. All I saw was a compact rectangular park with a concrete basketball court and a small baseball field with grass glinting silver beneath the midday sun.

My cell phone burbled, and it was Deb, calling from the rehab center: Could I come and get her in a couple hours? After what Karen told me, I felt conflicted, but Deb was my friend. How do you refuse a friend who's asking for help?

"Um, I guess I can do that, Deb." I took down the address and said I'd be there.

She was headstrong, that Deb. Even when very weak physically, as she clearly was when she stumbled out the front door of River Oaks Hospital that afternoon, she could be a bulldog of determination. There was a "my way or the highway" aspect to her personality that I was just beginning to understand.

Case in point: after Deb returned from rehab, she completely cut off the friends who had staged the intervention. She wouldn't talk to them, not even to explain why she was angry. I pleaded with her to reconsider. Maybe her friends had been wrong, maybe they'd been right, but they had acted out of love and concern. Surely, they had proven that love and concern during the years of stalwart care they had provided after Deb was shot. Couldn't she at least talk with them before breaking the connection?

No, Deb's mind was made up. "I'm not going to waste my energy on people who think they know better than me what's good for me," she said.

I couldn't fathom it. Here was Deb, who famously forgave the two strangers who shot and nearly killed us, refusing to forgive close friends who had turned their lives upside down to hold her back from the abyss of death.

I wasn't the only one who was puzzled. "I know she was angry with them, but I didn't understand that," Deb's sister-cousin Le'Trese told me. "What they did was help her have more life. What those boys did to y'all was more toward death. I don't have any insight on why Deb behaved that way. It's like the two things don't go in the same body."

A similar rupture took place between Deb and her mother. When Deb's father died in November of 2015, Deb spent his final days with him in the hospital. Despite the peculiarities of their relationship—him kidnapping her as a toddler, lying about her real mother, attempting to control her through financial assistance when she was grown—Deb loved him dearly. After he died, she asked her mother to accompany her to the funeral for emotional support. Her mother explained that her feelings about the man who had stolen Deb away from her all those years ago would prevent her from attending. Furious, Deb cut off her mother as uncompromisingly as she cut off the friends who staged the intervention.

It occurred to me that "The Truth Hurts, But Silence Kills," the slogan that the South African Truth and Reconciliation Commission used to encourage public support for their work, can apply to personal situations as well. When Deb's friends staged their intervention, it hurt them to tell their dear friend that she was an addict and that they were putting her in a rehabilitation facility against her will. But staying silent and doing nothing, they feared, would mean death—that Deb would die if she didn't kick her addiction. For her part, Deb certainly agreed with the importance of telling the truth, even when it hurt. She had done so in her City Council statement after we were shot, and she thanked me for doing so when I sorrowfully told her the back stories of the Scott brothers' violent, impoverished childhoods. But that didn't mean that it wasn't hard for Deb to hear her friends' truths about addiction.

Maybe hard truths are hard for all of us to hear. Maybe sometimes it's easier to tell the truth than it is to hear it.

Not long after her friends' intervention in Deb's addiction, Tuffy Nelson got arrested and charged with possession of heroin. The whole thing was bullshit, Deb told me. The police had stopped and searched Tuffy's truck without probable cause; the heroin belonged to a guy Tuffy had given a ride to, and that guy fled the scene. But given Tuffy's long criminal record from the days before he turned Good Samaritan, the district attorney's office was threatening to put him away for a long time, maybe life.

Deb was determined to prevent that, especially now that Tuffy had left his gangster days behind and become a positive force in the community. The only way to keep Tuffy out of jail, she decided, was to hire a private attorney. Otherwise, Tuffy would have to rely on the public defender's office for Orleans Parish, which was so chronically underfunded that the attorney in charge, Derwyn Bunton, had attracted national attention by publishing an opinion article in the *New York Times* explaining that he had stopped accepting certain felony cases—not because he didn't believe in every American's Sixth Amendment right to counsel, but because he did not want to contribute to the charade that he and his preposterously overworked staff could provide adequate counsel to the huge number of indigent defendants who needed it.

Deb needed to raise thousands of dollars for the lawyer, and she was hitting up everyone she knew, including me. I explained to her that it would be a journalistic conflict of interest for me to give money to someone I was writing about; it would make me look biased toward Tuffy's and Deb's version of events. What I could do, I said, was investigate Tuffy's case and perhaps write about it. This seemed to satisfy Deb, and I did write a piece for the *Daily Beast*, quoting Bunton and reporting that the underfunding of public defenders in Louisiana was so extreme that, in one instance, thirty separate defendants were herded into a courtroom to plead guilty en masse—after spending a total of thirty seconds each with their court appointed legal counsel.

Deb's mood darkened, however, as Tuffy's court hearing approached and his legal fund remained insufficient. She redoubled her efforts to squeeze donations from everyone she knew. She asked me again. I explained again that it would be a conflict of interest. She let it go for a week then called to make an identical request. Tuffy's court date was three days away, she told me; she simply had to raise the money. I explained once again that, as much as I sympathized, I couldn't do it.

"But nobody'd have to know," Deb replied. "Tuffy has a nonprofit group that funds his work feeding the homeless. You could send your check there."

"That wouldn't make it right, Deb," I said. "That would make it money laundering."

She shifted to guilt tripping. "So, let me get this straight," she said. "You don't care if this Black man who doesn't have legal representation goes to jail."

"That's not fair, Deb," I said. "Of course I care. But I've told you and told you, the ethics of journalism don't allow me to do what you're asking."

"So it doesn't bother you that Tuffy might spend the next five years in jail?"

"Deb," I said and stopped, at a loss for words.

There was a pause, an exasperated sigh on her end of the line, and then, for the only time in our relationship, Deb hung up on me.

I waited a week, hoping Deb would calm down. Then I sent her an email, trying once again to explain the conflict of interest, inquiring about Tuffy, and asking if she and I could try to talk things through. No reply. I had to travel overseas for work, but upon my return ten days later, I emailed again. Still no reply. I figured she must be really mad.

Finally, I called Tuffy. He told me his court hearing had been delayed again, so he was still a free man. He and Deb were working on raising money for the private attorney, but she'd been having serious health issues, including her opioid addiction. As a former crack addict himself, Tuffy recognized an addict when he saw one. He had tried to help Deb quit, he told me, like others had helped him quit, "but somebody who's an addict, they got to decide *themselves* they gonna quit." Tuffy emphasized, though, that Deb's addiction was an entirely different beast than his had been. He took crack to dance and have fun; she got hooked on opioids because she got shot and the resulting physical pain was impossible to bear without constant medication.

Tuffy had been with Deb in the hospital around this time, and Deb allowed him to listen in while the doctor explained her situation: despite the thirty-six surgeries she'd had since getting shot, her vital organs were still far from working properly; the initial damage was simply too great. And that damage, plus the aftereffects of all the surgeries, was causing ferocious levels of pain inside her body. The only way this pain could be kept at bay was through ample applications of heavy painkillers. The doctor said he was sorry this was the case, but there was only so much he and his colleagues could do about it.

"Deb couldn't help getting addicted," Tuffy told me. "She not a weak person, you know that. But the pain inside her body was too much for anyone to take. There was no way for her to deal with it but them pills."

When I asked Tuffy if he had spoken with Deb in the last couple days, he said he hadn't. And he was worried. In the past day or two, people had posted messages on Facebook, saying that Deb was in the hospital and people should pray for her.

The next morning, May 2, 2017, I was at San Francisco International Airport boarding a flight to New York when I got the call from Karen Gadbois.

"Mark, I'm very sorry to tell you this, but Deb died."

"Oh, no!" I shouted, startling the passengers standing in line around me. "No, no, no! When? How?"

"This morning," Karen replied. "She'd been in the hospital, she wasn't getting better, and her organs just shut down. I'm sorry."

I couldn't speak. My vision blurred. My insides felt at once deflated and on fire. I couldn't process what I was hearing.

"Mark, I'm sorry, I have to go," Karen said. "I have other people to call. We haven't made plans for the funeral yet, but I'll let you know as soon as I can."

"Thanks, Karen. Thanks for thinking of me. God bless you for everything you've done for Deb."

By talking with various friends and loved ones, I pieced together the timeline of events between my last phone call with Deb and her death. It turned out that Deb had been in the hospital on and off since she and I last spoke a month ago. Annie LaRock had been concerned when Deb didn't show up for seder. "I called and texted her to ask why she hadn't come, she didn't respond," Annie told me. "So I went to her apartment to check on her."

"What day was that?" I asked.

"Wednesday, April 12," Annie said. "I found her inside her front room. She was slumped over, with her back to the door. I told her to get up. She was semiconscious. She threw her arm up behind her as if she was trying to push me away. I said if she didn't get up, I was going to call the emergency medical services. She threw her arm back again to push me away. So, I called, they came, and then she got *really* pissed. She started yelling and trying to push them away, too. They restrained her and loaded her into an ambulance, literally kicking and screaming."

Deb spent the next ten days in the hospital, where doctors concluded that she had sepsis. Nevertheless, on Saturday, April 22, she somehow got herself released—again the bulldog determination. She was scheduled to receive an award the next day from Avodah New Orleans, an anti-poverty organization, and "she wanted to get that award," Annie recalled, "she was so proud of it." Displaying her princess side, Deb summoned Simone Levine, a friend who served on Avodah's advisory board, to fetch her from the hospital.

"When I got there, the nurse said, 'She's not discharged,'" Levine told me. "So I told Deb, 'I'm not doing this.' Deb said, 'If you won't, I'll call somebody who will.' So I did it."

The awards ceremony was held at Temple Sinai, the oldest Reform Jewish congregation in Louisiana; it followed the "repair the world" teaching Deb had embraced since discovering her Jewish heritage at age nineteen. Photos of Deb at the event show her looking haggard, clearly unwell. When it was time for her to address the crowd, Levine had to help her up to the podium.

A few days later, Keith Twitchell, Deb's landlord and former colleague, looked outside to see Deb standing in the yard, barefoot, slowly swaying from one foot to the other as if lost in a trance. This went on for two hours. An ambulance was summoned, again Deb thrashed in protest. The medical team restrained her and took her to the hospital. She never came out.

"Deb died a few days later," Annie said. "It was basically massive organ failure. The doctors did what they could, but one vital organ after another was just shutting down."

Deb's mother received a text from Andrea Queeley at 4:00 A.M. California time, Monday, May 1. "Andrea's text said, 'Deb in grave condition in hospital, told to notify next of kin,'" Deb's mom told me. "Then [Andrea] called me and said the doctors had told her they couldn't get Deb's blood pressure above forty-five. They had two key medicines at the maximum level and it wasn't helping. Her organs were failing, and they wanted to know, if her heart stopped, should they not revive her?"

Deb's mother was troubled by the fact that no one was with her daughter at the moment she died. Linda Usdin, who had been keeping vigil for days, had headed home minutes before for some much-needed sleep. Deb's friend Brianna Henry, who was covering the next shift, was on her way to the hospital but arrived too late.

"Deb was gone at 7:00 A.M. Pacific Time on May 2," her mother said.

In the end, then, one person did die from the Mother's Day second line parade shooting. But Deborah Cotton fought off death for nearly four years before she succumbed. Adding yet additional coincidences to the others already studding this story, Deb died three years to the day after she and I first met in 2014, and three hours before judges on the United States Court of Appeals heard Akein Scott's appeal of his life sentence. On the following May 12, four years to the day after the Mother's Day shooting, those same judges rejected Akein Scott's appeal, guaranteeing that he would spend the rest of his life in prison.

> *I'll fly away, in the morning*
> *I'll fly away*
> *Oh, my my, Hallelujah, by and by*
> *I'll fly away*

Black people have been getting buried with music and dance in New Orleans for three hundred years, since the first enslaved Africans arrived there in 1722. Today's second line parades are descendants of those early funeral rituals; the core elements are the same. The body of the deceased is carried forth, trailed by a line of family, friends, and well-wishers who walk slowly, purposefully. There is drumming and singing of mournful songs; there is sorrow and lamentation. When the final resting place is reached, words are spoken, and the body is laid to rest. The crowd does not disperse, however; it reforms and marches on. The music resumes, shifting to uplifting tempos. Dancing begins. And there is a party, where revelers celebrate the life of the departed and the continuation of life for everyone who is still here.

The music at Deb's funeral was, of course, supplied by the To Be Continued Brass Band. Assembled on stage at the historic Carver Theater on Orleans Avenue, all the band members except Juicy were wearing red T-shirts with the words, DEBORAH COTTON RIP printed in white across the front. Juicy wore a black suit as he stepped to the microphone at

11:35 A.M. on June 10, 2017. "We 'bout to celebrate the life of Deborah Cotton," he told a crowd of some 150 people. "Feel free to sing along. And whatever you need to let out, let it out."

TBC's first number was "I'll Fly Away," and never had I heard the song performed more powerfully. I had always thought of "I'll Fly Away" as a hymn, a country tune that praised the everlasting life promised to God's faithful. But the TBC's horns and drums gave the song an unexpected fervor, and the lyrics revealed an astonishment. Deb had died in the morning, just as the song's first verse described, but it was the third verse that startled. The singer envisions a reunion in heaven with a loved one: "Oh, how happy we shall be to meet, I'll fly away, no more cold iron shackles on my feet, I'll fly away." When Albert E. Brumley wrote the song, in 1929, he intended those iron shackles to convey an image of prison, which Brumley saw as a metaphor for humans' earthly existence. But iron shackles were undeniably also a symbol of the slavery that was imposed upon African Americans. Imposed but not forever, the song suggested, for one fine morning we'll fly away.

As TBC soared through the song, Tuffy rose from his seat and headed to the space between the stage and the crowd. Wearing the same DEBORAH COTTON RIP red T-shirt as the band, he started to dance. Stuttering his feet back and forth, his arms akimbo, he hopped, slid, and twirled from one side of the auditorium to the other. In the third verse, as Juicy sang about iron shackles, Tuffy flopped to the floor and briefly lay face down before popping up to kneel as if in prayer. At song's end, he stood, face somber, and pointed at the photograph of Deb on stage, as if to say, "That was for you, Deb."

A succession of speakers took the audience through the many facets of Deborah Dione Cotton's life, history, and identity, starting with her family. Her sister-cousin Le'Trese, dressed in white from head to toe, said, "Debbie's family always knew how fabulous she was, but we didn't understand how much impact she had on the rest of the world. Debbie was passionate about whatever she was involved with, and I encourage each of you to find

your purpose, your passion, and live your life with that purpose and passion. Debbie would like that."

Speaking for Deb's Jewish side, Linda Usdin said, "Deb approached
spirituality and religion as adventurously as she approached everything
else in her world. She was drawn by the concept of what Jews call Tikkun
Olam, repair the world." Linda then read the poem "When All That's Left
Is Love," by Rabbi Allen S. Maller:

> *When I die*
> *If you need to weep*
> *Cry for someone*
> *Walking the street beside you . . . .*
> *And when you say Kaddish for me*
> *Remember what our Torah teaches*
> *Love doesn't die*
> *People do*
> *So when all that's left of me*
> *Is love*
> *Give me away*

I was in tears by the time Linda spoke the final lines, and I wasn't the only
one. Andrea Queeley channeled the writer side of Deb by reading an amusing
excerpt from her book *Notes from New Orleans* about a neighbor who used to
walk his pet pig past Deb's front door. Deb's activist side was invoked with
a performance of Marvin Gaye's "What's Going On" by singer Erica Falls.
Her Christian side was celebrated by Sunni Patterson, who beckoned the
crowd to "stand up and take a deep breath," because she was going to talk
about "the F word—forgiveness." For Deb to forgive the young men who shot
her "was a revolutionary act" that each of us can emulate, Patterson said. As
we go through the tomorrows of our lives, she added, "Let's see each other
through Deb's eyes and ask ourselves, 'What would Deb do?'"

Deb's answer to that question was read by Asali Ecclesiastes as the service closed: "If I don't do anything else before I leave here, I need to have made my presence felt and do what I can to repair the world, do my piece to repair the world."

And with that, the TBC roared back into "I'll Fly Away." Before the first verse was finished, Juicy was leading the band off the stage down into the audience, second line parade style. As they headed down the center aisle, Juicy swung an arm around Tuffy's shoulders and gave him a hug. The second line was now officially beginning as the crowd filed out behind the band, through the lobby, and into the bright sunshine outside.

Waiting at the curb was a white horse hitched to a white carriage with glass windows, the definitive symbol of a luxurious second line funeral. The band, blowing hard, took their places behind the carriage as the crowd continued spilling from the theater. The back door of the carriage was opened and an urn carrying Deb's ashes was placed inside next to a vase of red roses, a bottle of champagne, and a half-smoked joint. Facing out from the walls of the carriage were large photos of Deb from various points in her life, beaming her effortless radiance.

As the TBC unleashed a final chorus of "I'll Fly Away," the driver slapped the reins across the horse's shoulders and the carriage began rolling. The procession crossed the neutral ground to the opposite side of Orleans Avenue and headed toward Treme, the neighborhood where jazz was born and Deb had lived. The weather was beyond splendid, a brilliant blue sky dotted with puffy white clouds and just enough breeze to keep a body comfortable. The crowd swelled as strangers joined the second line; the sight of a white horse and carriage signaled that something special was underway. Tuffy had stripped off his red T-shirt to reveal a white tank top, his bald head now beaded with sweat. Not far from him, I spied Lennard Epps, the friend of Little Manny Taylor who the police believed was the intended target of the Mother's Day shooting; Epps was wearing the same red T-shirt as Tuffy and the TBC.

As we turned left onto North Prieur Street, the TBC launched a new song, the band's polished rhythms augmented by homemade instruments that appeared among the marchers—the shrill of a referee's whistle, the *thunk-thunk-thunk* of a drumstick whacking a glass bottle, the clang of a cowbell. Deb's mother walked behind the carriage, her face creased with sadness and yet smiling. When the parade reached Claiborne Avenue's shade beneath Interstate 10, vehicle traffic halted without complaint in true New Orleans fashion.

Surrounded by this community spirit and glorious music, I felt transported back to Mother's Day of 2013 and the parade where this story began. That second line parade had begun beautifully and ended tragically, but on this day of laying Deb to rest it was comforting to see and feel that the ritual retained its majesty and healing power. As if to exorcise the violence that assaulted Deb and the rest of us four years ago, a vision suddenly appeared when the procession reached North Villere Street: silhouetted against the sky, a Black man dressed all in white was dancing along a building's roofline. The band halted as the crowd cheered him on, whooping and hollering. Then we threaded our way along the edge of Congo Square, the holy of holies where African American ancestors on long ago Sundays planted the seeds of the jazz music that has blessed every second line parade in New Orleans history.

Instead of entering the park, we turned left to arrive at Ursulines Avenue. There, the band halted in front of the house where Deb lived for most of her time in New Orleans, the cramped attic apartment with the sweet back porch overlooking Congo Square. The TBC began a new song, playing with even more energy and chanting a deep, sing-song lyric: *"Way-oh, way-oh, way-oh, way-oh."* From across the crowd, Lennard Epps frantically waved me over. Shouting to be heard over the music, he said, "This the song we got hit on. This the song they was playing when we got shot." It was "Shaka Zulu," the Hot 8 song Joe Maize had cited when recalling that fateful moment. Now, outside of Deb's old apartment, the TBC was reviving that tune to sing Deb's spirit into the next life.

Two blocks away waited Tuba Fats Square, a rectangle of grass where the second line concluded and the after-party commenced. Tuba Fats Square was created as a repudiation of official efforts to limit the playing of live music in Treme. Glen David Andrews, who grew up nearby, had spearheaded the campaign to save the land from gentrification and turn it to public purpose. At the far end of the plot was the Candlelight Lounge, for decades the home of the Treme Brass Band and the iconic New Orleans musician Uncle Lionel Batiste. It seemed a fitting spot for Deb's final send-off. If she were sitting on her old back porch, she would have heard the music wafting through the trees.

After a break, the TBC blasted into "Wild Magnolia," the song they cowrote with Andrews that called for removing Confederate statues from New Orleans. It was the first time I'd heard the song live, and five months into Donald Trump's presidency, it was a welcome tonic to all he represented. *"We gonna name Lee Circle, after Allen Toussaint,"* TBC sang. *"Tear those monuments down!"*

As the TBC delivered this war cry, a new generation of cultural warriors was stepping up. Two little kids who looked like they were four or five years old ran from their mothers' sides to the open space in front of the stage and began attempting the stutter steps and twirls of second line dancing. Once again, the music and heritage of African American New Orleans was melding beauty and despair, offering a lesson from the soul of the nation to all who would heed it.

I like to imagine that Deb was with us at that final send-off; it was her kind of party. To this day, I miss her terribly. But I console myself with the thought that the dead never really leave us, not if we keep them in our hearts, words, and deeds.

So say her name: Deborah "Big Red" Cotton.

Remember her name: A warrior for compassion, joy, and justice.

Honor her name: Do your part to repair the world.

Further Reading and Listening

Acho, Emmanuel. *Uncomfortable Conversations with a Black Man*. New York: Flatiron Books, 2020.

Baldwin, James. *If Beale Street Could Talk*. New York: Dial Press, 1974.

Baptist, Edward E. *The Half Has Never Been Told: Slavery and the Making of American Capitalism*. New York: Basic Books, 2014.

Barker, Danny, ed. Alyn Shipton. *A Life in Jazz*. New York: Oxford University Press, 1986.

Baum, Dan. *Nine Lives*. New York: Spiegel & Grau, 2009.

Bechet, Sidney. *Treat It Gentle: An Autobiography*. New York: Da Capo Press, 2002.

Beckert, Sven. *Empire of Cotton: A Global History*. New York: Alfred A. Knopf, 2014.

Berry, Jason. *City of a Million Dreams: A History of New Orleans at Year 300*. Chapel Hill: University of North Carolina Press, 2018.

Berry, Jason, Jonathan Foose, and Tad Jones. *Up From the Cradle of Jazz: New Orleans Music Since World War II*. Lafayette: Lafayette Press, University of Louisiana, 2009.

Blackmon, Douglas A. *Slavery by Another Name: The Re-Enslavement of Black Americans from the Civil War to World War II*. New York: Anchor Books, 2009.

Branch, Taylor. *Parting The Waters: America in the King Years 1954–63*. New York: Simon & Schuster, 1988.

Branch, Taylor. *Pillar of Fire: America in the King Years 1963–65*. New York: Simon & Schuster, 1998.

Branch, Taylor. *At Canaan's Edge: America in the King Years 1965–68*. New York: Simon & Schuster, 2006.

Burns, Mick. *Keeping the Beat on the Street: The New Orleans Brass Band Renaissance*. Baton Rouge: Louisiana State University Press, 2006.

Coates, Ta-Nehisi. "The Case for Reparations." *The Atlantic*, June 2014.

Coates, Ta-Nehisi. *We Were Eight Years in Power: An American Tragedy*. New York: One World Publishing, 2018.

Carter, Hodding, et al., eds. *The Past As Prelude: New Orleans 1718–1968*. New Orleans: Pelican Publishing House, 1968.

Cruden, Alex and Dedria Bryfonski, eds. *Perspectives on Modern World History: The End of Apartheid*. Farmington Hills, MI: Greenhaven Press, 2010.

Davis, David Brion. *The Problem of Slavery in the Age of Emancipation*. New York: Alfred A. Knopf, 2014.

Douglass, Frederick, with notes by Henry Louis Gates Jr. *Douglass Autobiographies: Narrative of the Life, My Bondage and My Freedom, Life and Times*. New York: Penguin Putnam, 1994.

Du Bois, W.E.B. *The Souls of Black Folk*. New York: Penguin, 2018.

Evans, Freddi Williams. *Congo Square: African Roots in New Orleans*. Lafayette: Lafayette Press, University of Louisiana, 2011.

Foner, Eric. *Reconstruction: America's Unfinished Revolution, 1863–1877*. New York: Harper & Row, 1988.

Ford, Dionne and Jill Strauss, eds. *Slavery's Descendants: Shared Legacies of Race & Reconciliation*. New Brunswick, NJ: Rutgers University Press, 2019.

Franklin, John Hope and Alfred A. Moss Jr. *From Slavery to Freedom: A History of African Americans*. New York: Alfred A. Knopf, 2002.

Garza, Alicia. *The Purpose of Power: How We Come Together When We Fall Apart*. New York: One World, 2020.

Gehman, Mary. *The Free People of Color In NOLA: An Introduction*. New Orleans: Margaret Media, 1994.

Glaude Jr., Eddie S. *Begin Again: James Baldwin's America and Its Urgent Lessons for Our Own*. New York: Crown, 2020.

Hersch, Charles. *Subversive Sounds: Race and the Birth of Jazz in New Orleans*. Chicago: University of Chicago Press, 2007.

Hochschild, Adam. *Bury the Chains: Prophets and Rebels in the Fight to Free an Empire's Slaves*. New York: Houghton Mifflin, 2005.

Jacobs, Harriet. *Incidents in the Life of a Slave Girl*. Mineola, MN: Dover Publications, 2001.

Johnson, Walter. *Soul By Soul: Inside the Antebellum Slave Market*. Cambridge, MA: Harvard University Press, 1999.

Kendi, Ibram X. *Stamped from the Beginning: The Definitive History of Racist Ideas in America*. New York: Nation Books, 2016.

Kmen, Henry A. *Music in New Orleans: The Formative Years, 1791–1841*. Baton Rouge: Louisiana State University Press, 1966.

Landrieu, Mitch. *In The Shadow of Statues: A White Southerner Confronts History*. New York: Viking, 2018.

Levine, Bruce. *The Fall of the House of Dixie: The Civil War and the Social Revolution That Transformed the South*. New York: Random House, 2013.

Lichtenstein, Grace and Laura Dankner. *Musical Gumbo: The Music of New Orleans*. New York: W.W. Norton, 1993.

McWhorter, John. *Woke Racism: How a New Religion Has Betrayed Black America*. New York: Portfolio/Penguin, 2021.

Nine Times Social and Pleasure Club. *Coming Out the Door for the Ninth Ward*. New Orleans: Neighborhood Story Project, 2006.

Obama, Barack. *A Promised Land*. New York: Crown, 2020.

Peck, Raoul, ed., from texts by James Baldwin. *I Am Not Your Negro*. New York: Vintage International, 2017.

Powell, Lawrence N. *The Accidental City: Improvising New Orleans*. Cambridge, MA: Harvard University Press, paperback edition, 2013.

Rawick, George P. *From Sundown to Sunup: The Making of the Black Community*. (Volume I of *The American Slave: A Composite Autobiography*.) Westport, CT: Greenwood Press, 1972.

Sakakeeny, Matt. *Roll with It: Brass Bands in the Streets of New Orleans*. Durham, NC: Duke University Press, 2013.

Shin, Bryan and Yohuru Williams, eds. *The Black Panthers: Portraits from an Unfinished Revolution*. New York: Nation Books, 2016.

Sparks, Allister. *Beyond the Miracle: Inside the New South Africa*. Chicago: University of Chicago Press, 2003.

Tanner, Lynette Ater, ed. *Chained to the Land: Voices from Cotton & Cane Plantations*. From interviews of former slaves. Winston-Salem, NC: John F. Blair, 2014.

Tutu, Desmond. *No Future Without Forgiveness*. New York: Doubleday, 1999.

Ward, Geoffrey C. *Jazz: A History of America's Music*. Based on a documentary film by Ken Burns. New York: Alfred A. Knopf, 2000.

Wilkerson, Isabel. *Caste: The Origins of Our Discontents*. New York: Random House, 2020.

Wilkerson, Isabel. *The Warmth of Other Suns: The Epic Story of America's Great Migration*. New York: Random House, 2010.

Zinn, Howard. *On Race*. New York: Seven Stories Press, 2011.

Musical Listings

"Amazing Grace," Treme Brass Band: https://www.youtube.com/watch?v =Ghupw_2va7Y/.

"AP Touro," Rebirth Brass Band: https://www.youtube.com/watch?v =hLmEATtknIM/.

"Back Stabbers—Rebirth Groove," Brothers of Brass: https://www.youtube .com/watch?v=MstailPay6Y/.

"Big Girl," The Hot 8 Brass Band: https://www.youtube.com/watch?v =_pFLGqpsIXs/.

"Blind Willie McTell," Bob Dylan: https://www.youtube.com/watch?v =_AIRdU6CPf0/.

"Bourbon Street Parade," Preservation Hall Brass Band: https://www.youtube .com/watch?v=JNJhCgcYvvI/.

"Bury the Hatchet," Glen David Andrews: https://www.youtube.com/watch?v =IpIUufaYisk/.

"Casanova," Rebirth Brass Band: https://www.youtube.com/watch?v =ZQYusEy4N-c/.

"Do Whatcha Wanna," Rebirth Brass Band: https://www.youtube.com/watch ?v=X_AOwrXev60/.

"Flee As a Bird/Oh, Didn't He Ramble," Louis Armstrong: https://www .youtube.com/watch?v=PqnpstPM6yU/.

"Gimme My Money Back," Treme Brass Band: https://www.youtube.com /watch?v=2KyvXtpY45I/.

"Hey Pocky A-Way," The Meters: https://www.youtube.com/watch?v=EEtX T9w9AYU&list=PLgu6eRj4_paRZekPWUkbNeSPFCuLYCHM8&i ndex=70/.

"I Don't F*ck with You, Don't F*ck with Me," TBC Brass Band: https://www .youtube.com/watch?v=yIAapSTVaZ4&list=PLgu6eRj4_paRZekPWUkb NeSPFCuLYCHM8&index=142/.

"I Wanna Dance with Somebody," TBC Brass Band: https://www.youtube .com/watch?v=L5sQ4o2ZE6E/.

"I'll Fly Away/Part-Time Lover," TBC Brass Band: https://www.youtube.com /watch?v=nDwKfBuJpRI/.

"In the Sweet Bye and Bye," Olympia Brass Band: https://www.youtube.com
    /watch?v=xlpg4dlMJC4/.
"It Ain't My Fault," Gulf Aid All-Stars, featuring Mos Def, Lenny Kravitz,
    and the Preservation Hall Brass Band: https://www.youtube.com
    /watch?v=6-hgqMys-Bs/.
"Just a Closer Walk with Thee," Rebirth Brass Band: https://www.youtube.com
    /watch?v=UcbsQUQ8fEM/.
"Let Your Mind Be Free," Soul Rebels: https://www.youtube.com/watch?v
    =awCy-529Q3g/.
"Lift Every Voice and Sing," Ray Charles: https://www.youtube.com/watch?v
    =QU8921j20e8/.
"Lord, Lord, Lord," Olympia Brass Band: https://www.youtube.com/watch?v
    =HlnDq_a_JLg/.
"Mardi Gras Day," Kermit Ruffins with Trombone Shorty: https://www.you
    tube.com/watch?v=tDhpXGpGw0w/.
"Mardi Gras in New Orleans," Professor Longhair: https://www.youtube.com
    /watch?v=LR82f0GJgXg&list=PLgu6eRj4_paRZekPWUkbNeSPFCuLY
    CHM8&index=73/.
"Mardi Gras in New Orleans," Tuba Fats' Chosen Few Brass Band: https
    ://www.youtube.com/watch?v=i9q5Sbj3km4/.
"Mardi Gras Mambo," The Meters: https://www.youtube.com/watch?v
    =v7hxqp2reVc/.
"My Feet Can't Fail Me Now," Dirty Dozen Brass Band: https://www.youtube
    .com/watch?v=ASGn9H5fdPM/.
"Oh! Didn't He Ramble," Louis Armstrong: https://www.youtube.com
    /watch?v=wzkCeWBuTv8/.
"Over in the Gloryland," Leroy Jones: https://www.youtube.com/watch?v
    =_9iZuUK7NvQ/.
"Paul Barbarin's Second Line," Dirty Dozen Brass Band: https://www.youtube
    .com/watch?v=ttWwSD-rdmY/.
"Red Dress," Big 6 Brass Band: https://soundcloud.com/user-60647372
    /red-dress/.
"Roll With Me, Knock With Me," Lil Rascals Brass Band: https://www.you
    tube.com/watch?v=T9pd8VWyibA/.
"Saint James Infirmary Blues," Jon Batiste: https://www.youtube.com/watch?v
    =M3qTwHRECmM/.
"Second Line (Joe Avery's Blues)," Wynton Marsalis Quintet: https://www
    .youtube.com/watch?v=0RqWGuWIM_g/.

Shaka Zulu, Hot 8 Brass Band: live performances only/no digital recordings
    available.

"Southern Man," Neil Young: https://www.youtube.com/watch?v=m5FCcDEA6mY/.

"Strange Fruit," written by Abel Meeropol, performed by Billie Holiday:
    https://www.youtube.com/watch?v=-DGY9HvChk/.

"Treme Song," John Boutté: https://www.youtube.com/watch?v=yEGQ27ieFh0/.

"When I Die, You Better Second Line," Kermit Ruffins: https://www.youtube
    .com/watch?v=b_awCl-qYM0/.

"When the Saints Go Marching In," Louis Armstrong: https://www.youtube
    .com/watch?v=17nXsv7o64k/.

"Why I Sing the Blues," B. B. King: https://www.youtube.com/watch?v
    =ccHrgxsO9z0/.

"Wild Magnolia," TBC Brass Band featuring Glen David Andrews:
    https://www.youtube.com/watch?v=iVCe0xrNLL0&list=OLAK
    5uy_nz238u17uH_rokgAGBXNWZI06KrrVnXEQ/.

"You Don't Want to Go to War," Rebirth Brass Band: https://www.youtube
    .com/watch?v=va7-CJiRuPU/.

Acknowledgments

My thanks go first and forever to Deborah "Big Red" Cotton, not only for the countless ways she helped and supported me in writing this book but for the life she led that inspired it. When Deb and I first met, she didn't know me from a can of paint, as people in New Orleans sometimes say. But she opened wide the door, sharing her thoughts and feelings, often on quite intimate matters, without hesitation or guile. Deb also encouraged numerous others of her acquaintance to speak with me, something many of those individuals normally would have been reluctant to do with a White reporter from out of town. I hope the finished book, despite its inevitable imperfections, would receive Deb's approval.

I also want to thank the many other people who spoke with me for this book, with a special shout-out to Kevin Allman, Deb's editor at *Gambit*, for facilitating my initial connection with her. I thank each of them for their time, their candor, and their implicit trust in me to tell this story fairly and accurately. A reporter is only as good as his or her sources, and the sources I've been blessed with in New Orleans were second to none. And special thanks as well to *Rolling Stone* editor Sean Woods, who endorsed the value of my reporting and provided crucial guidance about framing the narrative.

I also thank the staff at the Whitney Museum, particularly Ashley Rogers, and the Historic New Orleans Collection, particularly Jessica Dorman. Both of these institutions are performing valuable public service and, like many of their visitors, I learned a great deal from their exhibitions and artifacts.

I also thank my friends and colleagues in New Orleans, especially Fred Kasten and Jason Berry, for their tutelage in the incomparable musical past and present of the city, and Schuyler Hoffman and David Peterson for graciously hosting most of my New Orleans visits.

I'm grateful beyond measure to the good people at Pegasus Books, especially my brave and insightful editor Jessica Case. More than once while writing this book I wondered whether it would ever see the light of day. I now see, and rejoice, that those hours of darkness were a test of my fortitude, with Pegasus the reward awaiting me at the break of dawn. I'm likewise thankful to my longtime agent, Ellen Levin, who never gave up on this project when others would have.

Finally, I thank, as always, my family and dear friends for their boundless encouragement and faith in me. You know who you are.